Thapa Politics in Nepal

About the Author

Dr. K.L.Pradhan born in August 1955 is presently holding the post of Associate Professor in History Department, Government Aizawl College. He completed his graduation from Pachhunga Memorial Govt. College, Aizawl with Honours in History. He passed his MA (History) in 1979 securing 1st rank and a Gold Medal. He joined M.Phil. Prgramme and completed in 1982. He continued for Ph.D. degree which he obtained in 1987 from NEHU, Shillong. He started his career as Lecturer in 1984 and was placed in the present post in 2006. Besides his normal duties, Dr. Pradhan also hold the posts of Coordinator, UGC Sponsored Coaching Centre, IGNOU, Programme Officer, National Service Scheme and a Member of Internal Quality Assurance Cell. He is presently a Member of Board of Studies (undergraduate) , Mizoram University, Aizawl.

He is deeply involved in historical research. He published several research papers in journals. He is also the author of 'Brian Hodgson at the Kathmandu Residency (1825-1843) He did his Post Doctoral Research Programme under Indian Council of Historical Research, New Delhi and completed in 2005. He is presently working on "British Imperialism and Native Resistance- A case study of the Mizos" .He is a member of various historical research organisations. Besides, he takes active part in social services.

Thapa Politics in Nepal

With Special Reference to Bhim Sen Thapa
(1806-1839)

K.L. Pradhan
Department of History
Government Aizawl College
Aizawl, Mizoram

CONCEPT PUBLISHING COMPANY Pvt. Ltd.,
NEW DELHI-110059

ISBN-13: 978-81-8069-813-2

First Published 2012

Published and Printed by

Concept
Since 1974

Concept Publishing Company Pvt. Ltd.
Regd. Office:
A/15-16, Commercial Block, Mohan Garden,
New Delhi-110059 (INDIA)
Phones : 25351460, 25351794, *Fax* : 091-11-25357109
Email : publishing@conceptpub.com,
Website: www.conceptpub.com

Editorial Office:
H-13, Bali Nagar, New Delhi-110 015, India.

Cataloging in Publication Data--*Courtesy:* D.K. Agencies (P) Ltd. <docinfo@dkagencies.com>

Pradhan, K. L., 1955-
Thapa politics in Nepal : with special reference to Bhim Sen Thapa (1806-1839) / K.L. Pradhan.
p. cm.
Includes bibliographical references (p.) and index.
ISBN 9788180698132

1. Nepal—Politics and government—19th century. 2. Bhimasena Thapa, 1775-1839. I. Title.

DDC 954.96 23

Preface and Acknowledgements

This attempt to study Thapa Politics in Nepal with special reference to Bhim Sen Thapa from 1806 to 1839. There has no doubt been a considerable progress in historical writings in Nepal in recent years and they provide a valuable backgrounds or understandings of Nepal's political, social, economics, and her foreign relations with Tibet- China and British India. Chittaranjan Nepali has taken the pains to write a book on him: *Janaral Bhim Sen Thapa ra Tatkalin Nepal* (Janaral Bhim Sen Thapa and Nepal in his days) primarily based on Nepali documents. While he critically analyses the events of the period, he fails to consult the important documents preserved in the National Archives of India. Gyunu Dungel's *Mukhtiyar Bhim Sen Thapa ra Tatkal Nepali Sahitya,* (in Nepali) also tries to project Bhim Sen Thapa as a true nationalist who safe-guard, the independence of Nepal from the British influence. Ludwig F. Stiller's *The Silent Cry: The People of Nepal,* has given the detailed social, economic and political background of the period under review. Binaya Kumar Sharma's *Bhimsenlai Niyalda* (in Nepali) also explains the Darbar political conspiracies against the Mukhtiyar.

My own interest in this theme developed when I was doing my Ph.D. Degree way back in 1984. Since then I was looking for a moment to work on the Thapa's political activities under Bhim Sen Thapa. The opportunity came when the Indian Council of Historical Research, New Delhi, has accepted my research project in 2002 and awarded me the Post-Doctoral Fellowship.

The present work begins with an attempt to focus on the political system during pre-unification era; the process of unification under Prithvi Narayan Shah, various principalities and the political and social systems of the kingdom. The next chapter deals with the rise of Bhim Sen Thapa to power, his policy of expansion and consolidation and various works undertaken. The Gorkha militarism and war with the British India follow this. The Next two chapters deal with the policy of foreign relations with China and the disaffected Indian native states to form a confederation against the British and the administrative system under Bhim Sen Thapa. His relations with the British Resident assumes an interesting study particularly with Brian Hodgson, based on the archival records preserved have been explained analytically. The policy of the Resident towards the Nepal in general and Bhim Sen Thapa in particular has been focussed in details. It also explains the emergence of various contending factions in the Darbar who were working against each other to acquire power in the Nepali politics. The factors leading to the downfall and the subsequent events of political uncertainty has been studied in details in chapter eighth. In the conclusion, a critical attempt has been made to evaluate Bhim Sen Thapa's contributions to Nepal and particularly to the people of Nepal through rules and legislations. At the end of the volume, appendices, glossary and selected bibliography are appended.

The work is primarily based on unpublished and published documents preserved in the National Archives of India and Nepal, private diary, records, memoirs, accounts and contemporary writings where have been extensively used. At the time of collections of the data, I was fortunate to have free access to consult the archival materials preserved in Kathmandu and New Delhi. The Centre for Nepal and South Asian Centre and Tribhuvan University Libraries also gave me free access to consult the books and periodical journals kept in their respective libraries. I had the opportunity to discuss the subject matter with the Vice-Chancellor, Prof. Triratna Manadhar, and Dr. Sushil Kumar Thapa of Tribhuvan University, Shri Harihar Joshi, President of Nepal—Past and Present and the officials of the National Archives of Nepal. Discussion with them has greatly helped me to look at the project from different angles. During my stay in Kathmandu, Shri Hira Lama and Srimati Sushma of Sanepa, Kathmandu and my niece Kumari Promi Pradhan extended all possible help to me. I am very much indebted to them.

I am specially indebted to Shri Nirmal Kumar Pun for translation of all the documents written in Nepali into English and the valuable suggestions for improving the presentation and style of the work and for his constant encouragement to complete the project. Further, I would like to thank Dr. R. Thangvunga, Head of English Department, who has taken the pain to go through the manuscripts and offered me valuable suggestions.

This project could not have been completed if the Indian Council of Historical Research, New Delhi, did not grant the Fellowship to me. I am very much grateful to the officials and the Members of the Council. I also express my gratitude to the Government of Mizoram, Human Resources Development Department and Higher Education, Aizawl for granting me study leave and the Principal, Government Aizawl College for extending all possible helps for the completion of the Post-Doctoral Research Project. I owe a special thanks to my wife Lalthazuali for her untiring support.

Finally, my thanks are due to and are gratefully rendered to Shri Ashok Kumar Mittal of Concept Publishing Company Pvt. Ltd. for his courtesy and whole-hearted cooperation in the production of the book. Any suggestions for the enrichment of the subject matter will be gratefully welcomed.

K. L. Pradhan

Contents

Abbreviations

AR	:	Asiatic Researches.
BPP	:	Bengal Past and Present.
B.S.	:	Bikram Sambat.
Cf.	:	Compare.
CNAS	:	Centre for Nepalese and Asian Studies.
COD	:	Court of Directors.
FMPR	:	Foreign Miscellaneous Political Records.
FN	:	Footnotes.
FPC	:	Foreign Political Consultations.
FSC	:	Foreign Secret Consultations.
HJ	:	Himalayan Journals.
HM	:	Hodgson's Manuscripts.
JASB	:	Journal of Asiatic Society of Bengal.
JBORS	:	Journal of Bihar and Orissa Research Society.
NAI	:	National Archives of India.
NAN	:	National Archives of Nepal.
NEN	:	Narrative of Events in Nepal.
NWP	:	Papers Relating to Nepal War.
PIHC	:	Proceedings of India History Congress.
PT	:	Political Transactions.
QHR	:	Quarterly Historical Journal.
SRGB	:	Selection of Records from Government of Bengal.
TU	:	Tribhuvan University.

Glossary

Adalat	:	A Court of Law.
Adhiya	:	A crop-sharing system between landlord and the cultivator.
Amali	:	The chief revenue collection official of a district.
Amanat	:	A system of revenue collection through officials appointed by the government.
Baisi	:	Twenty two.
Bhansar	:	Custom House.
Bharadar	:	A high ranking official, a member on nobility.
Bhatha	:	Lands in the Tarai adjoining the Indian border.
Bandha	:	Lands mortgaged by the government to private individuals.
Beth-Begar	:	see jhara.
Bichari	:	A Jugde.
Birta	:	Land granted by the state to individual, general on a tax-free basis.
Bhota	:	Maintenance loans supplied to settlers under land reclamation projects.
Brahmins	:	Priestly class.
Chaubisi	:	Twenty-four.
Chaudhuri	:	A landlord in the Tarai districts or a market inspector or a headman of Newar communities in hill regions.
Chowkidar	:	Watchman.
Dhakareah	:	Off the roll soldier.

Dharmadhikar	:	Chief religious authority of the kingdom.
Dharmashastra	:	Hindu religious scriptures.
Dittha	:	A high ranking officer in the judicial heirarchy.
Dware	:	An official appointed at the royal palace to collect certain levies.
Fauzadar	:	A local functionary in the charge of revenue collection and other functions.
Feringhees	:	Foreigners.
Guru	:	Religious preceptor.
Guthi	:	Lands endowed to temples, monasteries and other religious and philanthropic institutions for similar purpose.
Hulak	:	A relay of porters.
Ijara	:	A contract for collection of revenue.
Ijaradar	:	Contractor—the holder of an ijara.
Itachapli	:	Criminal court.
Jagir	:	A land assigned to a government employee or functionary as emolument.
Jagirdar	:	A government employee: beneficiary of jagir land assignments.
Jhara	:	Compulsory labour, generally unpaid ,with such variations as Beth (agricultural labour) and Begar (porterage services)
Kachari	:	A Law court.
Kamara-Kamari	:	Slave.
Kapardar	:	The chief of the royal household.
Kharidar	:	A civil officer.
Kharita	:	It is a document similar to a letter patent of English Constitutional Law.
Khazanchi	:	Treasurer.
Kipat	:	A form of customary communal land tenure system prevalent among the eastern regions including Kathmandu valley.
Kiriya	:	Bonded slave.
Kot-Linga	:	The highest Court of Law in Nepal.
Kotwal	:	A chief police officer of a town or district.
Kut	:	A system of tenancy under which rent was payable in the form of a specific quantity of produce or sum of money.
Lalmohar	:	Royal proclamation in the form of letter.

Madhesi	:	People of plain.
Mukhiya	:	A village headman in the hill regions.
Mukhtiyar	:	It is a Persian word which means "competent to do", or the Commander-in-Chief.
Mohi	:	A tenant.
Mokaddam	:	A Parganna-level functionary who assisted in the collection of revenue in the Tarai.
Munshi	:	An official-in-charge of correspondence in English or Persian.
Naike	:	A leader or headman.
Nankar	:	Lands assigned to Chaudhuris and Mokaddams in the eastern Tarai district as their emoluments.
Nirkhi	:	Sales tax.
Pakho	:	Unirrigated hillside or high lands.
Pancha	:	Member of a Panchayat or local council
Parganna	:	A group of mauja joined together for purpose of revenue administration.
Pandit	:	A religious priest.
Panjani	:	Annual renewal of tenure.
Parbattiah	:	Hillman.
Patta	:	Land allotment certificate.
Patuwari	:	A village level functionary in the Tarai districts who maintained land and revenue records.
Peskhar	:	A judicial functionary in some Tarai districts.
Pota	:	Tax payable as some categories of Birta lands in Kathmandu valley.
Rajdhani	:	State capital.
Raikar	:	State-owned land.
Sipahis	:	Soldiers.
Subba	:	Headman of the Limbu community in the far eastern region.
Subedar	:	The Commander of a military company.
Sardar	:	A top ranking officer in-charge of military affairs.
Sunnad	:	Deed of grant by the government of office, privilege or right.
Thani	:	A village level revenue functionary in Jumla

		Mustang and other areas in the north-western Nepal.
Tharghars	:	Chiefs or selected caste who were in-charge of such functions as demarcation of Birta boundaries.
Thanedar	:	The chief of a police outpost.
Taksar	:	Mint.
Tuddikhel	:	A parade ground.
Zamindar	:	A landlord; an estate holder; a hereditary collector of revenue.

I

Introduction

Sandwiched between the two big powers, India in the south and Tibet-China in the north, the kingdom of Nepal is bounded by Mahakali in the west and the river Mechi in the east. The entire northernmost part, i.e. the great Himalayan region is mountainous where less than 10 per cent of Nepal's population resides with pastoral economy. However, it is traverse by at least eighteen passes: most important among them are Takla Khar, Mustang Kerung, Kuti, Halia Velong which formed the channels of communication with Tibet. Below this, in the mid-hills, comprises the valley of Chitlong to the south-west of Nepal within its subordinate Valley of Panauni, a tributary of the river Bagmati; the valley of Doon and Kupla; the valley of Nuwakot and the valley of Banepa. In this valley the capital of the kingdom—Kathmandu is situated.[1] It was the main centre of habitation and cultivation. About fifty per cent of Nepal's population resides in this valley. Father Giuseppe calls "its (Kathmandu) extensive plain of Nepal resembling an amphitheatre covered with populous towns and villages".[2] The next region consists of Churia Hills, Bhadar and Tarai along the southern border of Nepal. Tarai with its alluvial soil for cultivation and abundant forest resources forms immediate zone between the Gangetic plains and the Siwalik range.[3]

The earliest inhabitants of Nepal were the Kirats now represent the Limbus and Rais of eastern Nepal. The Lepchas of eastern part of Nepal are also said to have lived there. The Bhangi and Dotiyal ethnic groups of western Nepal migrated from Kumaon and Garhwal. The Chepang, a nomadic tribe living near confluence of rivers Kali, Seti and Trisul Ganga are an indigenous groups.[4] In the central valley of Nepal live the Newars. The western and west-central regions are inhabited by the Gurung, Magar and Bhutiyas of the Mongoloid origin. Tharus and Boksas who lived in swampy and malarious Tarai claimed to have migrated from India. The Sherpas and Bhotiyas of northern borderland are migrated from Tibet[5]. Regarding the ethnic identity and its origin, Leo E. Rose and T. Scholz write that "one can divide the groups into two rough categories (a) those who speak Tibeto-Burman languages have Mongolian facial features, live at higher altitude and in the northern parts of the country, and observe religious beliefs considerably influenced by Buddhism and (b) those who speak Sanskrit derived languages, have Indo-Aryan features, live at lower elevations in southern region and practise Hindu religious customs".[6] However, in due course of time, most groups in the hills have adopted many Hindu practices. In fact, it is not uncommon to find elements of Buddhism and Hinduism entwined in the numerous religious festivals celebrated throughout Nepal.

According to the oral tradition and available historical documents, the Kirats dynasty that had ruled the Kathmandu valley earlier were replaced by the Licchavi dynasty in the fourth and fifth century and the latter were the first Nepali dynasty of Indian (i.e. plains) origin. They ruled the country for a considerable period and developed a close and friendly relations with Tibet. In the process, Nepal became major intellectual and commercial entrepot between south and central Asia and also contributed significantly for spread of Buddhist religion and culture in the northern areas. During the Licchavi period, the hill areas to the east and west of Nepal valley witnessed considerable changes in politics and society.[7]

From the eleventh to eighteenth century A.D., the kingdom of Nepal was ruled by the Malla dynasty. The exact origin of the Malla is, however, still a subject of great debate in Nepal. It is presumed that like their predecessor Licchavi, they were Indian by decent high caste Hindu by self-identification. The presumption is further supplemented by the first legal and social code strongly imbued with Brahmanic Hindu principles introduced by the Malla King Jayasthiti Malla in the Kingdom.[8]

During the Malla rule, some basic political and social changes began to take place in the hill areas of south and west. By fifteenth century most of the hill areas of south and west of Kathmandu valley were ruled by Kshatriya Rajputs assisted by Brahman preceptors and advisors. The introduction of high caste Hindu elites into the central Himalaya hills led to establishment of two confederations of the Baisi and Chaubisi rajyas.[9]

History of modern Nepal as a unified political and social system is of a relatively recent development dating back only to the latter decades of the eighteenth century. Till mid-eighteenth century A.D. Nepal, as we know today, was divided into number of principalities. In the west of Kathmandu valley to Mahakali river, there were at least forty-six separate principalities and these were traditionally divided into two groups known as the Baisi and the Chaubisi rajyas, ruled by the Rajputs as well as several decentralised tribal polities.[10] Long before the Rajputs started streaming into western Nepal, small bands of Hindu had been entering the area from India as a result of Muslim invasion. These people found a ready haven and were eventually merged among the hill society. There, indeed, was no trouble for these immigrants as the Khash tribe of Nepal had many things in common. The bands of Rajput were also similarly absorbed. After the fall of Chittor in 1303AD, a large number of Rajput fugitives made their way into Nepal.[11]

The entry of Rajputs into central Nepal was greatly facilitated by the presence of Khashas who had already established their stronghold in the Karnali basin. The Malla (Khash) kingdom was basically feudal and these states maintained their independent status. For more than two hundred years this Malla kingdom had united more than half of greater Nepal into a large feudatory state.[12] indeed it was the Rajputs who had greatly contributed to the fragmentation of the Malla kingdom of Jumla. Stiller writes, "Though they were relatively few in number, they were of a higher caste, warriors and of a temperament that quickly gained them the ascendancy in the princedoms in the Jumla kingdom, their effect on the kingdom was centrifugal".[13] That apart, the ambition of the Rajputs often led them into treacherous activities against their very benefactors. "It is sad", but true as Francis Tuker states that "as these pages show, that the Rajputs was so often guilty of base ingratitude and treachery to gratify his ambition. Rajputs were fierce, ruthless people who would stop at nothing".[14]

The disintegrated Baisi rajyas in the Karnali region comprised of Jumla, Jajarkot, Accham, Rukum, Mushikot, Ropla, Bhajang, Dailekh, Banggafi, Dharma, Dhang, Malebam, Chitli, Sattala having its headquarters at Jumla. It also included Kumaon, Garhwal in the west and western Tibet to the north of the Himalayas. In the south, it controlled Surkhet in the inner Tarai.[15]

The Chaubasi rajyas in the Gandaki region included Palpa, Tanahu, Lamjung, Bhirkot, Nuwakot, Dhurkot, Parbat, Gahro, Rising, Chiring, Dhor, Gulmi, Hasma, Piuthan, Argakhachi, Sarta, Kaski, Dhanding and others. In the 16th century A.D. Lamjung, Tanahu and adjoining areas towards Kathmandu were ruled by the local chiefs. Toward the end of the first decade of the second half of the 16th century some conspirators in Gorkha who were not satisfied with their Khas rulers requested the Rajput ruler of Lamjung to allow them to set up his youngest son as the ruler of the Gorkha. With the permission, the conspirators launched their scheme and the ruler of Gorkha was killed, and Lamjung ruler's youngest son, Drabya Shah was installed as new king. Thus Gorkha was the last Hindu rajya to be established in the western hill region. However, the Gorkha was never included in the list of the Chaubasi rajyas possibly because the lines of affiliation, had been formalised before the rajya was brought under the rule of Hindu Dynasty.[16]

Among these forty-six rajyas, Palpa was the biggest and most powerful. It comprised of Butwal, an important trade centre, and an extensive area in the Tarai on lease from the rulers of India. In course of time, Gulmi and Kaski, who were under the influence of Palpa, had broken off and proclaimed itself an independent rajya. Further, the royal family of Palpa established an independent rajya in Tanahu, Makwanpur and later extended to Vijayapur in Chaudandi region in the east. Thus, the ruler of Palpa controlled the whole of central and eastern Nepal except Kathmandu valley.[17]

Besides these rajyas, the Kathmandu valley comprising the kingdom of Kathmandu, Patan and Bhatgaon were ruled by the Malla kings. The boundaries of the kingdoms were however not limited to the valley. Both the frontiers of Kathmandu and Bhatgaon reached Tibet in the north, while in the east they included parts of present Kabhurepalchok. Sindhupalchok and Dokhla district. In the west Nuwakot and Dhanding belonged to Kathmandu and Patan respectively. In the south of Kathmandu valley, the kingdom of Makwanpur touched the borders of Patan and included Tarai districts.[18] In the east the Kingdom of Chaudandi controlled the districts of Okhaldunga and Bhojpur in addition to Saptahari, Mahatari, Siraha, Dhanusa and Sarlahi district in Tarai. Further east, the kingdom of Vijayapur controlled the whole of far eastern hill districts of Dhankuta, Panchthar, Taplejung, Terhathum, Sunkhuwasabha and Tarai district of Morung, Sunsari and Jhapa as well.[19]

The above description of the political units into which the present kingdom of Nepal was divided during the eighteenth century is not intended to emphasise the multiplicity or even the small size of most of them from the point of later political development which had greater significance. The process of territorial expansion and disintegration had, by the middle of eighteenth century, proceeded to an extent which made difficult for any rajyas to encroach upon its neighbours without inviting retaliation in kind from one or more other rajyas. Territorial expansion was, therefore, possible only if any rajyas was able to achieve the support or at least the neutrality of surrounding rajyas.[20]

Gorkha was a small enclave in the Gandaki region.In fact, it was ruled by various kings/chiefs belonging to Magar, Gurung and Khadka. The rulers of the Gorkha were too poor with little revenue resources to acquire. In spite of its small size and poor revenue, the Gorkha was fortunate to have numbers of outstanding statesmen, as its kings. Ram Shah (1606-1636) introduced first legal code which had tremendous impact upon the surrounding areas and became important factor in the subsequent expansion of the Gorkha empire. The Gorkha rajya was encircled in the west by Kaski, Lamjung and Tanahu. They were much stronger and commanded economic resources which later helped the Gorkhas to expand towards the east, north, and the south. During Ram Shah's period, these rajyas reached the frontier of Kathmandu at Nuwakot and of Tibet at Rasuwa.[21] According to Gorkha Vamsavali, the Gorkha had planned to conquer Kathmandu valley during Narbhupal Shah's (1716-1743) period. An attempt was made to invade Nuwakot in 1737 but without success. It was under Prithvi Narayan Shah, who ascended the throne of Gorkha Kingdom on 3rd April, 1743, made extensive preparation to conquest the three Malla kingdoms of Kathmandu valley.[22] Though young, he was endowed with a vision and boundless ambition. He set his house in order, organised his troops and launched on a career that was destined to bring all Nepal under his banner. Sir Francis Tuker writes:

> The Gurkha army was now being organised by its young leader for the great talk ahead of it... In the case of the Gurkhas, it was the company of some one hundred and fifty men, each company having a band of about ten men and an establishment of "artificers"... The armament came to be mainly firelocks but in place of bayonet these highlanders carried khora and khukri. The bow and arrow were still in use, on both sides, in the days of Prithvi Narayan.[23]

Prior to the campaign, Prithvi Narayan Shah secretly visited India and procured firearms and technicians to train the local manufacturers of arms and ammunitions. Further, before he actually embarked upon conquering Nuwakot, he sent emissaries to Kaski, Lamjung, Tanahu and Palpa to promote friendship. With the neutrality of this rajyas, Prithvi Narayan Shah annexed Nuwakot in 1744. It gives a privilege to Gorkha's participation in the profitable trade between Tibet and India.[24] The Malla kings had no other alternative but to accede the new role of Prithvi Narayan Shah because the main route between Kathmandu and Tibet run through newly annexed Nuwakot.[25] In 1748, the Gorkha king subjugated Sidhupalchok, Khaburepalchok, and other areas of importance in the east. The Himalayan passes of Kuti and Kerung also came under tne control of Gorkha. The conquest of Makwanpur in 1762 enabled Prithvi Narayan Shah to control eastern Tarai and Shindhugati through which Kathmandu valley maintained contact with India. And in March 1767, Kirtipur was, without much resistance conquered which gave the Gorkha king his first strategic foothold in the valley. The success further gave Prithvi Narayan Shah to concentrate his efforts on the conquest of the three Malla kingdoms. By controlling over the territories adjoining Kathmandu valley, he made it possible to impose economic blockade. The kingdom of Kathmandu was thus finally overran by the Gorkhas in September, 1768 without shedding a single drop of blood. In the subsequent years, Patan and Bhadgaon were conquered without any difficulty. Thus, after defeating them Prithvi Narayan Shah shifted his capital from Gorkha to Kathmandu and laid down the present kingdom of Nepal.[26] In 1715, when he died, the kingdom of Nepal comprised, whole of eastern Tarai i.e. Morung, Sunsari, Jhapa, Siraha, Sarlahi, Mahottari, Bara Oarsa and Rautahat; eastern and central inner Tarai i.e.

Sindhuli, Udaypur, Chisapani and Makwanpur apart from (Kathmandu Valley) and reached the boundary up to river Teesta. By 1789, the Chaubasi and Basi rajyas in the western region had all been annexed and the frontier extended to Mahakali river in the west. In 1790, Kumaon area was also conquered.[27]

Nepal, as Hindu state, the source of all royal power and prerogatives were derived from the ideal embodied in the Dharmashastra, *Manusmriti*.[28] It is, however, recorded that the monarchical system of government can be traced from Lichhavi and Kirati dynasties. Like ancient and medieval periods, the Maharaja of Shah dynasty was the head of the state and exercised supreme authority in legislature, executive and judiciary. He was supreme commander of the army. His decisions were always final and binding to all citizens. He was regarded as an incarnation of Lord Vishnu in Nepal.[29] The position of the monarch was further strengthened after the unification of Nepal under Prithvi Narayan Shah. All the officials of the kingdom, Anchal, military and the newly acquired territories were appointed by the king himself. He waged war against the enemies, concluded peace treaty, make friendship with the neighbouring states. It was prerogative which no one could deny. All the documents pertaining to wars, dissoluting, foreign relations, introduction of new laws and customs were promulgated with suffixing the royal seal-Lalmohar. He also acted as the Chief Judge and decided the civil and criminal cases according to the principles of Hindu Dharma. The Maharaja had the right to deport any person who offend against the state, pardon the offenders and grant permission to return from exile.[30] The Maharaja also undertook to reform the existing social evils like; gambling, slavery etc. For these, the Maharaja was assisted by a "Thar Garh" *Bharadars who were mainly drawn from the family based aristocracy.

Nepal has usually been defined as an absolute monarchy in theory, but limited in practice, because there are some theoretical limitations on the power of the king manifested in Hindu tradition. But there is a question that the practical limitations on the powers of the king have had greater effect, at times transforming the Shah rulers into a mere puppet in the hands of dominant faction in his own Darbar.[31]

Likewise, the institution of the Bharadars were probably been established during the Lichhavi period to help and advice the king in his administration. In the Gorkha rajya, prior to the unification of Nepal, the Bharadars were mainly drawn from the influential persons of high caste i.e. Pande, Pant, Aryal, Khanal, Rana and Bohra known as the "Thar Garh". These Bharadars had played important role in the process of the unification of the country under the leadership of king Prithvi Narayan Shah and were later appointed in different posts of importance in the Darbar. The Bharadars, a consultative body in the kingdom became the single most important organ in the process of decision-making of the states. They were the king's Councillors or Ministers and "together ran the administration, fought wars, manoeuvred diplomacy and concluded or broke peace and treaties in the name of king".[32]

In the beginning, the structure of Bharadars was hierarchical with loose definition of its function based on family. But the meeting usually comprised of all high government officials, elders of the national elite families. According to Hamilton, there were twelve or thirteen members of them; one Chautriyas, four Kazis, four Sirdars, two Subedars, one Kapardar and one Khazanchi.[33] Whereas Regmi writes that there were four Chautriyas, four Kazis and four Sirdars.[34] But numbers of Bharadars considerably increased in 1799, when Rana Bahadur Shah abdicated the throne in favour of his minor son Girwan Juddha. According to Copper Plate inscriptions of Rana Bahadur Shah, there were ninety five Bharadars in the Darbar.[35] The assent of the Bharadars on major policy issues was essential and winning their consent was a very delicate process in view of the factional rivalries. Hence, it was seldom possible for them to organise successful coalition government. Among them, there was constant struggle for power. The Darbar politics was largely conspiratorial in character and marked by an obvious proclivity for violence. Opposition was sometimes eliminated through assassination but not often by expulsion.[36] Besides, hill Brahmins elites who had dominated the Darbar, served both as support base for and as a check upon the royal and Bharadars. They fulfilled these functions without direct involvement in the politics. Their role as Guru or priests to the royal families gave them a fairly high position in the administrative decisions and they later monopolised the state legal system. The another section, Newar elites who managed the affairs of the Malla Darbar, were excluded from the Gorkha system. However, because of their economic and administrative skills, they were accommodated. It became the norm for Newars to hold a near monopoly on key second level position in the central administration and played important role in decision-making of the state. They were less conspicuous and thus appeared to be less threatening than the Bharadars families.[37]

The emergence of a new aristocracy and the hereditary monarchical system brought new complication and tensions in Nepali political life. And the most unfortunate was the division among the royal families. The King, having more than two wives, their respective sons and the collateral branches of the Shah family always tended to work at cross-purposes making manipulation of the royal family by some faction or the other, both possible and rewarding. The system was further complicated by the fact that a minor was on the throne from 1777 to 1847.[38] The process of the government during this period has been remarked as "were actually controlled by the regent and/or Mukhtiyar (Minister) and the alliance of political faction provided them with a support base".[39] The period also witnessed administrative malpractices and nepotism. The Bharadars were so divided among themselves and Maharaja being minor, that the country was at time on the verge of anarchy. Towards the end of eighteenth century, intense power struggle between the various factions characterised the central politics in the Darbar the scene being dominated alternatively by the Pandes and the Thapas.[40]

The rajyas to the west of Kathmandu with social and political structure akin to the Gorkhas were rapidly absorbed. Others were left with a measure of local autonomy as chiefdom. Unlike western hills, the eastern region was inhabitated by the tribal communities with ill-defined decentralised administrative system. Very little is known of the manner of their absorption by the Gorkha, but apparently they were left with a measure of autonomy considerably greater than those of other chiefdoms.[41]

The territorial expansion of the Gorkha kingdom and the transfer of capital to Kathmandu under central control, for the first time not only brought communities and territories with diverse political and social systems but also of new elite culture. A large number of families from Gorkhas established themselves in Kathmandu permanently and became leader at least in the beginning of the Shah Darbar. Other high caste families from other conquered rajyas soon followed suit and became part of new elite and, in course of time dominated the Shah Darbar. Thus the Gorkha conquest brought under central control for the first time, communities and territories ruled by desperate government based upon different economic and administrative system and social, political, cultural and political concepts—Hindu, Buddhist, Newar, Islamic and Kirati.[42]

However, the political unification of the country did not lead to the emergence of a nation in true sense. Prithvi Narayan Shah had, in far western hill areas, generally followed the policy of subjugating rajyas without actually annexing their territories. Some of them accepted the status of vassal under the Gorkhas.[43] Thus, the territorial expansions rather than consolidation of the areas, already brought under new regime, delayed the process of national integration. The political unification only created the basic territorial and political framework. Their administrative consolidation did not attract much attention. As a result, administrative divisions were made according to the boundaries of the displaced rajyas, thus, preserving the basis for old loyalties and centrifugal tendencies. And the communal and geographical divisions further remained unaffected due to the difficulties of transports and communications. While the process of unification was going on Prithvi Narayan Shah died in 1775.[44] He was succeeded by his son Sinha Pratap Shah to become the king of Nepal. During the minority of the king, the administration of the country was carried out in his name by his mother Queen, Rajendra Laxmi as regent. Immediately, the regent embarked upon to fulfil the dream of Prithvi Narayan Shah to unify the country. To achieve the objective, she had strengthemed Nepalese army and suppressed the rebellion of those who tooks advantages of the political instability of the state. She ruled for about nine years and died in 1786, and the regentship was passed on to Chautaria Bahadur Shah who returned from Betiah, India.[45] Bahadur Shah to strengthen his position in Darbar, immediately concluded a matrimonial alliance with the powerful Raja of Palpa. Then with the help of Bharadars, he was able to extend the Gorkha kingdom towards west after annexing Gulmi, Chandrakot, Khanchi, Arjunga, Adha, Baklung, Piuthan, Jumla, Accham, Doti, Surkhet, Dailekh and others. By 1790, the territories of the kingdom of Nepal reached up to river Mahakali in the west. To the south-west, the Nepali soldiers captured Almora and continue to proceed toward

Srinagar.[46] However, the Gorkhas had to divert its army to defend the northern frontier from the Chinese advance at Dhaibung. War broke out between the Gorkha and the Chinese on the issue of debased coins. However, there are diverse views regarding the cause of war. According to Chinese historian Wein Yuan, the cause was due to the Gorkha taking the plea of the increase of taxes on merchandise and admixture of dust on the table salt, send troops and invaded the frontier.[47] It was also recorded that the war broke out primarily because of currency. Traditionally, the Nepalese coin was considered legal tender in Tibet. During the last Malla king, the coins had become too debased which prompted Prithvi Narayan Shah to issue new pure currency with the view to develop trade. However, the Tibetan insisted that the exchange ratio of the new pure currency and the old debased coin must be at par which the Gorkha fairly refused.[48] According to Col. Kirkpatrick, "from ancient time Tibet and Nepal had close union. Pure Mahendra Mulli (Nepali coin) coinage of Nepal was current money in Tibet during the reign of Jai Prakash Malla, the Mahendra Mulli became much debase so when Nepal passed into Gorkhas, hand. Tibet was full of debase money...without any settlement and there was no transaction for a few years. So, many conferences were proposed by the Gorkhas, but the Tibetans turn deaf ear, nor the Nepalese were allowed to proceed for China to put their case before the Chinese Emperor. Thereupon, the hostilities began".[49] However, the real reason seems to be that the Gorkha found the quarrel over currency a good pretext to expand their kingdom and to raid the rich monasteries in Tibet.[50]

Till 1791, the Chinese Government did not interfere. This prompted the Gorkhas to attack Tibet on later's failure to pay annual tribute and also on the pretext of ill-treatment of the Nepalese traders by the Tibetan authority. The Gorkhas occupied the Kuti pass and looted the rich monastery of Digarche. It immediately aroused the enmity of the Chinese Emperor who dispatched huge force consisting of seventy thousand Chinese soldiers to punish the Gorkhas perpetrators. It was under this circumstances that Chauturia Bum Shah sought the British help against the Chinese. Lord Cornwallis, the then Governor General of the East India Company refused to give any military help but sent Col. Kirkpatrick to Nepal as a mediator. The later, however did not reach in time, but enable to extract a Commercial Treaty with Nepal on 1st March,

1791.[51] Yet the Treaty was not implemented due to stiff opposition from the king and the Bharadars.

In the meantime, Rana Bahadur Shah who attained the majority desired to take the reign of the administration of the kingdom in his own hands. The Bharadars were also disappointed with the attitude of the Regent and his pro-British policy. Thus with one stroke, Bahadur Shah was deposed and later imprisoned. Then the young Raja immediately constituted a new Bharadars to run the administration. He appointed Ranodhoj Shah as chief Chauturia and Bidur Shah as Chauturia. To help them, four Kazis were elected and among whom Damodar Pande was the most influential.[52] Notwithstanding the post of Chief Kazi was held by Kirtiman Basnet. These Kazis were to work under the direction of King and the Chauturias.[53]

Maharaja Rana Bahadur Shah soon manifested strange signs of royal eccentricity and was unpopular with the Brahmin faction in the Darbar. In 1797, Bahadur Shah died in prison which did not lessen the strength of the opposition faction against him. Further, the army remained largely under the influence of several Bharadars including Damodar Pande. The opposition to young Raja was greatly strengthened in 1798 when he openly excluded his eldest son Ranodhoj Shah by a high caste Chhetri wife from succession to the throne and established a heir apparent—his infant son Girwan Juddha by a Brahmin wife, a marriage which violated basic caste principle and shocked the Hindu elite of Nepal.[54] Rana Bahadur Shah was far from being conventional and conservative in his life and behaviour, causing grave offence to the Brahmin community. His marriage to Kantivati, the daughter of a Brahmin was considered illegal according to Hindu law. Such was the situation in the Darbar, and fearing the opposition from the Bharadars, Rana Bahadur Shah abdicated on 23rd March, 1799 and placed his son Girwan Juddha on the throne and appointed Maharani Rajyeswari as regent.[55] He then retired to Deopatan, a vicinity of Kathmandu along with his two Ranis. After abdication he became a Swami (Nirvananand). But the renunciation from politics lasted only for a few months and by Autumn of 1799, he again attempted to re-assert his authority against the Bharadars through the help of people. He even restored the priesthood of Tapleju temple to Pandit Amritananda Upadhya. Further, he directed the people of Laibu, Dhanchok and Thankot to proceed to Patan. When such situation developed, the Bharadars immediately shifted the young Maharaja to Nuwakot from where the administration of the state machinery was run.[56] Thus, twin government was established in Nepal. From Deopatan Swami Maharaja issued royal order to all military companies to safeguard the minor king against the obnoxious Bharadars. To counter such move, the Bharadars also issued instructions to all the military personnels in the name of young Maharaja not to obey the orders of the former and asked them to proceed to Nuwakot. Not only these, the regent Maharani had also issued an order to the Gorkha soldiers to be vigilant against the Bharadars.[57] A civil war seemed imminent until it became apparent that most of the army officials sided with Bharadars. Discretion suggested a temporary withdrawal from the political arena in Nepal for Swami Maharaja and his supporters. Perplexed by the intrigues, on 1st May, 1800, Swami Maharaja set out for Banaras (India) with a retinue including his uncle Bal Bhadra Shah, Bhim Sen Thapa, Rangnath Pandit, Dalbhanjan Pande, Balhnar Singh Kanwar and others. He was also accompanied by his Queen Rajyeswari[58].

Swami Maharaja's presence in India where he could both serve as focus for dissident factions and bargain the British authority for restoration of power was an awesome to the security of the regime in Kathmandu.[59] This situation was considered by the British as an excellent opportunity for furtherance of political and commercial interest of the company. A British military official Capt. Knox was accordingly deputed to Banaras to wait upon the arrival of Swami Maharaja and to offer his service as a mediator in the latter's dispute with the Bharadars. The Ex-Maharaja's principle objective in the complicated intrigue that ensued was to re-assert his authority in Nepal and punish the Bharadars who had forced him to exile in India. On 6th November, 1800, Swami Maharaja proposed to the British agent if the British agreed to restore his throne, he would pay to the company 37/½ per cent of the revenue derived from the hill and 50 per cent from Tarai.[60] Such proposal though profitable to the company was not acceptable as it would obligate the latter to guarantee the Shah dynasty in future. Rather, the Company would help the ex-Maharaja to restore his authority in Kathmandu on condition that the latter had to concede a trading post at Kathmandu for commercial purpose.[61] Swami Maharaja immediately consulted Bhim Sen Thapa who categorically rejected such proposal. The failure on the part of the British to extract favourable concession from the exiled Maharaja, they turned towards the Kathmandu Darbar. It was concluded that it was preferable to pressurise the *de facto* government in Nepal into an agreement than to undertake the task of restoring exiled Raja to an insecure throne over the objection of the powerful elements in Kathmandu. Meanwhile, in Kathmandu, Damodar Pande and other influential Bharadars were also busy in manoeuvre to keep the ex-Raja and his supporters permanently in India and firmly establish their position in the Darbar. To fulfil this objective, a negotiation was concluded between the representatives of Nepal and the British at Patna. On 26th October, 1801, a treaty of Commerce and Alliance was accordingly signed.[62] It was however, of a political nature. The most controversial clause of the treaty for Nepal was the provision allowing establishment of a British Residency at Kathmandu. A hot discussion on this subject erupted almost immediately after the appearance of Resident Capt. Knox in the capital.[63]

Meanwhile, the political setting of Nepal was taking a dramatic turn. The administration was in the hands of the weak and feeble junior Maharani which gave an opportunity to all contending factions to conspire against each other. Taking advantage of the political instability in the Darbar, the ex-Raja immediately ordered Rani Rajyalaxmi to proceed to Kathmandu. She was clearly instructed with utmost caution to dissolve the recent concluded treaty with the British. She was, however, compelled to camp at the border village. In the meantime, chief Kazi Kirtiman Basnet and other Kazis were assassinated and Damodar Pande was suspected of it.[64] In February, the junior Maharani fled from the Darbar and Maharani Rajyeswari assumed the regency of the minor Raja and Damodar Pande was appointed as Chief Kazi. Within a short span of time, the new regent ordered to pay off all the dues to the Company for the allowances of the ex-Maharaja. The attitude of the Bharadars was neither friendly toward the British. The political development in the kingdom led Capt. Knox to conclude that he was *persona non-grata* and should better leave the country before the situation turned worse. This suspension of diplomatic contacts did not have salutary effect as expected and the Governor General Lord Wellesley formally abrogated the treaty of 1801 on 24th January, 1804.[65] It was decided that the ex-Raja be left at liberty to return to Nepal unconditionally. In the following month, ex-Raja Swami Rana Bahadur Shah prepared for Kathmandu with his followers. Damodar Pande after receiving the news of such movement, immediately sent troops to prevent latter's entry into Nepal. However, the army who were deployed turned in favour of the ex-Raja and Damodar Pande was arrested. Then, Rana Bahadur Shah took the charge of administration as Mukhtiyar.** The regency was also taken away from Maharani Rajyalaxmi and Bhim Sen Thapa was made one of the Kazi.[66]

The brief period of Rana Bahadur Shah's Muktiarship had important development in the internal and external politics. He was the first royal member in the Shah dynasty who had surrendered his position as a king and worked for his minor son Girwan Juddha as Mukhtiyar. It was his policy to prevent the British influence in the Darbar which resulted in an anti-British sentiment among the Bharadars. While he was in Banaras, he saw one native state after another entered into Subsidiary Alliance, surrendering their independence. Since the abrupt termination of relations with the British, he feared that the former would play any kind of intrigue or even wage a war against Nepal to establish its influence.[67]

Once he assumed the power in his minor son's name, he immediately paid attention to strengthen the Nepalese army. He also clearly perceived that his remaining in power solely depended on the support of the soldiers. However, the greatest obstacle to strengthen Nepalese military capacity was the country's limited financial resources. Since there was no other alternative, he reluctantly proposed the confiscation of Birta land. It was recorded that abundant lands were awarded to the Brahmins as well as for religious purpose, i.e., Guthi. In search for new sources of revenue, the system under which rent-free land grant (Kusa-Birta) had been given to Brahmins, was modified and these lands were either expropriated by the state or brought within the ambit of the taxation system. In fact, the Birta was awarded to the Kazis, Sirdars and other military officials in lieu of emoluments. He clearly understood the negative impact of the confiscation of Birta-extended to these officials. Hence, he was compelled to take such measure against the Brahmins. This episode is known as "Baisathi Haran" in the history of Nepal.

Meanwhile, the death of Damodar Pande, imprisonment of Prithipal Sen and increasing influence of the Thapas in the Darbar led to the factional rivalries. The anti-Mukhtiar politics led by Sher Bahadur Shah (illegitimate brother of Rana Bahadur) hatched a conspiracy against the Mukhtiyar. The Darbar remained explosive. The Mukhtiar's efforts to use the newly acquired authority against his enemies, however, culminated in his own assassination in April 1806.[68] In the crisis that followed, Kazi Bhim Sen Thapa effectively removed the leaders of opposition actions. It was estimated that around fifty to fifty-five officials were either murdered or executed at the aftermath of the incident.[69] Bhim Sen Thapa became the master of the situation and the Thapa family emerged as the most dominant political faction in the Darbar. With the rise of Bhim Sen Thapa to power, began another epoch in the political history of Nepal.

Notes

1. Thapa, D.P. and Thapa, N.B., *Geography of Nepal,* Calcutta (1969), pp. 1-15; Bose, S.C., *Geography of Himalayas,* New Delhi (1984), pp. 153-173; Hodgson, B.H., *"On Physical Geography of Himalaya",* Journal of Asiatic Society of Bengal, (1849), pp. 761-781; Mason, K., *A Note on the Nepal Himalaya,* Historical Journal (1934); Karan P.P. and Jenkins, J.W., *The Himalayan Kingdom—Bhutan Sikkim and Nepal,* Princeton (1963) pp. 79-88.
2. Guiseppe, Father, *An Account of the Kingdom of Nepal,* Asiatic Researches, Vol. II (1799) p. 309. et. seq.
3. Pradhan, K.L., *Brian Hodgson at the Kathmandu Darbar,* New Delhi, (2001 BS) p. 1. Hunter, W.W., *Imperial Gazetteer,* Vol. XIX, Oxford. (1896).
4. Bista, D.B., *People of Nepal, Kathmandu,* 1967, pp. 1-45.
5. *Ibid.,* Sinha, A.C., *Studies in the Himalayan Communities,* New Delhi (1984), pp. 2-4.
6. Rose, Leo E., and Scholz, T., *Nepal Profile of Himalayan Kingdom,* New Delhi (1980) p. 71.
7. *Ibid.,* pp. 72-73; Also see Singh. *Iman, Kirat Itihas, Sikkim,* (1952) p. 72; Bajracharya, D. *Licchavi Abhilekh, Nepal,* (n.d.) p. 419.; Rahul Ram, *The Himalayan Borderland,* New Delhi (1970).
8. Hasrat, Bikramjit, *History of Nepal. Punjab* (1971), pp. 134-143; Regmi D.R., *Modern Nepal, Calcutta* (1961), pp. 1-42.

9. Stiller, F. Ludwig, *The Rise of the House of the Gorkha,* Patna (1973), pp. 1-50. Regmi D.R. *op. cit.,* pp. 1-42, Hasrat B.S. *op. cit.,* 134-143.
10. Rose and Scholz, *op. cit.,* p. 9, Regmi, M.C. *A Study of Nepali Economic History,* New Delhi (1971) pp. 1-14.; Faige, F.H. *Regionalism and Nationalism Unity in Nepal,* California (1975).
11. Basnet, L.B., *"Nepalese or Gorkha",* A pamphlet, Sikkim (n.d.) p. 247.
12. Pandey, R.N., *"A Short History of Doti State, Western Nepal",* Nepal Review (1969), p. 247.
13. Stiller, F. Ludwig, *op. cit.,* 45.
14. Tucker, Sir Francis, *Gorkhas, the story of the Gorkha in Nepal,* London (1957), p. 20.
15. Regmi D.R. *op. cit., 49;* Karki, Y. Singh. *Biswas Parichaye,* Kathmandu, (2031 BS), p. 107. Kirkpatrick, W., *An Account of the Kingdom of Nepal,* London (1911).
16. Hamilton, Francis, *An Account of the Kingdom of Nepal,* Edinburgh (1819) p. 106; Joshi, Bhawan Lal and Rose, Leo E., *Democratic Innovation in Nepal,* California (1966) p. 5.; Shah, Rishikesh, *Nepali Politics: Retrospect and Prospect,* Delhi (1975), p. 49.
17. Regmi, M.C., *op. cit.,* p. 4.
18. Chenjong, I. Singh, *Kirat Kalin Bijayapur,* Kathmandu (2023 BS); Pande, A.R. *Bhim Sen Thapa Kalma Nepal,* Kathmandu (2037 BS) unpublished, pp. 1-14.
19. *Ibid.;* Regmi, M.C. *op. cit.,* p. 4.
20. *Ibid.*
21. Chatterjee, Bhola, *Recent Nepalese Politics,* Calcutta (1967) pp. 14-15: Yogi, N. Nath *Gorkha Vamsawali,* Banaras (1964), pp. 95-113.
22. *Ibid.*
23. Tucker, Sir Francis, *op. cit.,* pp. 44-48.
24. Stiller, E. Ludwig, *op. cit.,* p. 27: Pant, N. Raj and others, *Prithvi Narayan Shah ko Upadesh,* Kathmandu (2025 BS), pp. 726-27.
25. *Ibid.,* pp. 973-974; Tiwari, Ramji (ed.) *Aitihasik Patra Sangraha,* Part-II, Kathmandu (2021 BS), pp. 79-82.
26. Regmi, M.C., *op. cit.,* p. 7.
27. *Ibid.,* p. 8: Thapa, S.B. *op. cit.,* pp. 15-16.
28. Stiller, FLudwig, *The Silent Cry: The People of Nepal,* Kathmandu (1976), p. 165: Shrestha, M.K., *A Handbook of Public Administration in Nepal,* Kathmandu (1965) pp. 1-3.

29. Pradhan, K.L., *op. cit.*, p. 4.
30. Manadhar, T. and Baid, T.R., *Crimes and Punishments in Nepal,* Kathmandu (1985), pp. 122-123: Bajracharya, D. and Shrestha, *op. cit.*, pp. 141-147.
 * 'Thar Ghar' denotes Influential Persons of six High Caste.
31. Rose, Leo E. and Scholz, *T. op. cit.*, p. 21.: Adhikari, *op. cit.*, p. 19.
32. Regmi, D.R., Vol. II, *op. cit.*, p. 279.
33. Hamilton, E, *op. cit.*, pp. 108-109: Krikpatrick, W., *op. cit.*, pp. 197 and 203.
35. Nepali, C.R. *General Bhim Sen Thapa ra Tatkalin Nepal,* Kathmandu (2013 BS) pp. 118-123.
36. Pradhan, K.L., *op. cit.*, p. 7.
37. *Ibid.*
38. Shrestha, M.K. *op. cit.*, pp. 2-3.
39. Rose, Leo E., and Scholz, T. *op. cit.*, p. 22.
40. *Ibid.*: Malla, Govind, *Prajatantra ko Produrbhau,* Kathmandu (1976) p. 220.
41. Stiller, E. Ludwig, *op. cit.*, p. 44.: Regmi, D.R., *op. cit.*, pp. 60-62.
42. Regmi, M.C., *op. cit.*, p. 12.
43. Yogi, N. Nath, *Itihas Prakashma Sandhipatra Sangraha,* Banaras (1960) p. 4.
44. Shrestha, Hariyal, *Naya Nepal Parichaye,* Kathmandu (2035 BS) pp. 83-84.
45. Nepali, C.R., "*Chautariya Bahadur Shah ko Nayaki Kal,*" Sharada Issue No. 1 (2014 BS) and *Rana Bahadur Shah,* Kathmandu (2057 BS), pp. 1-19.
46. Regmi, M.C. *op. cit.*, pp. 10-11.
47. Tucker, Sir Francis, *op. cit.*, p. 58.
48. Kirkpatrick, W. *op. cit.*, p. 338.
49. *Ibid.*
50. Chaudhuri, K.C., *Anglo-Nepalese Relations from the Earliest Times of the British Rule in India till the Gurkha War,* Calcutta (1960) p. 65: Schulyer, Camman, *Trade through Himalayas,* Princeton (1951), p. 113.
51. Aitchison, C.U., *A Collection of Treaties, Engagement and Sunnads Relating to Indian and Neighbouring Countries,* Vol. II, Calcutta (1906), pp. 103-105, also see Appendix-A.
52. Chaudhuri, K.C. *op. cit.*, pp. 101-105: Ramakant, *Indo-Nepalese Relations,* New Delhi (1968), p. 13.
53. Nepali, C.R., *op. cit.*, pp. 118-123. The instructions read us

"During the king's minority all should live in harmony. They should conceal no plot. They would work together with good hearts. Unless prevented by illness, all should be present at one court to conduct business. Except in consultation together they should not conduct any kind of business with other persons. Let them not say there is work, or that they are not well, when they are well, and telling such lies stay at home. Let them seek advice from the military caste on military matters only, but in other matters let them take advice of other people. Put wise counsellors in the Court. Let them be industrious. Whatever work must be done, let it be done quickly once it has been understood. Whatever happens, in improving the Country, increasing income and strengthening the country, listen to the simple people also and carry out any necessary requests they make".

54. Jain, M.S. *Emergence of New Aristocracy in Nepal,* Agra (1972) pp. 2-3 *et.seq.:* Bhandari, D.R., *Nepal ko Aitihasik Vivechana, Banaras,* (1959) p. 209.
55. Nepali, C.R., *op. cit.,* pp. 1-19.
56. *Ibid.*
57. Pande, A.R., *op. cit.,* pp. 20-21,
58. *Itihas Prakash,* Vol., pp. 64-65: Ramakant. *op. cit.,* p. 13 *et.seq.*
59. *Ibid.,* also Rose, Leo E. *op. cit.,* p. 72.
60. *Ibid.,* p. 78.
61. Aitchison, C.V., *Op. cit.,* pp. 105-108. *See* Appendix-B, Stiller, F.L., *op. cit.,* p. 230. Hunter, W.W., Life *of Brian Hodgson,* London (1896), p. 9.
62. Nepali, C.R., *op. cit.,* p. 56. Oldfield, *op. cit.,* p. 287.
63. Dungel, Gyarav., *op. cit.,* p. 21, Ramakant. *op. cit.,* p. 15.
64. *Ibid.,* also see Dhanlaxmi R. *British Attitude to Nepal's Relations with Tibet, China, New Delhi* (1981) p. 25; Tyagi, S., *Indo-Nepalese Relations,* Delhi (1974), p. 49.
65. Nepali, C.R., *op. cit.,* pp. 10-12.
66. Landon, P., *Nepal 2 Vols. Kathmandu* (1976 Reprint), pp. 82.
67. Oldfield, *op. cit.,* p. 303; Nepali, C.R., *op. cit.,* pp. 74-76.
68. Shrestha, S., *op. cit.,* pp. 31-34; Ramakant, *op. cit.,* pp. 17.
69. Dungel, G., *op. cit.,* p. 23.

** Lal Mohur appointing Rana Bahadur Shah as Mukhtiyar Quoted in Nepali, C.R. *op. cit.,* p. 180. Appendix-I.

II

Bhim Sen Thapa: Early Life and Career

Lives of great persons are ever inspiring. Their lives are full of confusions, hardships and struggles. Like the maxim 'morning shows the day to come', sign of ample talents are visible even during their childhood. Family environment is the first foundation for progress of those great personalities who contributed in national building. Liberal thinking and ambitions are fostered in family environment. The feeling of nationalism is germinated at a very tender age in the mind of worthy son of a nation.[1]

The first ever person to become Mukhtiyar from outside the royal family in the history of Nepal was Bhim Sen Thapa. His activities, right from his childhood indicate that he was endowed with unsurpassable talents, and sharp intelligence. In fact, historians have not chronicled his true life at all. It is surprising to note that no research scholar has taken any interest on this aspect of Bhim Sen Thapa's life. Foreign historians are keen to reproduce Nepal under Bhim Sen Thapa's rule while Nepali historians have become egoistic of his achievements leaving many informations undugged. History should aspire to sketch actual events, informations and facts and interpret in the context of history. Only then the hidden facts will be revealed which in true could enlighten future generations.[2]

The Hindu Puranas have classified mankind into four castes—Brahmin, Kshatriya, Vaisya and Sudra, Their nature of works are distributed accordingly. The Brahmins perform the religious rites and also acted as advisors and preceptors to the king. The duty of Kshatriya is to defend and rule the country. On the basis of such tradition, the Kshatriyas are still ruling Nepal. Nepal is a country inhabitated by the Rajput Kshatriyas who fled from India due to the Muslim invasion. Among them Kshatriya Khas is also included, who ruled Karnali region and several of the Baisi and Chaubisi rajyas. A very interesting feature that had permanent effect on the society of that particular area and later on the whole of Nepal was the introduction of the caste system. As such, the supremacy of the Brahmins and the Kshatriyas in the political and social arena have perpetuated for ages. They not only occupied high posts in civil and military administration but also at village levels. Till date, the Jimmawals, Mukhiyas, Talukdars and Amalis either belong to Kshatriyas or Brahmin castes.[3]

Before we analyse the role played by the Thapas in Nepali politics, particularly of Bhim Sen Thapa, it is imperative to find out who these Thapas were. When Prithvi Narayan Shah undertook the task of unification of the kingdom of Nepal, the Bharadars from different caste like, Pande, Basnet, Rana, Pant, Arjal and Bohra known as 'Thar Garh" played dominant role, for its success.[4] Although the Thapas were excluded from this, they played significant role in the process of on going unification. These Thapas primarily belonged to the Khas Chhetri and Magar Thapa.[5] Their appearance could be traced in the Karnali region when the Malla kingdom was firmly established under Prithvi Malla in 1413 AD. They were skilled and abled soldiers and it was not difficult for them to get employment and in course of time were appointed as sardars. The disintegration of Karnali kingdom after the death of Abhaya Malla and subsequent establishment of Baisi rajya did not effect them from occupying the posts of Bharadars.[6]

While one section of the Thapa settled in the Baisi valley, another section of the Thapas migrated towards the east. They were readily employed in the recently established Chaubasi rajyas, Malla kingdoms of Kathmandu valley and the Sen kingdom of Bijaypur in the east. In 1703, when the king of Bhaktapur Bhupatindra Malla and Kantipur king Bhaskar Malla concluded a peace and friendship treaty, Bir Bhadra Thapa and Damodar Thapa stood as witnesses. Gradually, other Thapas also occupied the prestigious posts in the Malla Darbar and *Bijayapur* Darbar.[7]

In 1559, when Drabya Shah established the Shah Kingdom in Gorkha, he got support from the "Thar Garh". As already stated, the Thapas like Basnets were not included in the above category.[8] However, like the Basnet, the Thapas also got entry into the Shah Darbar during Prithvi Narayan Shah, whereas the Thapas became powerful faction in the Darbar of Rana Bahadur Shah. These Thapas were Khas Thapa and Magar Thapa. During Narbhupal Shah (1638-1685) numbers of Thapa Bharadars were listed.

Within the Khas Thapa, there are, Godar, Bagale, Thakuryal, Deoja and others. According to Gorkha chronicles, the Bagale Thapa became prominent when they lived in Jumla.[9] Later on they proceeded towards east. However, according to available documents and records, Bhim Sen Thapa's ancestor could be traced from Bir Bhadra Thapa's time. The documents further ascertained that when Prithvi Narayan Shah started the process of unification of Nepal, under his banner, Bir Bhadra Thapa played an important role. He was the leading Bharadars when Nuwakot was annexed to Gorkha kingdom in 1744. There are ample evidence of his services under Prithvi Narayan Shah.[10]

Bir Bhadra Thapa had three sons—Jiwan Thapa, Bangsaraj Thapa, and Amar Singh Thapa. The eldest son Jiwan Thapa died in 1757 in the Kirtipur battle with Kalu Pande.[11] The youngest son Amar Singh Thapa led many battles against the independent principalities within Nepal and also against the Tibet. In 1759, he was elevated to the post of Sardar in the Shah army. Amar Singh Thapa had five sons and all of them had contributed one way or other in the political history of Nepal. When his eldest son Bhim Sen Thapa became the Mukhtiyar of Nepal in 1806 he was posted at Palpa as administrator.[12]

It has become a matter of serious study as how an ordinary person like Bhim Sen Thapa, who was not within the ambit of privileged sub-caste, could hold the highest post in the Shah kingdom. Before we discuss his contributions and achievement during 31 years of uninterrupted rule, it is pertinent to trace his early life.[13] According to documents available in the National Archives, Kathmandu shows that Bhim Sen Thapa was born in August 1775 at Pipal Thok.[14] His mother's name was Satyarupa Maya. However, most of Nepali historians have claimed that he was born at Borling, Gorkha No. II which is one day journey from Gorkha Darbar. The following story gathered from the native inhabitants clearly shows that he was indeed born at Pipal Thok. The statement is further supported by various traditions and the remains of old building.[15] In 1831, at the peak of his power he constructed a water spring near Raniban which still exists. His father also erected a 'Bhimsen Temple' at the same place. The

Temple bell donated by Bhim Sen Thapa can still be seen. The young prince Rana Bahadur Shah visited Gorkha in 1785 in connection of investiture with the sacred thread ceremony. It was at this time that Bhim Sen Thapa met the young prince and cemented a bond of friendship which lasted many years to come[16].

Bhim Sen's early childhood is still shrouded in mystery. Since no written documents are available, one has to rely on the tradition of the period. According to it, Bhim Sen did not enjoyed luxury of lift. His father, Amar Singh Thapa was Sardar in the Shah army and had to move from one place to another. As an eldest son, he had to support his mother in all domestic works as well as to look after his brothers. As a result of this, he did not receive any formal education. However, he might have received basic education at home through tutor. In those days, the privileged classes used to engage Brahmins to educate their offspring at home, and generally they were taught Sanskrit. In spite of this, one can find all the qualities of a great and abled man in his life. He appears to be clever, farsighted, politically conscious and diplomatic on practical life.[17]

According to the Gorkha Vamsawali, Bhim Sen Thapa had four brothers—Nain Singh, Bhaktawar Singh, Amrit Singh and Ranbir Singh. And from his step-mother, he had two brothers—Ranbam and Ranzawar. All of them contributed distinguished services in the process of expansion and consolidation of the kingdom. Due to lack of any records or documents, it is very difficult to ascertain when did Bhim Sen Thapa entered into matrimony. Some historians argue that he had two wives and a concubine, whereas Samsher Bahadur Thapa claims that he had only one wife.[18] The stone inscription at Bhimbiswar Mahadev Temple situated at Bungkot testifies that Bhim Sen Thapa had indeed three wives. From them he had one son who died at the tender age in 1796 and three daughters, married accordingly as Lalita Devi to Uday Bahadur, Janak Kumari to Samser Bahadur and Dhirga Kumari to Dal Bahadur Pande. In spite of this, he felt emptiness within because of lack of his own son. To fill the void caused by the death of his only son, he adopted his brother Nain Singh's son Sher Jung Thapa.[19]

In 1798, his father Amar Singh Thapa took him to Kathmandu and enrolled him as Maharaja Rana Bahadur Shah's bodyguard. Since then he lived at Thapathali.[20] In 1804, when he was appointed to the post of Kazi, he shifted his Residence to Bag Darbar near Tuddikhel. From here, he carried on the administration of the kingdom till 1837 when he was removed from the Mukhtiyarship. Although the Thapas did appear in the Gorkha Darbar during Prithvi Narayan Shah's rule and before him, their uninterrupted rising can be attributed from the time of Rana Bahadur Shah. and the progress and development made by them could be counted from Bhim Sen Thapa.[21]

From the beginning, Bhim Sen Thapa was loyal to the king and the country. As the intimacy grew more and more, Bhim Sen became most trusted person of the young king. In spite of all adversaries that befell on Rana Bahadur Shah, he never deserted him. He was always with his benefactor. When Rana Bahadur Shah abdicated his throne to his minor son Girwan Juddha, Bhim Sen Thapa accompanied him in his exile at Banaras.[22] Here, in Banaras, Bhim Sen Thapa got an opportunity to study in depth, the Indian native states and the growing powers of the East India Company and their motives. An English writer remarks on Bhim Sen Thapa that "he was the first Nepalese statesman who grasped the meaning of the system of protectorate which Lord Wellesley had carried out in India. He saw one native state after another came within the net of British Subsidiary Alliance and his policy was steadily directed to save Nepal from similar fate".[23] Alarmed with such development, Bhim Sen Thapa had vigorously pressed Rana Bahadur to return to Nepal and take the reign of power in his own hands.[24]

Meanwhile, political development in Kathmandu turned more complex. The administration of the kingdom was in the hands of the junior Maharani which gave an opportunity to all contending factions to conspire against each other. The situation became worse when a numbers of Kazi, including one of the Regent's most favourite, Kazi Kirtiman Basnet was assassinated and the Pande faction led by Damodar Pande was suspected for it. Damodar Pande was made the chief Kazi. After gaining considerable power, he tried to establish pro-British policy and sought to keep ex-raja Rana Bahadur under British surveillance at Banaras. In 1801, he had concluded a Treaty of friendship with the East India Company which was purely political in nature. The chief Kazi promised to fulfil the clauses and welcome the first British Resident, Captain Knox in the Darbar. In 1803, Maharani Rajeshwari returned to

Kathmandu at the instance of ex-Raja and assumed the post of regent of the minor king.[25] She closely studied the prevailing political situation and found that almost all the Bharadars were against the Treaty of 1801 and the arrival of the British Resident in Kathmandu. Further, anti-British feelings were openly displayed.

While such political development in Kathmandu was gaining ground, Bhim Sen Thapa was secretly working to get support from the Bharadars. He maintained a close contact with Sher Bahadur Shah, Bidur Shah, Bhaktawar Singh and others through letters. He even employed spies to get informations from the Darbars. He called his father, Amar Singh Thapa from Kumaon for his advise.[26] By now, ex-raja Rana Bahadur Shah clearly perceived the situation and the conspiracy of the Bharadars in the Darbar and motives of the East India Company. Fortunately, at Kathmandu Darbar, a heated dispute on the subject of permanent British Residency erupted. As the man held responsible for the Treaty, Damodar Pande's position was severely undermined and his supporters deserted him in large numbers to the side of Rana Bahadur Shah. The Darbar's opposition to the issue had become so bitter by March, that Capt. Knox decided to return to India. The suspension of diplomatic ties did not have salutary effects as expected and Lord Wellesley finally abrogated the Treaty on 24th January, 1804. The Governor General further resolved that the ex-raja Rana Bahadur Shah should be freed to return to Nepal unconditionally. He, along with his followers, immediately repaired for Kathmandu.[27] They reached at the outskirts of the capital—Thankote where Damodar Pande and his troops tried to prevent the entry of ex-raja to Kathmandu. With sheer diplomacy, Bhim Sen Thapa managed to draw all the troops in ex-raja's favour and Damodar Pande was arrested on the spot.[28] Then Rana Bahadur Shah took the reign of power in his own hands and became the first Mukhtiyar from the royal family departing from the usual tradition. Bhim Sen Thapa was awarded the post of Kazi in the Darbar in 1804.[29] In this context, Baburam Acharya has remarked, thus "... when a new Bharadari was being constituted Ranodhoj Shah, Sher Bahadur Shah, Pran Shah and Bum Shah were appointed as the 1st, 2nd, 3rd and 4th Chautaryas, respectively. Bhim Sen Thapa could have become the chief Kazi then, as whole process of overhauling was carried out on Bhim Sen Thapa and Sher Bahadur Shah's consideration. But he (Bhim Sen Thapa) did not wish to be elevated to the post of chief Kazi outright. So he remained 2nd Kazi appointing his brother's father-in-law Ranjit Pande, who could be used as a puppet, as the chief Kazi. Bhim Sen Thapa enlisted themselves in the same rank and pay. He consolidated his position by including Amar Singh Thapa (elder) and his sons in the Thapa caucus".[30]

The above facts project Bhim Sen Thapa as a person of complex personality. Did he really become 2nd Kazi but not Chief Kazi after Ran Bahadur Shah took the reign of power in his hands? Was he only pre-occupied with maintaining monopoly in Bharadari by his family members and relatives? Were Sher Bahadur Shah and Bhim Sen Thapa the complete authority in over-hauling of Bharadars? It seems it was essential on the part of Bhim Sen Thapa to consolidate his position so as to guard himself from rival factions. Contemporary politics was full of rivalries and conspiracies, whoever could grasp opportunity, became powerful. But valid written documents about Bhim Sen Thapa serving as 2nd Kazi, is found nowhere. It is possible that he wanted to show himself aloof from active role in politics appointing his relatives as Kazis to serve his purpose. While these events indicate his shrewdness, it also project him as narrow minded. The Lal Mohur granting him power in 1804 A.D. do not prove he being the second Kazi.[31]

During the brief period of Rana Bahadur Shah's Mukhtiyarship, Bhim Sen Thapa manipulated the policy of the Darbar to strengthen Nepal army. In 1805, he suggested, to confiscate the Birta. Survey regulations promulgated for this area i.e. Kathmandu valley in 1805 refer to land confiscated from Brahmins, Sanyasis Khas and other communities. According to the order issued by King Girwan Juddha in 1804: "After we entered Nepal i.e. Kathmandu valley our great-grand father (i.e. Prithvi Narayan Shah) scrutinised Guthi land endowments made by the Malla kings, abolished those that were to be abolished, and confirmed those that were to be confirmed".[32] During 1805-06, the requirement of military campaign undertaken in Jamuna-Sutlej region forced to take such drastic measures. While confiscating the Birta land instructions issued as:

1. All land grants made by former kings as well as by their queens and crown prince shall be confirmed, provided they had accepted Kathmandu's sovereignty and had not

been displaced. But the area in excess of the figures mentioned in the grant shall be confiscated.

2. Land grants made without royal authority by officials deputed from Kathmandu shall be abolished.
3. In case documentary evidence of title is not available and the adjoining landowners have no knowledge of either the donor or the beneficiary, the land shall be confiscated.
4. Even in case documentary evidence of grant is not available, land shall not be confiscated if the adjoining landowner takes oath that the grant was authentic.[33]

Lands granted as Birta in the eastern Tarai during the self-imposed exile of ex-king Rana Bahadur Shah from May 1800 to January 1804 were all confiscated.

On the basis of above, Rana Bahadur Shah confiscated the Birta lands belonging to Brahmins and land allotted to religious guthi. Those who were reluctant to surrender their Birta, forces were used against them.[34] This episode is known as "Baisathi Haran" in the history of Nepal. Some historians allege that such action of Rana Bahadur Shah was an act of insane. Bal Chandra Sharma in his 'Nepal ko Aitihasik Rup Rekha' writes that the incident was due to the death of queen Kantivati whom he loved dearly and executed it before he left for Banaras on exile.[35] Oldfield also wrongly states that birta confiscation was carried out in 1814-16 during Anglo-Gorkha war by Bhim Sen Thapa to meet war expenditures.[36] Both the explanations are flawed. However, it is true that the Birta confiscation made the Mukhtiyar Rana Bahadur Shah unpopular with the Brahmins and his close relatives.

The growing popularity of Thapa faction under the leadership of Bhim Sen Thapa was not welcomed by the opposition led by Sher Bahadur Shah. The latter in connivance with rival faction hatch a conspiracy against Rana Bahadur Shah to oust him from power. Bhim Sen Thapa secretly learnt about it. To obliterate the opposition move, Mukhtiyar summoned Sher Bahadur Shah, his half-brother and his supporters. When the latter refused to comply with Rana Bahadur to proceed to the war front, an order was issued to arrest him on the ground of anti-government stance. Then ensued a scuffle in which Mukhtiyar Rana Bahadur was assassinated by Sher Bahadur Shah in 1806.[37] The latter was immediately killed by Bal Narshing Kanwar, the father of Jung Bahadur

Rana. In the crisis that followed, Bhim Sen Thapa, one of the closest of the Mukhtiyar acted quickly and effectively removed the opposition faction. Around fifty-five men were either murdered or executed in the aftermath of the assassination, and the Thapa family emerged as the dominant faction in the Darbar.[38] Rana Bahadur had two surviving widows—Swarna Prabha who performed sati immediately after her husband's death and Rajeswari Devi the eldest queen who had been imprisoned at Helambu, was forced to perform sati on the 9th day after the death of Rana Bahadur. Lalit Tripura Sundari is called 'Pattraggi' and not 'Pattarani' because she married to a ruler who had renounced kingdom.[39] Rana Bahadur Shah was persuaded to marry Tripura Sundari with a view to solve próblem of Regency. Maharaja Girwan Juddha Bikram Shah then immediately appointed Maharani Tripura Sundari as a regent and Bhim Sen Thapa the Mukhtiyar. The royal orders were issued in this effect ordering that all Chautariyas, Gurus, Purohits, the civil and military officials would henceforth follow the instructions given to them in his (king) name by the Mukhtiyar. In case of non-compliance of the orders, Bhim Sen Thapa was given free hand to pur.ish the person according to the nature of crimes.[40]

This is the first incident of its kind that a non-royal family member had occupied the highest post of civil and military administration of the country. Once he was bestowed with the power, Bhim Sen Thapa immediately transferred old and influential Bharadars to far-flung areas in the west and east of the kingdom. And in their places, loyal Bharadars and his close relatives were appointed. The institution of Bharadar, once powerful consultative body, now become a mere 'yes men' body. Their counsel and advise were unaccountable. He also appointed his father Amar Singh Thapa as administrator of Palpa. In 1811, he was appointed General.[41]

It was important for the new Mukhtiyar to understand the fact that Gorkhas led continuous career of fighting ever since their advent in the central Himalayas. Military became their profession and cherished social value. It became necessary for each and every Bharadars to appease the soldiers so as to stay in power. It is a fact that for the last few generations, king had been minor and the real power was in the hands of Mukhtiyars. Each contending faction tried to secure this coveted post and control the army which necessitated keeping them in good humour. Bhim Sen Thapa, indeed, clearly perceived that his position in the Darbar could only be secured if he maintained good rapport with the army.[42] At the same time, he apprehended that the British in India would invade Nepal on slightest pretext to extend their influence in Nepal and beyond its frontiers. These internal imperatives and external pressures drove him towards a martial expansionist policy of expansion, he immediately set out to consolidate his position by reorganising the Nepalese army on the line of European military system.[43] As already stated, the economic condition of Nepal in the beginning of 19th century was on the verge of collapse due to royal family feud, instability of the government and very low return of the revenue collections. It was reported that the Government had to collect revenues in advance. In such circumstances, it was seldom possible for new Mukhtiyar to maintain strong and huge regular army or increase any new battalion. Thus the accumulation of funds from the Birta confiscation in 1805 were solely utilised for reorganisation and development of the army.[44] The Gorkha army consisted of two sections—bhara and jhara. Bhara denoted regular troop who were recompensed through jagir land grants and cash salaries, Jhara referred to irregular conscripts who did not receive any remuneration.

To train the Nepalese army on the line of modem warfare and tactics, Bhim Sen Thapa secretly engaged the French military officials. The code of conducts were imparted on European system and their dresses were also similar to that of the French army. He also introduced the different ranks and files in the army. Not only he reorganised the existing system but made it more attractive jobs to the youth to join the army by increasing various facilities. Well furnished barracks and Jhara (porter) were also provided to carry their amenities, in times of war or peace.[45] The post-unification period witnessed a great demand on the part of the Government for labour service. The expanding size of the kingdom and its continuous military expeditions necessitated the transportation of military and other equipments over long distances. There was an increased demand for labour in the production of munition as well as the constructions, repairs and maintenance of forts, roads and bridges. The Government, therefore, found it expedient to fulfil its labour needs on a compulsory bases.[46] All the adult males of all castes appears to have been under obligation to render compulsory and unpaid labour service to the state. Exemption was granted only through royal order. Apart from this, exemptions were granted to the families of high officials, nobility, temple attendance, and others. The Brahmins were also granted exemption in 1813 from compulsory labour.[47]

The other area of Bhim Sen Thapa's interest was the Hulak system. This was a primitive postal system. It used to carry the Government mail and goods from one district to another or even from capital (Kathmandu) to the remotest parts of the kingdom. The key points on this road were Doti, Accham, Dullu, Dailekh, Piuthan, Pokhara, Gorkha, Nuwakot and Kathmandu. The services of Hulak between Kathmandu and the western front were first introduced in 1804 for transportation of mail. In due course the scope of such services was extended so as to cover the transportation of arms, ammunition and other military supplies. At each strategic points military escort under control and supervision of administrator were provided to protect the Hulaki. These arrangements insured the uninterrupted movement of mail and military equipments. To carry these, jhara porters were engaged in relays so that no person was required to provide the services beyond the limits of his village. They were directed by a naike who was responsible for keeping villagers informed in time of their turn in rotation. However, the maintenance of the system was more complicated than expected. In May 1808, it was reported that due to non-availability of adult porters for hulak services, minor children were engaged:

> We have received reports that at place where the number of Hulaki households is small and not enough porters are available, you seize the sons and daughters of the subjects, beat them and force them to carry loads even when the subjects offer to increase the number of relays. (Henceforth), increase the number of relays for the transport of Government stores, arms and ammunition in villages where (the number of Hulaki households) is small...Any person who beats the wives, sons and daughter of the subject for transporting his own supplies, other than those of the government, shall be awarded severe punishment.[48]

It was further reported that the difficulties faced by the people were aggravated by the general tendency of Bharadars and other influential persons to utilise it for their personal requirements. Orders were issued to carry only arms and ammunitions of government stores. However, they were intimidated and oppressed by the officials. Since their services were required regularly and permanently they were exempted from the obligation of jhara services elsewhere. The facilities provided to them, however, varied from one place to another. Some were allotted land under Adhiya tenure and some were compensated for their services in the form of cash wages.[49] Regulations promulgated in July 1809 for the reorganisation of Hulak service in the western regions read as:

> In areas west of Dharmathali (in Kathmandu) and east of the Bheri river, inspect whether or not Hulak outposts for the transport or mail have been established as mentioned in the previous order. According to this order, Hulaki porters had been granted a 50 per cent concession in the Walak levies, in addition to full exemption from (other) compulsory labour obligations and taxes on their homesteads...
>
> In areas west of the Bheri river and east of the Jamuna river make an estimate of the amount required for payment to Hulaki porters employed for the transport of mail on the basis of the sum sanctioned in the previous order and the sum required according to arrangements made this year for different areas and submit a report accordingly.[50]

The next aspect which needs to be studied in the post-unification scenario of the kingdom of Nepal is bondage or slavery which were rampant during the early 19th century A.D. due to rural indebtedness. Although the farmer owned no land, he possessed tenancy rights on the land he tilled on the basis of regular payment of rents. In case of failure of crops, he had to take loan from money-lenders at an exorbitant rate of interests and offer as guarantee, his own labour and his family. Often, indebtedness led to bondage. A debtor was compelled to work for the money-lenders under this system in fulfilment of his debt obligations in the capacity of bondman or Bandha. Karl Marx has observed: "Usury centralises money wealth while means of production are dispersed. It does not alter the mode of production but attaches itself firmly to it like a parasite and make wretched. It sucks out its blood, enervate it and compel reproduction to proceed under even more pitiable condition".[51] However in the case of Nepal, the non-existence of private property rights in the land also meant that tax arrearers could not be met through foreclosure of defaulter's title to his land.[52] It, therefore, often resulted in enslavement. It was reported that, sometimes, the district officials and revenue functioneries enslaved the ryots families who failed to pay taxes and other, and sold them in India.[53] Further acute poverty often led to slavery. In Dullu Dailekh, the farmers used to sell their children to the purchasers from plains as well as from Tibet and sometimes even kidnapped the children of others for such sale.[54]

Further, enslavement resulted due to administrative victimisation and tyranny. Such reports were received by Kathmandu. Slavery was, thus, a consequence of factors deeply rooted in the economic and social fabric of the society. Therefore, large numbers of people were enslaved in different parts of the kingdom. In this regard, Edwin T. Atkinson writes in 1808 from Garhwal that:

> At the foot of the pass leading to Har-Ka-Pairi is a Gorkhali post, to which slaves are brought down from the hills and exposed for sale. Many hundreds of these poor wretches, of both sexes, from three to thirty years of age, are annually disposed of in the way of traffic. These slaves are brought down from all parts of the interior of the hills and sold at Hardwar from ten to one hundred rupees each.[55]

During the Shah rule from 1804-1815, an English official estimated around 2,00,000 persons were enslaved in Garhwal. Stiller in his "Silent Cry" writes that "slavery in Nepal was not as harsh as it was in other areas, does not alter the fact that it was slavery".[56] He further adds that "Slavery was a social evil in the sense that society accepted it as a response, extreme but valid, to the question of indebtedness.

Slavery had its roots in an economic system that put undue pressure on the farmer. If the analysis is carried further, it becomes

…at the primary cause of this increased economic pressure … the escalating demands that the military forces of Nepal we… making on the economy from 1804-1806.[57]

The Gorkha Government took measures to mitigate the plight of common people. Royal orders were promulgated from time to time prescribing the collection of taxes and fine in cash but had little effect. In 1807, revenue officials were directed to recover all outstanding in cash. It also directed that all persons enslaved on the ground of default in payment of taxes and fines should be freed and that the ryots should no longer be enslaved for non-payment of taxes. The freedom of slaves was, of course, an impossible task.[58] In 1812, a general ban on traffic in human beings was ultimately imposed in Garhwal Sirmur and other areas. In spite of all the efforts of the government, it did not effectively check enslavement in the future and the suffering of the farmers perpetuated.[59]

Another measure adopted by Bhim Sen Thapa was land reclamation and settlement. Nepal was an agricultural society and the majority of the people were engaged in the agricultural production. In the formative years of his Mukhtiyarship, much attention was not given to the policies and programmes aimed at increasing production and developing national economy. Maxims of Prithvi Narayan Shah states that "the palace will become strong if the subjects are fat".[60] In his general view the people were only store house of the king whose real strength depended upon the proper control of the army and the people. He, therefore, gave due importance to land reclamation and settlement in the wastelands of Tarai to increase revenue and to meet the growing need of military expenditures. Taking the notion from him, Mukhtiyar Bhim Sen instructed the officials stationed at the borders to ensure that the people continued to occupy the lands adjoining the borders. The regulation pertaining to this effects further authorised the local functionaries to procure settlers even from India and allot wastelands to them for reclamation whenever possible. It further instructed them to make necessary arrangement for irrigation facilities at the expense of the Government.[61]

At the beginning, the government undertook the reclamation of wastelands through forced labour under its direct supervision and control. But due to non-availability of tenants, the wastelands were allotted to individual peasant on contract basis with exemption of tax. The Government also provide irrigation channels and extended loan to the settlers. In spite of many shortcomings, the system benefited both the Government and individual. While Government carried the benefit of land reclamation without any investment, the peasant found it profitable enterprise. In view of such profitability, the Bharadars including Mukhtiyar took up contracts for land reclamation of wastelands in Tarai in 1808.[62] The Government records revealed the considerable achievement in this policy particularly in eastern Tarai. In 1811, the Darbar appointed officers to coordinate the policy all-over the state.[63] However, due to the shortage of manpower and effective mechanism, large areas of cultivable lands remain waste in the district of Morung, Rautahat and elsewhere.

Closely connected with the land tenure system, the trade and commerce of Nepal was another important aspect which Bhim Sen Thapa was interested. His policy was primarily based on the principle of Prithvi Narayan Shah* who believed that foreign (English) traders would impoverish the people if they were allowed into the country.[64] His policy was therefore, elimination of foreign interests from internal and external trade. The East India Company had been trying to open trade routes to Nepal and thence to Tibet. Many important missions were dispatched from 1774 to 1801 but failed to achieve any success. Traditional trade relations with Tibet was maintained through the local traders.[65]

The Gorkha Government under Bhim Sen Thapa was afraid least the commercial contacts with the English should have adverse political consequences. But this did not mean that trade relations between Nepal and India were entirely cut off. Indian traders continued to operate in the interior markets of the country. In fact, traders from India were encouraged to open shops wherever possible, both in the hills and in the Tarai.[66] Nepal Government had imposed restriction only in the case of valuable commodities.

Bhim Sen Thapa sought to provide necessary facilities and encouragement to the native traders. The collection of duties, earlier stationed in the border areas were shifted to the interior to avoid inconvenience for the traders. Local custom officials were warned not to harass the traders. The people of Asi and Panchasaya of Jumla district were granted exclusive rights to trade in Dang and Salyan, and the people of Gam, also in the same district, in

Achham and Bajura. Border trade between Nepal and Tibet was subject to a number of similar restrictions.[67]

To expand the internal trade, the local officials were directed to open new markets at suitable places. After 1807, the Government undertook the experiment of opening new market under its direct control and supervision in Tarai and inner Tarai. Market towns were thus established at Hitura in Makwanpur, and at Bhadaruwa in Saptari district in 1809.[68] Revenues appropriated from these sources increased the income of the government. The main reason behind the opening of markets in the southern borders, in fact, appears to have been to monopolise the trade which the Tibetans used to conduct directly with the English. Bhim Sen Thapa realised that:

> "If Tibetans and Firangis (i.e. foreigners or, in the contemporary context, Englishmen) meet and trade with each other, our ryots and traders will lose their employment and the results will not be good".[69]

Therefore, the native traders were strictly forbidden to deal directly with the English. The frontier administrators were instructed to develop and expand markets in the border areas to increase revenue, facilitate land reclamation and settlement and protect from external encroachment.

In 1811, arrangements were made to export timber from the forest of Chituan to Calcutta on governmental level. At the same time, it made efforts to diversify agricultural and other product in order to expand the export trade. Apart from these, the government undertook to develop minting coinage and mining under the state control.[70]

Bhim Sen Thapa also felt the need of proper communications and transport. He was mainly guided by two considerations: to isolate Kathmandu valley from the south (India) and open up line of communications westward in order to meet military needs in Kumaon, Garhwal and the Jamuna-Sutlej region. He clearly perceived the military strategy of the kingdom whose line of defence was based along the Churia hills and thus, keep isolate Kathmandu valley from the south. The Government of Nepal was not in favour to open many routes connecting Kathmandu valley with the plains.[71] The local administrators were firmly told to close all tracks in the strategic areas around Kathmandu valley. To check the infiltrators, passports regulations were introduced. According to the regulation, the local traders as well as the general public who desired to leave Kathmandu valley through the Churai route should be permitted only after proper scrutiny of the passports. The local officials were warned that:

> In case you permit any person, irrespective of his status, leaving this side to proceed onward even though he does not have (a document bearing) the signature of the passports authority, we shall beheaded you.[72]

All these policies and programmes undertaken by Bhim Sen Thapa in the early part of his career were series of economic and military measure primarily designed to meet the short term exigency. In fact there were numerous defects which resulted in abuses in respect of land reclamation and settlement and market system.

Notes

1. Pande, A.R. *op. cit.*, pp. 35-36.
2. Dungel, G. *op. cit.*, pp. 1-5 and 10.
3. Pande A.R. *op. cit.*, 37.
4. Shrestha S., *Mathbar Singh Thapa,* Kathmandu (2046) p.11; Acharya, Baburam; *Shri Punch Bada Maharaja Prithivi Narayan Shah* (Sangchhipta Jiwani) Kathmandu (2024 BS), p. 4.
5. Tiwari Ranji and Others (Ed), *Atihasek Patra Sangaraha, Part II,* Kathmandu (2021 BS), pp. 44-45.
6. Yogi Narahani Nath, *Itihas Prakash,* Vol. 11, Part I, Kathmandu, (2013 BS), Khanal, M.P., (Ed) *Medieval Abhilekh,* Kathmandu (2030 BS), p. 17.
7. *Ibid.,* Also see Chenjong, Iman Singh., *op. cit.,* p. 79.
8. Shah, R.K., *Nepal and the World,* Kathmandu (1955), p. 54.
9. Thapa, S.B., *Ranbir Singh Thapa,* Kathmandu (2033 BS), pp. 5-9; Yogi, N.N., *op. cit.,* Vol. 1, pp. 119-21.
10. Bajra, D.B., and Shrestha, T.B., *Shah Kalin Abhilekh,* Kathmandu (2936 BS), pp. 290-292; Pant, N., *Shri Panch Bada*

Prithvi Narayan Shah ko Dibya Upadesh, Kathmandu (ND 2010 BS), p. 727.
11. Yogi, N.N., *op. cit.,* p. 120; Pande, Sardar Bhim Bahadur, *Rasta Bhakti ko Ekjalak* (2041 BS), pp. 111-117.
12. Dhungel, G. *op. cit.,* p.11.; Shrestha, S., *op. cit.,* pp. 32-35.
13. Pande, A.R., *op. cit.* pp. 35-54.
14. National Achirves, Nepal's Documents (ND) quoted by Dungel, G., p. 149.
15. *Ibid.,* p. 17.
16. *Ibid.,* p. 10; Pande, A.R. *op. cit.,* p. 46.
17. *Ibid.* See Also Bajracharya, D., *Triratna Saunderya Gatha,* Kathmandu (2019).
18. Thapa Sher Bahadur, *op. cit.,* p. 10.
19. *Ibid.,* Also see Pande, Bhim Bahadur, *op. cit.,* p. 247.
20. Nepali C.R., *op. cit.,* p. 16.
21. Dungel, *op. cit.,* p. 17.
22. Thapa, S.B., *op. cit.,* p. 21.
23. Shrestha, S., *op.cit;* pp. 26-27.
24. Thapa, Ramesh Jung, (ed.) *Prachin Nepal,* Kathmandu (2030 BS), pp. 1-28.
25. Landon, P., *op. cit.,* p. 82. Hunter W.W., *op. cit.,* p. 99.
26. Tyagi, S., *op. cit.,* p. 48.
27. See chapter I, pp. 16-17.
28. Thapa, Samser Bahadur, *op. cit.,* p. 23.
29. Bajracharya D., *op. cit.,* p. 43.
30. Yogi, N. Nath, *op. cit.,* Vol. I, p. 42.
31. Nepali C.R., *op. cit.,* pp. 252-253.
32. Acharya Baburam, *Bhim Sen Thapa ko Uthan, "Rooprekha"* No. 4. Kathmandu (2017 BS), pp. 37-38.
33. Nepali C.R., *op. cit.,* pp. 252-253.
34. Confirmation of Guthi lands: Bhim Sen Thapa's Documents, August 1804, No. 2/144.
35. *Ibid.,* Land Survey Regulations, April-December, 1805 Nos. 5/567; 6/162-192; 19/257-421; 20/216-359; April 1805, Nos. 5/501-514.
36. *Ibid.,* January 1806, No. 6/695, July 1806, No. 6/858.
37. Sharma Balchandra, *op. cit.,* p. 244.
38. Oldfield., Vol. 1. *op. cit,* p. 303.
39. Nepali, C.R., *op. cit.,* p. 32.
40. Bajracharya, D., *op. cit.,* p. 46.; Shrestha, S., *op. cit.,* p. 31.
41. Jain, M.S., *op. cit.,* pp. 4-5, *et.seq.*

42. Hunter, W.W., *op. cit.*, p. 98; Nepali C.R., pp. 83-84.
43. Bajracharya, D., *op. cit.*, p. 48; Sharma Binay Kumar, *Bhim Sen Lai Niyalda,* Kathmandu (2059 BS)
44. Yadav, Pitambar Lal; *Nepal ko Rajnatik Itihas*. Nepal (2040 BS), p. 142. Bhandari, D.R., *Nepal ko Udvau Tatha Bikash ko Bislesan Matka Itihas,* Kathmandu (2046 BS), pp. 391-398.
45. Sharma, B., *op. cit., 5.* Nepali C.R., *op. cit.*, pp. 64-66.
46. Regmi, M.C., *op. cit.*, p. 102.
47. *Ibid.*, p. 103.
48. For details of Hulak Service, Dr. Karky Jaya, *Nepal ma Hulak Byabastha, Ek-lekh:* 1804-1939 (unpublished) Bhim Sen Thapa Documents, May 1808, No. 36/81 Also see Appendix-C. The Documents further states that:
"We have received reports that at places where the member of Hulali Households is small and not enough porters are available, you seize the sons and daughters of the subjects, beat them and force them to carry loads even when the Subjects offer to increase the number of relay...Any person who beats the wives, sons and daughters of the Subjects for transporting his own supplies, other than those of the Government, shall be awarded severe punishment".
49. *Ibid.*, No. 2/230-50; 2/290-306; Regmi. Research Series, (4 April 1972): 69.
50. Regmi, M.C., *op. cit.*, pp. 113-120; Stiller, FL., *op. cit.*, 62-66.
51. Roy Chaudary S.C., *History of Modern India,* New Delhi 1983, p. 338.
52. *Ibid.*
53. Regmi, M.C., *op. cit.*, p. 118.
54. Bhim Sen Thapa Documents, September 1808, No. 36/164; June 1807, No. 20/404.
55. Edwin, T. Atkinson, *The Himalayan District of the Western Province of India,* Allahabad (1884) Vol. II, p. 620.
56. *Ibid.*
57. Stiller, F.L., *op. cit.*, p. 65.
58. Bhim Sen Thapa Documents, June 1807, No. 20/404.
59. *Ibid.*, September 1812, No. 40/349-354.
60. Prithvi Narayan Shah's Dibye Upadesh, *op. cit.*, pp. 19-26.
61. Regmi, M.C., *op. cit.*, p. 143.
62. Bhim Sen Thapa Documents, June 1808, No. 36/120; April 1810, No. 39/139 and May 1810, No. 39/215.

63. *Ibid.*, July 1811, No. 40/245.

* Prithvi Narayan Shah's, Dibye Upadesh, *op. cit.*, pp. 15-19. He had cautioned that the Kingdom of Nepal was sandwiched between two giant powers (India and China), and advised his followers not to develop intimate relations with either of them.

64. Chaudhuri, K.C., *op. cit.*, pp. 71-72: Markham, C., *op. cit.*, p. 127.
65. Dutta, K.K. *Survey of India's Social and Economic condition in the 18th Century (1707-1808)* Calcutta, (1961), p. 178.
66. Bhim Sen Thapa Documents, October 1807, No. 6/1048; February 1815, Nos. 24/644-647.
67. *Ibid.*, November 1809, Nos. 40/136-141.
68. Shankarman, R.(ed.) *Shahkalin Aitihasik Chhitti Patra Sangraha,* Kathmandu (1966), Vol. 1, p. 33.
69. Bhim Sen Thapa Documents, August 1811, No. 40/254 and September 1811, No. 40/266.
70. *Cf.* Prithvi Narayan Shah's Dibye Upadesh, *op. cit.*, p. 29.: Giuseppe, Fr, *An Account of the Kingdom of Nepal,* Asiatic Researches, Vol. II. No. XVII (Reproduced) February 1970. He writes that "within a distance of four days journey from Nepal (i.e. Kathmandu Valley) the road is good in the plains of Himalayas, but in the mountains, it is bad, narrow and dangerous". Hamilton, *op. cit.*, p. 180. Also see Henry T. Princep, *History of the Political and Military Transactions in India during the Administration of the Marquess of Hastings—1813-1823,* London (1835), p. 457.
71. Bhim Sen Thapa Documents, June 1804, No. 2/101.
72. *Ibid.* Sections 2 and 8.

III

Bhim Sen Thapa and Gorkha Militarism

In this chapter, an attempt has been made to analyse Bhim Sen Thapa's expansionist policy and Gorkha confrontation with the British India in 1814-16. Before we study the Gorkha militarism in details, it is imperative to find out the exact political status of Nepal during the period under review. Divergent views on Nepal political status are expressed by historians and others. What was the political status of Nepal in the nineteenth century A.D. when the powerful countries subjugated the weaker ones through the policy of a state aimed at establishing control beyond its borders over people unwilling to accept such control. The control may take the form of (a) direct annexation, (b) colony, (c) protectorate, (d) condominium, (e) sphere of influence, and (f) concession. The main objective is the exploitation of the people, the wealth and the natural resources of the subjugated land for the benefit of the imperialists getting raw materials, market, investment opportunities, military bases and soakpits for surplus population. In regard to Nepal, how was it treated by the British Government with which it had treaty relation or by the Chinese Government to whom it send periodic mission? Was it treated as independent country by its neighbours? These questions are relevant, for the status of a country is to be found "somewhere in the relation which obtain between the nation in question and all the other nations which may affect it or which it may affect".[1] Asian law and usage in terms of European expression very often "present a paradox for students of historical jurisprudence"[2]. Sovereignty, suzerainty, vassalage, tribute etc. are some of European expressions frequently used to characterise the status of Asian countries, but they hardly correspond to the precise nature of the usage, practice and law prevailing in these countries. In tune with the concepts of Western jurisprudence, some questions have been raised regarding the status of Nepal in relation to India. For example, was Nepal a feudatory of Ashok's empire? Was it a tribute paying kingdom on the frontier of Samudra Gupta's empire? Was it included in the vassal states of Chinese empire? Obviously these are the moot questions and the answers can never be unanimous.

Western historian like Aitchison in his book shows Nepal as an independent state.[3] Digby[4], Wright[5], Sherrings[6], Waddell[7], Brown[8], Oconner[9] etc., are firmly of opinion that Nepal was an independent state. However, there are some historians and writers who made confusing statements: 'Nepal is the largest of all the independent states in India'.[10] Imperial Gazetteer of India also refers Nepal as 'a Native kingdom' and 'an independent territory'. It has further included Nepal along with five native states[11] having direct political relations with the Government of India. It comments that "Nepal differs from other Native states in that it is independent in respect to its internal administration. Its foreign relations are, however, controlled by the Government of India; it is bound to receive British Resident; and it cannot take Europeans into its service without the sanction of the Government of India".[12] The same Gazetteer mentions Nepal "a Native state on the northern frontier of India. The political status of Nepal is somewhat difficult to define. It may be said to stand intermediate between Afghanistan and the Native States of India".[13] Brain Hodgson who spent eighteen years in Nepal also characterised it as 'the only independent one now left in India[14]'.

Perceval Landon, in his *Bibliotheca Himalayaica,* Volume II deplores the unfortunate mistake made by the compilers of the Imperial Gazetteers and categorically pointed out that "the Government of India had no right of interference or intervention or even of offering advice in Nepal, because it was an independent state". [15] The Government of India, Foreign Department no doubt upheld the status of Nepal as an independent state. One British official reiterates that "Nepal is not absolutely independent, in the fullest sense of the word, but on most respect we (the British) have treated her as an independent state, having power to declare war and make treaties. She is nominally tributary to China, but the Chinese Government evidently regarded her as lying outside the limits of empire".[16] In fact, the Chinese nominal sovereignty was first recognised after the Gorkha-Tibetan War (1788-92) and reiterated in the treaty of 1856 "did not lead to any strengthening of her actual position in Nepal".[17] The periodical missions from Kathmandu to Peking were nothing but means of profitable commercial transactions. Thus, throughout the 19th century, the Government of India totally ignored the paramountcy of China and acknowledged the independence of Nepal. She enjoyed an independent national life, and possessed the power of making war, concluded treaties and send envoys without hindrance from the British Government.[18]

Mukhtiyar Bhim Sen Thapa once consolidated his authority in the Darbar, immediately adopted the policy of expansion towards the hill areas to the west of Kumaon. To lead this military campaign he had chosen able and shrewd Kazi Amar Singh Thapa who had vast experience in this area.[19] With the Gorkha soldiers, all of the hill territory up to the Sutlej river was either expropriated or brought under direct control of the Gorkha dynasty. During the campaign, reinforcement of Gorkha soldiers were dispatched under Kazi Nain Singh Thapa, the Mukhtiyar's brother. The Gorkha thus came into conflict with Raja Sansar Chand, who held the territory east of Sutlej, but whose capital was at Kangra situated on the west bank of the river. By early 1809, almost all the territory had been conquered with the exception of Kangra.[20] Later they even crossed the river to attack Kangra fort. For more than two years the fort was surrounded by the Gorkha soldiers. Yet, they failed to seize it. Raja Sansar Chand took refuge to the Sikh kingdom and requested military help to drive away the Gorkhas from his territory. Initially, Raja Ranjit Singh was reluctant to offer such help least it would alienate the Gorkha. He was indeed interested to control the Sutlej river basin and Kashmir. When the Gorkha continued to attack Kangra and decided to proceed further towards Kashmir, a Sikh army attacked the Gorkha force besieging Kangra and drove them back to across the river Sutlej. This happened on 24th August, 1809. Ranjit Singh did not want to antagonise the Gorkha in view of the British threat to his empire. He rather suggested an alliance between the Gorkha and the Sikh under which Sutlej would become their boundary.[21] Kazi Amar Singh Thapa immediately sent the Sikh's proposal to Kathmandu Darbar for acceptance. But the Darbar, at Mukhtiyar Bhim Sen Thapa's behest, rejected the offer. This was the last obstacle between the Gorkha and their ultimate objective, the valley of Kashmir which at that time was independent, faction ridden and 'ripe for plucking' by any determined aggressor.[22] Had Gorkha succeeded in conquering Kangra and extended direct influence in Kashmir, her power would naturally have increased and 'Greater Nepal' from Bhutan in the east to Kangra in the west would have established. In this respect, Leo Rose writes: "A unified hill state, subordinate to the Gorkha dynasty appeared to be an imminent possibility, an achievement that might well have altered the future not only for Nepal but of India".[23]

The defeat of Gorkha soldiers at the hand of the Sikh army in 1809 made Mukhtiyar Bhim Sen Thapa more cautious in pursuing the policy of expansion. In fact, it was the conquests of Gorkha in the west of Kumaon that resulted in dispute with the British over certain villages—in the plains which had been subject to the hill Rajas prior to their submission to Nepal. The hill Rajas immediately sought British's protection and accordingly Major General Octerlony was directed to remonstrate with Kazi Amar Singh Thapa against the violation of the boundary which had been adopted for that quarter by mutual consent. The latter was apprised that he could not be permitted to extend his conquests below the hills. In spite of this, Kazi Amar Singh Thapa assumed that all the territories of these Rajas including those in the plains now belonged to Gorkha dynasty and occupied these areas in 1810 AD.[24] The British's continuous remonstration for immediate retreat of Gorkha troops from the lands and relinquish the claims of the villages had desired effect on the Darbar. Kathmandu was anxious to avoid any hostilities with the British until their own preparations were further advanced. Orders were dispatched to Kazi Amar Singh Thapa to comply with the demand of British and the Gorkha army were withdrawn from the disputed areas.[25]

The border friction between the British and Nepal had been noticed when series of encroachments began in 1804. It was recorded that in 1808, the Gorkha official posted at Morung had forcibly seized the zamindari of Bhim Nagar in the district of Purnea. Morung had been for years an asylum for robbers who after committing crimes on the plains retreated beyond the jurisdiction of British police. Instead of surrendering of these criminals to the British police for trials, they were given protection.[26] When the Kathmandu Darbar did not relinquish the territory, the British Government resolved to recover the lands by force. It was further reported by the Magistrate of Tirhut that at different periods between 1787 and 1812 more than two hundred villages have been usurped by the Gorkha along the borders at different times. In the district of Bareilly, the Gorkha had occupied five out of eight divisions of the Pargana of Khyrapur. They claimed an extensive tract in the district of Moradabad. Then there were extensive encroachments on Sarun and Gorakhpur districts which led to war in 1814. All these forced encroachments of the Gorkha were communicated to Bum Shah, the Subedar of Almora to evacuate them. Yet, the Gorkha claimed that the lands having belonged formerly to the Raja of Kumaon, conquered by the Gorkhas, had a right to these lands.[27]

However, the real bone of contention between the Gorkhas and the British was Butwal and Sheoraj. The first indication of British attitude towards Nepal was the occupation of Butwal by the Gorkha army in 1804. It had been established as a working principle between the Company and Nepal at the time of Prithvi Narayan Shah that as long as the Darbar was willing to continue the Zamindari payments on the lands they took from the hill Rajas, they might continue to cultivate them. Such arrangement was made on the portions of the Makwanpur Tarai as late as 1801. On the basis of this, the Darbar instructed its officials at Palpa to occupy the low lands. A Gorkha troops, thus entered the villages in Company's possession. On 18th August, 1804, the Governor General wrote a letter to the Maharaja of Nepal demanding immediate withdrawal of the Gorkha troops from the low lands of Butwal. The letter also sought to adjust the matter peacefully; to liquidate the arrears of revenue of Seoraj and also demanded to produce documentary proof of its claim of Seoraj.[28] In reply, the Darbar denied the right of British Government to interfere with respect to Seoraj; asserted Nepal's right by virtue of succession. In November 1805, the Gorkha troops occupied two-thirds of the district of Butwal to the west of Tarai. Sir George Barlow, who was entrusted to the matter, came to the conclusion that both Butwal and Seoraj ceded by the Vazier of Oudh to the company in lieu of large sum of money and the Company did not interfere in the internal affairs of those Rajas. On the contrary, the Gorkhas in the wake of their policy of expansion towards the south exterminated these Rajas and assumed their titles. This brought the Nepalese in contact with the Indian Zamindars who in turn also gradually came to be subjected to Bhim Sen Thapa's policy of expansion. The Indian Zamindars also encroached on the Nepali territory and often made exaggerated complains when their own territories were encroached upon.[29] Princep remarks that:

> ...unless when the encroachment was gross and easy of proof, it was vain to hope to interest the British Government in their favour. That Government (British) was, in the first place, no loser by the usurpation, for the public revenue was fully secured by the perpetual settlement and by the increased value of the entire estate against any loss for partial aggression. Moreover, it was on principle, distrustful of the pretensions of its own subject, which were generally exaggerated[30].

Meanwhile, notice was served to the Darbar to instruct its officials and troops to evacuate the lands in question.

This was followed, in 1810, by the enunciation of the principle of limitation; viz., that all land in the Tarai were the right of the British Government, while the Nepal Government must confine its possessions to the hills. Since then the Darbar received a steady flow of complaints of encroachment and usurpations. Finally, the friction along the border was focused on the areas of Butwal and Rautahat. Nepal had been in possession of Butwal area for many years which the British Government claimed had belonged to the Nawab Vazier of Oudh and the later ceded to the company.[31] In Rautahat, the British claimed twenty-two villages on the basis of thirty years uninterrupted possession but which, in fact, Nepal had seized on the basis of prior claim. When the matter became serious, both the Governments agreed to investigate the borders in question. Darbar appointed Kishan Pandit to represent the Government of Nepal while the Governor General deputed Major Paris Bradshaw to represent the British claims.[32] In 1813, both the investigating officers produced their reports supported by available documents etc. According to their findings, decision would be easily made, at least in theory; the party at fault in the border dispute. However, it is very difficult to attribute the delinquency to each party. Both the governments were absolutely convinced that their claim was just and proper. The Commission failed to yield any solution to the problem. By this time Lord Hastings had assumed the office of the Governor General of India who was much irritated about the growing influence of the Gorkhas in the Himalayan region.[33] He did not give much thought to the propriety of the claim and tradition of amicable settlement between the two governments. The considerations that influenced him were the large frontier of Nepal, which had a strong and disciplined army and a peculiar geographical advantage. While the British provinces in the north were exposed with no natural barrier. Thus, he had determined to cripple the power of Gorkhas through remonstration and, if required, by waging war. He wrote,

> we are not through a point of honour of demanding atonement for the wanton invasion of our territories, brutal massacre of our policemen and the studied cruelty to tying to a tree and shooting to death with arrows the native officer whom we had appointed to preside over the district; though the helplessness of obtaining from the government any disavowal of such a complicated outrage, must have made us look to war, even on that ground. But we were at issue with a nation so extravagantly presumptuous in representing its own strength; and so ignorant of our superior means; that the Gorkha Commissioner had on a former occasion remarked to ours, the futility of debating about a few square miles of territory, since there never could be a real peace between the two states, until we should yield to the Gorkhas our provinces north of Ganges making the river boundary between us: as heaven had evidently designed it to be.[34]

Lord Hastings, therefore, assumed a very rigid attitude on the matter of border dispute. There can be no doubt that the border problem was very real yet it was important to retain some sense of proportion. The Butwal Tarai, according to Major Bradshaw's report was only a wasteland and yield revenue less than 15,000 rupees a year from twenty-two villages. Though the land in question had comparatively small value to the British Government, it had become very important to the Gorkhas for whom it formed part of the real fruit of their conquests. The hills were poor in comparison to the fertile lands of Tarai and large section of virgin land had been assigned to the Bharadars and military commander, both in payment and as reward for their part in the expansion and unification of Nepal.[35] Some British officials were certain that if Nepal was deprived of her Tarai possession, Nepal's military potential would be seriously weakened. The fact is that the Anglo-Gorkha war of 1814-16 originated out of this border issue, yet a peaceful settlement would have provided an ideal solution for both governments, and war could have possibly be averted if both of them were not adamant on their stand. However, the situation was further aggravated in 1813 when the Gorkha troops tried to occupy several villages in the territory of the protected Sikh chiefs.[36]

It has generally been commented by historians that the Anglo-Gorkha war occurred solely due to the aggressive attitude of the Gorkha Darbar and its policy of encroachments. But a closer study of the situation and the British policy in wider perspective of eastern Asia and China would clearly expose the British intention of bringing the Himalayan States under its influences. Several attempts were made to open trade routes. Mission under Bogle and Turner were sent by Warren Hastings for this purpose.[37] In 1792-93, Lord Macartney went to China to seek commercial treaty, but got only some trade privileges. This unsuccessful venture compelled the British Government to turn towards northern frontier of India. The Gorkha territory, stretched from Sutlej in the west to Teesta river in the east, naturally attracted their attention.[38] Thus expedition under Kinloch in 1767; Kirkpatrick mission to Kathmandu as a mediator in 1791-92; trade mission under Maulavi Qadir Ali in 1795 and the Treaty of Commerce and Friendship, 1801 and Capt. Knox's appointment as Resident were executed.[39] All means of diplomacy had been tried with utmost care. The failure of these initiatives led the British Government to change its policy to open the doors of Nepal for trade and commerce led to declaration of war on the pretext of the border disputes. Further, the British were induced by Kumaon and Garhwal where natural resources and mineral deposits were found abundantly. And through Kumaon, direct communication could have been established with Tibet via Taklakot. Meanwhile, due to mismanagement and highhandedness of the Gorkha officials, the people of Kumaon and Garhwal were trying to overthrow the

Gorkha rule. It gave an opportunity to the British Government to play with the people against the Gorkhas.[40]

Since the time of Kinloch's expedition, the Gorkha Darbar had followed the policy, formulated by the founder of modern Nepal, Prithvi Narayan Shah. He instructed that the Gorkha should maintain friendly relations with British India but keep them out of the hills. because Europeans were looked upon with distrust and suspicion. A Campucian missionary was asked to leave Kathmandu.[41] All his descendents strictly followed the principles except Bahadur Shah and Damodar Pande who had maintained close relationship with the British to fulfil their ambitions. The Gorkhas had always regarded the Himalayan foothills, their strongest line of defence. It was an established policy to close off the less easily defended trails into the hills and to settle families of loyalty on those that were open. Further, the movement of outsiders through the hills was severely restricted.[42] The real objective of such restriction of movement of the outsiders was to prevent from acquiring valuable informations and secret routes by the British Government into the hills. The Darbar at the instance of Mukhtiyar Bhim Sen Thapa introduced passport system, to check the infiltration of unauthorised persons.[43] Every fort along the borders, were entrusted to check not only the people but also the commodities. This was essential because of the growing power of the British in India who might influence the people against the Government. Bhim Sen Thapa was aware of the British's clandestine policy which was used against the native states of India from time to time.[44]

When the dispute of Tarai lands emerged between Nepal and the British Government, the Darbar's claim was based on their conviction that the right which former hill rajas had exercised over the Tarai were real right. In those cases, where the hill rajas had exercised direct control over the land was indisputable. However, in other cases, the hill rajas had owned tenure rights based on a regular payment of rent to a raja in the plains. The Darbar held, as did most people in the south Asia, that tenure rights were real rights. Such tenure rights were contractual and considered valid as long as the contracting party paid the prescribed rents. The system was recognised by the British Government. In fact, Nepal had paid tribute to the British Government for such rights in the Makhwanpur Tarai in the Treaty of 1801. Prior to this, the East

India Company recognised this position in Bijayapur and Chaudandi Tarai to the east of Makhwanpur.[45] It also accepted Prithvi Narayan Shah's promise to fulfil the obligations of these two kingdoms towards the Company on the provision that the later did not interfere in the Gorkhali military action there.

In spite of all these developments Lord Hastings issued an 'ultimatum' to the Maharaja of Nepal to surrender Butwal and Seoraj lands within 25 days from the date of the letter. At the same time, the Magistrate of Gorakhpur was instructed to march with troops to occupy the lands if the reply of the Kathmandu Darbar was evasive or negative. The Commander-in-Chief of the British army was apprised of the possible confrontation with the Gorkha army and accordingly instructed to make seventeen companies of Native Infantry available under the command of Lt. Col. Richardson at Gorakhpur.[46]

The Maharaja, in reply to the 'Ultimatum' entirely evaded the demand of the British Government on the plea that the Border Commission under Lt. Col. Bradshaw did not settle the dispute but expressed his desire to send an agent to Calcutta for solving the pending differences. Meanwhile, the specific period of 25 days having been expired, the Magistrate of Gorakhpur directed the troops immediately to proceed into the disputed lands, which they occupied without any resistance from Gorkha troops. However, taking advantage of the rainy season, which was unbearable to the British soldiers, a party of Gorkha troops under the leader, named Munraj committed first act of hostilities on 29th May, 1814.[47] The act of atrocity resulted in killing of eighteen and wounded four British officials at Butwal and Chilwa Thana. Due to unhealthy season, the British Government could not send reinforcement. Lord Hastings consequently sent a letter to the Maharaja urging him to punish the perpetrators of the murders but the later did not pay much heed to the request. Since the relations between the two-governments continued to deteriorate. Lord Hasting added:

> The British Government has long borne the conduct of the Nepalese with unexample patience, opposing to their violence, insolence and rapacity, a course of proceedings uniformly just and moderate. But forbearance and moderation must have their take up arms in defence of its rights, its interest and honour, will never lay them down,

> until its enemy shall be forced to make ample submission and atonement of its outrageous conduct, to identify it, for the expense of war and to afford full security for the future maintenance of those relations, which he has so shamefully violated.[48]

Yet, the letter of the Governor General produced trepidation in the Nepalese Darbar. The question of war and peace was fully discussed in grand Darbar. One section of Bharadars represented by Bum Shah Chauria, Guru Rangnath Pandit, Kazi Dalbhanjan Pande and General Amar Singh Thapa advocated the policy of peace and moderation to avoid war with the British at this juncture. Instead, they appealed to Maharaja to establish proper administration in the recently conquered territories in the west. If circumstances compelled, they assured that the Gorkha army would certainly defeat the British, but it was not proper time to confront the enemy. Kazi Amar Singh Thapa even cautioned that if Nepal enter into the war, the people from the recently subjugated territory would revolt against Nepal.[49] He pointed the case of Almora where Bakta Thapa, the administrator's highhandedness created an anti-Gorkha sentiment and the same situation prevailed in Garhwal.[50] He rather proposed to return the lands usurped by the Gorkha troops in the border. He alleged that those who were in favour of war with the British did not have any military experiences. During the deliberation of the issue, most of the upper echelons of the Darbar were unanimous in their decision to avoid the war. Even Guru Rangnath Pandit, sided with them but was not ready to surrender the land to the British at any cost.[51]

One section of Bharadars led by Mukhtiyar Bhim Sen Thapa was in favour of war with the British. He recollected the British's sinister plan since the time of Prithvi Narayan Shah till the abrogation of the Treaty of 1801. They tried every possible means to open the doors in Nepal. The failure of the initiatives led the British to use another alternative i.e., war and bring Nepal under its political influence.[52] Bhim Sen Thapa accepted the challenge of the war on the basis of three fundamental considerations as mentioned by Stiller:

1. The increasing British knowledge of the secrets of the hills.
2. The state preparation of his army.

3. The possibility of powerful Indian Princes siding with Nepal to defeat the British and, perhaps, even to drive them out of Nepal.[53]

Thus, in the grand assembly of the Bharadars in the Darbar; Bhim Sen Thapa addressed to the Maharaja that

> Through the influence of your good fortune and that of your ancestors, no one has yet been able to cope with the state of Nepal. The Chinese once made war, but were reduced to seek peace. How then, will the English be able to penetrate into our hills?...The small fortress of Bharatpur (which Gen. Lake had failed to take in 1805) was the work of man, yet the English being wrested before it, desisted from the attempt to conquer it. Our hills and fortress are formed by the hands of God and are impregnable. I, therefore, recommend the prosecution of hostilities. We can make peace afterwards as may suit our convenience.[54]

After long deliberation, the dye was cast in favour of war. The most important point that emerged from the debates in the Darbar was that sense of grievance against the British on the border issue did not figure prominently. The Bharadars who were against had pointed out that "there was no injury done to Nepal that called for an appeal to arm" and those in favour of war advocated it on the grounds other than the protection of their just territorial claims.[55]

The Gorkha army had been trained in the battle and forged through numbers of campaigns. However, with the defeat against Kangra in 1809, the Darbar found it was no longer capable of expansion towards west. Expansion of territories to the north and east was not practical because of the connections Bhutan and Tibet enjoyed with the Chinese Emperor. The result of this impasse was that the army's fighting edge gradually declined. It was also true that non-acquisition of new lands restricted the size of army. Thus the existing army needed to be trained and well-equipped. The frontier's Gorkha officials were instructed to repair the forts and their arsenal.[56]

When it became obvious in the middle of 1814 that British invasion in Nepal was imminent, Mukhtiyar Bhim Sen Thapa dispatched secret missions to the Indian native Princes to form a confederation against the British. Pandit Padmamani Sharma was sent to Gwalior to apprise of the intention of the Gorkhas against the British to drive them out from India. The Gwalior Bharadars indeed accepted such proposal on the condition that other native princes also join hands. The Marathas were impressed with the Gorkhas' stand against the British. But the Sindhia alone did not feel competent for the task Bhim Sen Thapa was asking for.[57] Prudence urged him to insist on greater guarantees than Mukhtiyar Bhim Sen Thapa could offer him. However, at the end, all of them agreed to join only if Ranjit Singh would join the alliance. The clash between Amar Singh Thapa and Ranjit Singh on the issue of Kangra in 1809 would create some problem to bring the later into an alliance against the British. But Mukhtiyar Bhim Sen Thapa required alliance and overtures were to Ranjit Singh by Kazi Amar Singh Thapa.[58]

The negotiation between Kazi Amar Singh Thapa and Ranjit Singh was undertaken by Kharidar Prithvi Bilas Upadhaya who was his agent at the court of Sikh Kingdom. The Kharidar was clearly instructed of three basic proposals that: a possible division of the Gangetic plain from Delhi to Calcutta between the Sikhs and the Gorkhas and the Marathas; a suggested outline of the attack that could be made on the British and finally an appeal to Ranjit Singh in the name of Hinduism to drive the British out of India. It was a foregone conclusion that if Ranjit Singh was to join hands with the Gorkhas, the Marathas were already committed to join. Whether the proposed alliance would work against the British or not would be decided in the course of war.[59] However, Lord Hastings took more realistic view of it. He took stern measures to prevent any such alliance from interfering in his plan for Nepal. To counteract the Gorkha, Sikh and Maratha alliance, Lord Hastings prepared elaborate plan as:

1. The British protection was offered to the tiny state of Bhopal, where the Sindhia could first be expected to begin military activity. This step had as its sole purpose the delaying of Maratha activity in the area for a time, and was based on the Governor General's confidant's expectation that Nepal war would be brief.

2. In view of this, the whole disposal force of the Madras army was brought to the northern border of that presidency in order to be available for immediate action, should the Marathas make any effort to join the Gorkhas or to take advantage of the Nepal war to attack Bengal.
3. On the other hand, to ensure the brevity of the Nepal war, the Bengal army was heavily committed to that front. According to the official reports, there was a total of 46,629 British troops in the field at one time against Nepal. This represented over half of the total force available to the Bengal army, and left a thin covering of troops to handle all, normal military activity or even dualities in the half million square miles of the presidency as well as to man the quarter master services for the Nepal war.
4. Lord Hastings set out to raise an additional three regiments for the regular and six provincial corps to fill the gaps created by this heavy assignment of men to Nepal war.
5. Two additional King's regiments were summoned from the Cape and Mauritius to assist in handling the situation in India.[60]

Of his efforts, Princep concludes "although the greater part of the force of the Bengal Presidency was known to be occupied in the hill country, and daily account of reverses in that quarter must have been eagerly circulated, the Marathas were nevertheless deterred by the formidable aspect of the British preparations from resenting in any way this undisguised and direct counteraction to their view".[61]

When Mukhtiyar Bhim Sen Thapa was forging an alliance with Indian Native states, he also tried to get support from the Chinese Emperor. A letter addressed to the Chinese Emperor was sent through the Amban at Lhasa informing that the British were planning to invade Nepal in order to force a passage to Tibet, and alleged that the British had promised to pay Rs. 60,000 to 70,000 as a reward if Nepal allow them to proceed.[62] The Amban doubted the content of letter and rejected the request for financial assistance. The Amban replied that "there is no tradition of giving monetary aid by China. We Ambans cannot submit such requests to the Emperor...From now on never make such requests in your letters".[63] Yet, the Amban had sent a report to the Peking court summarizing the contents of Kathmandu's letter. Bhim Sen Thapa also approached various Tibetan high officials urging them to persuade the Ambans to support Kathmandu's request for aid. Instead of helping the Darbar's request, the Dalai Lama's regent advised Kathmandu to settle the dispute with the British Government on the best terms possible.[64] However, Bhim Sen Thapa was not a man who gave up so easily. He repeatedly wrote to Amban for assistance. Irritated Amban curtly wrote to Darbar that "the Emperor (Chinese) is not concerned with whether or not you are associated with the British or whether or not you honour the British...When you fight with the British, this happens outside our borders. The soldiers of the Emperor cannot go there we Ambans realise that the king is only a child and that you do not know how to work; so we have not submitted these embarrassing letters to the Emperor." They further commented that the Emperor's instruction was "they can join the Feringhi rule if they like so long as they send us tribute and so long as the Feringhi do not cross Tangut (Tibetan) frontier."[65]

Mukhtiyar Bhim Sen Thapa's appeal to the various Native Indian states for assistance also bore no fruits as those of China and Tibet. Thus, when Lord Hastings declared war on Nepal on 1st November, 1814, he had to fight the British army with the available resources.[66] The Gorkha soldiers displayed extraordinary bravery, four out of five British Generals showed grave incompetence. General R.R. Gilespie's soldiers were beaten while assaulting a small fort of Kalanga near Dhera Dun under the command of Balbhadra Singh. The British army was also chased from Jythak; General Wood was defeated at Jaigarh. In another encounter the British lost over a thousand men. Only General Octerlony did not suffer defeat at the hands of the Gorkha army. The initial success of the Gorkha soldiers in repulsing the advance of the British army encouraged the native states of India. In the north-west, Maharaja Ranjit Singh expressed anti-British feelings. The Pindari chief, Amir Khan openly started reorganising his troops in the Central India. Even the Sindhia's attitude towards the British was hardly conciliatory and it was at this time when the seed of next Marathas war sown. The repeated failures and the onset of unfavourable season meant a protracted and expensive war for the British. However in April-May 1815, the British army overran Nalapani, Deothal, Almora, Kumaon, Garhwal and the territory west of Jamuna. Kazi Amar Singh Thapa, deserted by his troops, was compelled to surrender the whole of the territory west of Kali river. A convention to this effect was signed on 15th May, 1815 with Gen. Octerlony.[67]

The defeat of the Gorkha soldiers and the loss of considerable territory in the Tarai compelled the Kathmandu Darbar to sue for peace. Accordingly, Guru Gajraj Missur, Chandra Sekhar Upadhya and Rudra Bir Shah were deputed as representatives to negotiate with the British officials. Taking advantage of the situation, the British placed before them various demands including the cession of whole of Tarai and establishment of Resident at Kathmandu. The demands were more than the Nepalese could readily concede. Guru Gajraj categorically expressed his inability to accept such demands. Rudra Bir Shah also affirmed his view that the cession of Tarai "would ruin the state of Nepal as principal chiefs (Baradars) and great part of soldiery drew their subsistence from Jagirs situated in that tract".[68] Considering the nature and importance of Tarai lands, Lord Hastings expressed that a sum of two lakh of rupees per annum in a form of pension would be given to the Bharadars and others whose jagirs were situated in that areas. The Darbar representative, unable to accept the British proposals, returned to Kathmandu for further consultation with the Maharaja and Mukhtiyar. Guru Gajraj even warned that such a sacrifice would be extremely unpopular among all the subjects and would provoke even the friendly Bharadars to join hands the Thapas faction for united defence.

The situation in the north-west and Central India became tense. At the same time, the Chinese's interest in Nepal further hastened Lord Hastings to modify the demands. He informed the Kathmandu Darbar that the British Government in India was ready to delete the clause concerning the Resident at Kathmandu and give up those part of lands between Kosi and Gandak except those portions which were according to him strategically essential for maintenance of a good boundary. Guru Gajraj returned to Sagauli on 28th November, 1815 and signed the documents of the Treaty on 2nd December, 1815 and promise to get ratify by the Maharaja of Nepal within fifteen days. The British government on their part ratified it on 9th December, 1815.[69] However, the Treaty was not ratified by the Maharaja in time because the faction in the Darbar, who still advocated war got support from Kazi Amar Singh Thapa and his family, who returned from war front. He advised the Maharaja not to ratify the treaty. He warned that if the British come to know the weakness of Nepal they would certainly subjugate the entire country. He considered the establishment of Residency as the first step towards subjugation. It can be asserted that the main fear of the Gorkhas was the ulterior motives of the British. Even at this juncture, the Nepalese Bharadars expected some sort of help from the disaffected native princes of India and Chinese.[70]

The non-ratification of Treaty of Sagauli by the Maharaja of Nepal led open hostilities once again. The second campaign did not last long. The seizure of Makwanpur and advanced towards the hills compelled the Darbar to send Guru Gajraj and Chandra Shekhar Upadhya with formal acceptance of the Treaty of Sagauli. It was accepted by General Octerlony on 4th March, 1816. Thus ended the Anglo-Gorkha War and the clauses of the Treaty were implemented which became the future course of Indo-Nepalese ralations.[71]

The defeat of the Gorkhas at the hands of the British army in the war need to be analysed thoroughly. The situation reveals that Mukhtiyar Bhim Sen Thapa had underestimated the power and military capacity of the enemy. The availability of the British soldiers, who had recently returned after the Napoleonic War, gave much impetus to the British in the war of 1814-16. It was also found that the British Government had borrowed a sum of rupees 2.5 crores from Nawab of Oudh to meet the war expenditures. The Nepal Government had to content with whatever the resources they had in their hands.

Further, the informations collected by Kirkpatrick in 1792 on Nepal's fortifications and routes; Hamilton's observation of military capacity of Nepal in 1801, Knox's collections of Nepal's internal and external defences and Major Bradshaw and Dr. Rutherford's report about passess and routes and on Kumaon tremendously helped the British East India Company in formulating plans (strategies) and mobilising its resources to invade Nepal.[72] It appears that whatever knowledge Bhim Sen Thapa had gathered on British power was limited and outdated. Another factor that contributed to the defeat of the Gorkha was that the recently conquered territories in the hills and plains sided with the British hoping to get back their lost territories after the war. Finally, Nepal failed to get any military and financial assistances, either from China, with whom she had allegiance, nor from the Indian native princes. The British, on their part, convinced the native princes and the Nepali Bharadars through the divide and rule policy.[73]

Thus the war ended with the defeat of the Gorkhas and had to sign a peace treaty. The most important provision of the Treaty of Sagauli (1816) contains nine articles dealing with various aspects such as cession of considerable portion of territories to the British, establishment of a permanent Resident at the Court of Nepal (Darbar) and others. Before discussing the nature of the implementation of the Treaty, one has to see whether the Treaty was dictated peace or not. Most of the Nepali historians alleged that it was purely an imposed peace agreement much against the wishes of the Gorkha sentiments. But it was not entirely correct as the British had initiated the peace process even during the war and also agreed in principle to relax some of the terms and conditions. Throughout the war, the Gorkha peace emissary had been present in the fort of Makhwanpur with the ratified treaty in hand. Immediately after the surrender of fort, the ratified treaty signed by the Maharaja was handed over to General Octerlony. Some of the clauses were made essential for peace, while others were relaxed with a view to bring about a speedy termination of the war and to make the Treaty acceptable to the defeated Gorkhas.[74]

According to the treaty of Sagauli[75], there were five articles where no relaxations were made. For example Article 2 states that 'the Raja of Nepal renounce all claims to the lands which were the subject of discussion between the two country before the war' as indispensable. The article 4 the surrender of the territory west of Kali river was put before the Gorkhas as an accomplished fact. This cost the Nepalese one-third of their territory and actually brought them to their knees. 'This was deemed necessary to cripple the Gorkha military power' and to secure passage for the British trade to China. It further checked Gorkhas on her eastward expansion and a guarantee was exacted from them not to molest the Raja of Sikkim. The Article 7 imposed the Gorkhas not to employ any European and American without the permission of the British Government. It was always inserted in the British treaties with Indian native states as a means to counteract the influences of the added importance.

The most resented clause of the treaty was the establishment of permanent Resident at the Court of Kathmandu Darbar. The

Gorkha, right from Prithvi Narayan Shah's time, had a genuine apprehension that the Resident would interfere in the internal politics of the states and lead to the annexation of their country.[76] The Gorkha envoy opposed this particular clause but cooled down when Lord Hastings ordered 'that all other points of the treaty were more or less open to subsequent discussion but they (Gorkhas) must take Resident or war'.[77] It was this very clause which made the people of Nepal jealous and discontent for decades. And the apprehension of the Darbar came true when the British resident had actually interfered the internal politics of Nepal in 1840-42.[78]

To sum up the nature of obligation of the Treaty, the provision can be classified into three parts: (a) the article relating to the territorial arrangements, (b) the articles restricting Nepalese freedom of action in foreign affairs, and (c) the articles on the establishment of permanent Resident. The first category of articles 2, 3, 4 and 5 deal with the territories to be ceded to the East India Company by the Nepal Government and pension to the Bharadars. The next category 6 and 7 imposing restriction on Nepal Government to expand towards Sikkim and employ any Europeons and Americans without the permission of the British Government. And, finally, an article relating to the Resident had aroused a lot of controversy. This office in Nepal had generally been confused with the Resident in Indian states.[79]

The Treaty was implemented. The Nepal Government evacuated troops from the forts and territories ceded to the East India Company. Minor problems in the east of Mechi rivers were also amicably settled. But the matter of Tarai was entirely different. During the negotiation of peace, the Nepalese agents told the British representative that Gorkha would never consent to surrender the whole of Tarai. It was their main source of income and jagirs of Bharadars were located in this tract. Tarai also provided a rich cultivable soil. The Darbar told to the British agent that the Treaty did not specifically define the extent of Tarai, hence, bulk area of forest belonged to Nepal. The British Government knowing the feelings of the Gorkhas, instructed the Resident to make a few more relaxation concerning the clauses of cession. By 15th July, 1816, the Darbar promptly ordered the evacuation and with it, the whole Treaty came to be legally implemented.[80]

Notes

1. Tieh Tseng Li, *Tibet Today and Yesterday,* New York (1966) Part II.
2. Sinha, N.C. *Asian Law and Usage in European Expansion: Some Illustrations from Tibet,* Man in India, Vol. 46, No. l, January-March (1966).
3. Aitchison, C.U. *op. cit.*, Vol. II.
4. Digby William, *India and Nepal,* London (1890), p. 3.
5. Wright, D., *History of Nepal,* Calcutta (1966 Reprint) p. l.
6. Sherring, A.C., *Western Tibet and British Borderland,* London (1966), pp. 1-2.
7. Wadell, L.A., *Among the Himalayas,* London (1900), p. 304.
8. Brown, P., *Picturesque Nepal,* London (1912) p. 1.
9. O'Conner, F., *On the Frontier and Beyond,* London, p. 54.
10. Ghosh, L.N., *The Modern History of Indian Chiefs, Rajas and Zamindars, etc,* Calcutta (1879), p. 24.
11. *The Imperial Gazetteer of India,* Vol. VII (1881), p. 103.
12. *Ibid.,* Vol. IV (1908), p. 92.
13. *Ibid.,* Vol. XIX (1908), p. 25.
14. *Ibid.,* p. 38.
15. Landon, P., Vol. 1, *op. cit.,* p. 101.
16. FSC June 1884, Bo. 438. Letter from Resident to Government of India.
17. Majumdar, K., *British Attitude to Nepal's Relations with Tibet and China, Bengal Past and Present,* (1967), p. 67, Majumdar remarks that "the Quinquennial mission from Kathmandu to Peking were nothing but "means of profitable commercial transaction".
18. FSC, September, 1876, No. 131, Letter from Government of India to the Resident of Kathmandu.
19. Nepali, C.R. *op. cit.,* p. 79: Gyawali, S., Amar Singh Thapa, Darjeeling (1943), pp. 46-47; Rose Leo E., *op. cit.,* p. 79. A recent writer remarks that "the policy of the Company under Sir George Barlow (1805-06) and Sir John Shore (1806-13) was essentially pacific with little or no interest in the Himalayan regions. This enabled Bhim Sen Thapa to embark on extensive military campaign towards these territories, Pradhan, K.L. *op. cit.,* p. 10.
20. Sharma, B. *op. cit.,* p. 249.

21. Gyawali, S. *op. cit.*, pp. 39, 47-48.
22. Bist, S.D., *Shahi Sainik Itihas Kathmandu* (1963), pp. 83-86.
23. Rose Leo E. *Nepal Strategy for Survival*, London, 1973, p. 80.
24. Stiller, L.F. *The Rise of the House of the Gorkha*, Patna (1973), p. 328: Also see FSC 15th April, 1813 No. 19, letter of the Governor General to the Raja of Nepal, 7th May, 1813.
25. Rose Leo, E. *op. cit.*, p. 81.
26. Princep, H.T. *op. cit.*, Vol. 1, pp. 59-60 Campbell's sketch-1808, quoted in Hasrat, Bikramjit, History of Nepal, *op. cit.*, p. 182.
27. *Ibid.*, *pp.* 182-183; Abstracts from Lord Moira's Secret letters to the Court-BISL (l) 1778-1859. (Series-1).
28. For details of Gorkha aggressions see Princep, H.T. *A History of the Political and Military Transactions in India during the Administration of Marquees of Hastings (1813-23)* London 1825. Chaudhuri, K.C., *op. cit.*, pp. 150-163.
29. Ross-of-Bladenburg, The Marquees of Hastings, Oxford, 1898, p. 57.
30. Princep, H.T. *op. cit.*, 64.
31. Stiller, L.F. *op. cit.*, p. 328.
32. Hasrat, B.J. *op. cit.*, pp. 254-256.
33. Rose Leo, E., *op. cit.*, pp. 82.
34. Princep H.T. *op. cit.*, pp. 11 and 60-61.
35. Cox, J.L. (ed.) *Papers Respecting the Nepal War*, London, 1824.
36. *Ibid.*
37. Chaudhuri, K.C. *op. cit.*, p. 140:, Markham, C.R. Narratives of *the Mission of George Bogle to Tibeter*, Trubner and Co.(1876), p. 137.
38. Pradhan, K.L. *op. cit.*, pp. 8-10: Lamb, Alister, *Britain and Chinese Central Asia Road to Lhasa* 1767-1905, London (1960), pp. 38-60. Chaudhuri, K.C. *op. cit.*, pp. 38-60.
39. Rose, Leo E., *op. cit.*, pp. 75-79; Ramakant, *op. cit.*, p. 21.
40. *Ibid.*, Sharma, B.C. *op. cit.*, p. 255.
41. Yogi N. Nath, *Prithvi Narayan Shah Dibya Upadesh*, *op. cit.*, p. 12.
42. Campbell's Sketch.
43. Nepali, C.R. *op. cit.*, pp. 170-171; Regulations on Passports System issued to the Frontier offices; Regmi, M.C. *op. cit.*, p. 165.
44. Tyagi, S., *op. cit.*, p. 50.
45. FSC 30th June, 1802, No. 10 A.; Treaty of October 1801, Art. V.

46. Princep, H.T., *op. cit.*, A.2, p. 75.
47. Hasrat, B.J., *op. cit.*, p. 184.
48. Campbell's Sketch.
49. The General views of the Bharadars are recorded in Appendix I of Princep's *Political and Military Transactions*, n. 41; Nepali C.R. *op. cit.*, p. 49.
50. Sharma, B., *op. cit.*, p. 253; Gyawali, S. *op. cit.*, p. 66. Nepali, CR. *op. cit.*, pp. 85-86.
51. Princep, H.T. *op. cit.*, n. 41. pp. 59-61.
52. Hunter, W.W., *op. cit*, p. 99.
53. Stiller, L.F., *op. cit.,p.* 335.
54. P.T. Para 20.
55. Princep, H.T. *op. cit.*, pp. 456-61.
56. Nepali, C.R., *op. cit.*, p. 112.
57. Letter of Ramdoj Thapa to Bhim Sen Thapa 1814, published in Nepali, C.R. *op. cit.*, pp. 285-91.
58. *Ibid.*
59. Letter of Amar Singh Thapa to Kharidar Prithvi Bilas, 1815, vide Nepali *C.R. op. cit.*, pp. 94-101; Rose, Leo E., *op. cit.*, pp. 80-81.
60. Princep, H.T., *op. cit.*, pp. 35-58.
61. *Ibid.*
62. Nepali, C.R., *op. cit.*, pp. 301-302: Letter to the Chinese Emperor from Maharaja of Nepal: Yogi, N.N., *op. cit.*, p. 78.
63. Itihas Prakash, *op. cit.*, Vol. 1, pp. 78-92.
64. Nepali, C.R., *op. cit.*, pp. 311-312. Letter from Regent of the Dalai Lama, Tibet to Maharaja of Nepal (nd): Yogi, N.N., *op. cit.*, pp. 79-80.
65. Parker, E.H., *"Nepaul and Tibet"*, Asiatic Quarterly, VIII (1899), p. 72.
66. Rose, Leo E., *op. cit.*, p. 87: Nepali, C.R., *op. cit.*, pp. 89-95.
67. Thompson and Garratt, *Rise and Fulfilment of British Rule in India,* London (1935), pp. 256-257: For details of the Indo-Gorkha war, see *North and Northeastern Frontier Tribes of India, Compiled by Intelligence Branch Division of the Chief of the Staff Army Headquarters India* (1983 Reprint) Part I, Ch. I, pp. 1-38: Pemble, John, *The Invasion of Nepal,* Oxford (1971): *HRRK.* pp. 100-101.
68. Hunter, *Military Sketches of the Gorkha War in India in the Year 1814, 1815 and 1816,* London (1822): *HRRK*, pp. 776-777.

69. Ramakant, *op. cit.*, pp. 32-33: *NWP*, p. 841.
70. Edward Thompson, *The Life of Charles, Lord Metcalf*, London (1937) p. 164.
71. *NWP*, p. 947.
72. Stiller, F.L., *op. cit.*, pp. 334-335: FSC 16th August, 1814, No. 5, 30th June, 1802, No. 11: 15th January, 1813, No. 46: 9th August, 1814, Nos. 10 and 11; 16th August, 1814, No. 10.
73. Nepali, C.R. *op. cit.*, p. 103; Dungel, G. *op. cit.*, p. 27.
74. Stiller, F.L., *op. cit.*, p. 20; Ramakant, *op. cit.*, Ch. II, pp. 38-41.
75. Rose, Leo E., *op. cit.*, p. 88.
76. Aitchison, C.U., *op. cit.*, Vol. III, pp. 173-175.
77. Pradhan, K.L., *op. cit.*, p. 108.
78. P.T., Para-52.
79. Pradhan, K.L., *op. cit.* Ch. VI., pp. 113-138.
80. For details see Ramakant, *op. cit.*, Ch. XII.

IV

Bhim Sen Thapa's Foreign Policy: 1816-1833

The late war had greatly undermined the prestige and position of Mukhtiyar Bhim Sen Thapa in the Darbar. He led the nation into a major war and defeat for which he was accountable. What he actually desired was to drive the British from the sub-continent and form a formidable confederation which did not materialise. Instead, Nepal had not only been stripped off her one-third territory, but also was hemmed on the three sides by the British.[1] It practically meant an end of all the hopes of their most cherished martial profession. A permanent Resident had been posted at Kathmandu to monitor the political activities of the kingdom. Bhim Sen Thapa accepted his folly and was fully conscious that another confrontation with the British would reduce Nepal to a status of a protectorate state.[2] Meanwhile, there was growing opposition in the Darbar to replace Bhim Sen Thapa from power. The Resident reports the political situation that:

> The body of Bharadars of chief people of the state, with the bulk of the people, are represented, however, as very inimical to (Bhim Sen Thapa), and may be considered as range, therefore with the Raja's mother and the Goroo (Gajraj Misra), who appears to possess the right on their side and to have the true interest of the Raja and the state at heart; while the executive power support by the army, must be considered as with Bheem Sen.[3]

Yet, Bhim Sen Thapa remained in power. The reasons are not far to seek. The death of King Girwan Juddha shortly after attaining majority and left a minor son Rajendra Vikram Shah on the throne and the unflinching support he enjoyed from the regent queen grand-mother Tripura Sundari paved the way for him to remain in power. During the deliberations of the retrocession of the Tarai; Nepal-China affair and involvement of Nepalese with Sindhia, Bhim Sen Thapa had deliberately allowed the influential Bharadars to have their share in the post-war decision making. It gave him an opportunity to judge the opposition's strength while allowing them in the discussion. He possessed an ability to gauge when it was prudent to let the Bharadars have its way to suit his own interest. He controlled the Darbar by manipulating the various factions and allowed them to commit themselves to a course of action of national interest but cautious when the issue of his position was threatened. Whenever there was opposition from the power groups, he turned towards army for support to maintain his position in the Darbar. As a skilled politician, he possessed tolerant ability 'to manipulate coalition.'[4] Further, in order to make the support mere effective, he capitalised on a situation of confusion and fear of further British intervention in the internal politics of Nepal, which proved to be much stronger after the war than it had been before.[5]

The prevailing political situation in the Himalayan regions prompted Bhim Sen Thapa to formulate such policy which would serve his own purpose or interest. He kept the soldiery busy throughout the kingdom and rumours were spread that he was only waiting the arrival of foreign aids against the British. At the same time, he recognised British's strength and tried to avoid open hostility and to render the Treaty of Sagauli as little productive as possible for the British but to gain maximum out of their generosity. He accepted the entire treaty under the compulsion and promised to fulfil the Treaty obligations at least in theory. [6] Towards China, he assured to maintain and preserve the traditional friendship through the periodical mission. Thus, the survival of Nepal as a 'nation' became Bhim Sen Thapa's core policy. He knew that peace was the best policy to preserve the sovereignty of his country intact.

Thus, Bhim Sen Thapa formulated two basic objectives. The restoration of parts of all of the territories lost in the Sagauli Treaty and the withdrawal of the British Resident from Kathmandu. To achieve the objectives, he followed a policy of rendering the Treaty as much as nugatory as possible.[7] He took advantage of every opportunity to evade and revise the issue. During the course of negotiation for the Treaty of Sagauli, the Darbar pointed out that the subsistence of Nepal wholly depended on the Tarai and cession of three large stretches of the Tarai which constituted practically whole of Nepal's Tarai holdings was unacceptable to the Gorkhas.[8] In exchange for this, the Treaty granted Nepal two lakhs of rupees annually to be used as pensions to the Bharadars. It was made clear to the British that they could not survive without Tarai and that they would never accept a Treaty that deprived them of it. The British officials also realised that such a responsibility would involve the Government in serious troubles. The amount of rupees two lakhs would appear as a debit on the company's accounts and every year two lakh of rupees would have to be extracted from other sources of income to pay for it. Further, the climate was extremely unhealthy and administration most expensive and troublesome. Even the frontier officials were not in favour of retaining the Tarai lands. Thus the Governor General decided to return parts of the Tarai lands, except these situated between the river Kali and Rapti, to Nepal. In return it wanted to abolish Article 4 of the Treaty concerning pensions.[9]

The Governor General-in-Council finally resolved that:

> our commitment to pay Nepal two lakhs of rupees a year indemnity for the Tarai land taken from them a mistake. We can rectify this. When Gardner presents his credential as a 'gift', which will nullify our commitment to pay the two lakhs of rupees. This will protect our position and please the Nepalis, who place a high value on land and are reluctant to accept the pension.[10]

The Resident was accordingly instructed to communicate the decision of the Council to the Darbar. The Nepal Government wanted to regain as much Tarai as possible including all the productive lands that had been taken. Both the officials discussed the proposal, studied the sketch maps with the proposed boundary to be erected about four miles south of the northern points on the border. The proposal was turned down by the Darbar as the land to be restored would fall within the forest and return, little cultivated land never yield revenue of two lakhs rupees a year. They suggested that the border should be put further south.[11] The Governor General had no objection to accept the Darbar's proposal provided the basic objective were safeguarded that the British would retain all land that the Gorkhas had taken from the British subjects and establish a buffer between the Nepal border and the twenty two villages formerly in dispute. Therefore, the Resident was advised not to follow the two koses line rigidly and come to an understanding with the Darbar on principles and then take away only the lands which were essential for the British subjects.[12] Finally, it was agreed between Mukhtiyar Bhim Sen Thapa and the Resident that instead of two koses taken from the southern-most projection, only half kose throughout the length of the area to be restored to Nepal will be reserved by the British.[13] In due time, the Darbar wondered why the payment of two lakh rupees in pensions must be stopped if the return of part of land were truly a 'gift' from the Governor General. They pointed out that the value of the land to be restored was not equal to the two lakhs and suggested that if they had to choose, they might well opt for the continuance of the pensions.[14]

Lord Hastings decided that the tracts situated between the over Kosi and Orriah and between Tanavi and Gandak will also be given back to Nepal at the time of demarcation of the border.[15] He also granted the old boundary except at the disputed portion.[16] The disputed land literally meant the twenty-two villages of Naunore and other which were subject of dispute since 1812, were to be restrained by the British Government. On the basis of negotiations Resident Gardner prepared a memorandum of the retrocession of the Eastern Tarai and the annulment of pension.[17] On 14th September, 1816, the Governor General remarked on the restoration of Tarai and annulment of pensions that "when the Court of Nipaul becomes apprized of the full extent of the proposed restitution as stated in my letter of the 24th ultimo, it is possible that it may relinquish of receiving the amount of the pensions exclusive of the acquisition of the territories in the tract which it will gain". He further stated that:

> it may be hoped, therefore that they find their actual recovery of territory will so considerably surpass the expectations they could have indulged at the time when

> your conference with Gijraj Misser and Chunder Seecur on this subject of the pensions took place, they will consider those acquisitions as sufficient equivalent for the pensions.[18]

The document was presented to the young Maharaja Rajendra Vikram Shah on 8th December, 1816, the day of his accession[19]. The Maharaja acknowledged and expressed his satisfaction in a formal note. The return of extensive areas of land to Nepal included tracts of land that had never been held by the Nepali before.[20] Thronton attribute the act of the Governor General as:

> Vanity was the original source of all the error of Lord Moira in connection with the Nepaul war; it caused him to rush into it without due preparation; and it most characteristically reappeared, at the close of the campaign, in his notable project of giving the disputed lands back to the Nepaulese; by which act, though it set at naught all the principles of commonsense, and converted the war into an idle but dismal farce, he hoped to secure the reputation of being magnanimous and liberal.[21]

Immediately after the restoration of the Eastern Tarai to Nepal, the British demanded evacuation of the western Tarai from river Rapti to river Kali which was to be handed over to Nawab of Oudh. The Darbar also appointed its representative, Rudra Bir Shah Chautariya to supervise the evacuation. By January 1817, the British made certain concession to the Darbar by offering the title of holding of Bearee, a Bhutia pargana to the Darbar. The Nepalese evacuated the western Tarai without any more dificulty.[22] Yet, a controversy arose on the Gorakhpur frontier. The British Government claimed lands situated at western limits of Gorakhpur and the river Rapti. The Nawab of Oudh naturally claimed this territory. Actually. the British gave this tract to Nawab in exchange of one crore rupees of war loan that he gave during Anglo-Gorkha war.[23] Thus to compensate the Gorkhas, restoration of land between Gandak and Tanavi was immediately announced which was formerly to be done by the Magistrate of that fron tier at the time of survey and demarcation of the boundary. By 23rd July, 1817, the land in question was peacefully settled and handed over to the Nawab of Oudh.[24]

The demarcation of the boundary assumed an important aspect. The British Government, considering the necessity urged the Nepal Darbar for immediate demarcation of the frontiers. Bhim Sen Thapa did not understand the matter properly. He felt it necessary to interpose a trip of land between the border and the twenty two villages. Borders for him as well as for the Nepal river, ridges, mountain ranges and the extent of one's military control. Boundary lines were alien to his thinking. It was indeed difficult for anyone from Asia to grasp the concept of boundaries as it is today. Bhim Sen Thapa realised the importance of the boundary lines along the frontiers. He realised that the late war was partly due to such factors. A good and secure boundary free from all disputes is necessary for development of a country. At the same time, the British Government repeatedly pressed the Darbar for a proper survey and demarcation of the borders.[25]

On 7th December, 1817, the Darbar nominated the boundary commission under the leadership of Bum Shah Chautriya and Rudra Bir Shah. They were directed to proceed for the western Tarai. The British on their part deputed Lt. Grant. He was given clear instructions that everything up to the foot of the hills belonged to Oudh and beyond that to the Nepalese.[26] Both the representatives were abled to demarcate the boundary from Arrah to the river Chirolee only and postponed for the next good season.[27] In November 1817, as scheduled, both the parties proceeded with their works. However, dispute arose on Nepal-Oudh border. In fact, it was satisfactorily adjusted in March 1817 by both the representatives.[28] Taking advantage of the carelessness of the Oudh authority; the Gorkha did not evacuate the lands. The matter became more complicated when the British requested for complete evacuation of all territory up to foot of the hills was ignored by the Darbar. Rather they deployed two armed company to occupy the tracts. The British Government immediately demanded evacuation of those portions and the submission of the dispute for decision. The Resident was also asked to withdraw from Nepal in case the Darbar fail to meet the demands.[29] The remonstration had desired effect on the Darbar who agreed to withdraw from the lands situated between the projecting ridges. On 23rd July, 1819, Bhim Sen Thapa agreed to give up all as demarcated by Lt Grant. The principle of the foot of the hill was strictly adhered to throughout the demarcated line. Thus by the winter of 1819-20 the survey and demarcation was completed.[30]

The survey and demarcation of the boundary from Kosi to the western limits of Gorakhpur was based entirely on different footing. Here, the general principles of restoration and demarcation of the boundary was carried as follows. The Nepalese were to be restored all the lands which could have possibly been given without hazarding the frontier and future adjustment of the exact line of boundary. The actual line as stood in 1812 should be taken for considerations. Accordingly, the Magistrate of Gorakhpur, Sarun and Tirhut were appointed boundary commissioners of their respective districts. Lt. Col. Bradshaw was made incharge of Butwal and Seoraj. The demarcation of the frontiers of Sarun, Tirhut and Gorakhpur were completed in March and May 1817, respectively with the Nepalese officials. However, in the case of tract laying between the river Orriah and Gandak unilateral decision was taken by the British in December 1817, as the Darbar did not depute their commissioners during the period of demarcation.[31]

As regard to the boundary between river Kosi and Mechi, it was peacefully settled after the Darbar agreed to send its commissioner on the spot.[32] Here, the old frontier was confirmed and demarcation was completed in February 1818. The last important boundary to be settled was between Nepal and Sikkim. This portion was clearly demarcated by the river Mechi, but the problem soon arose as the river was divided itself into two branches before entering into India. Capt. B. latter, the political agent in Sikkim held that the old Mechi should be confirmed as the boundary. It was not clear in 1817, because Resident Gardner was reluctant to add that any discussion of this sort would create trouble, because the Treaty of Sagauli did not clarify whether old or new Mechi would be boundary and it would be impossible to satisfy the Darbar on this point.[33] The matter was kept pending till 1830's when it gave rise to a serious and prolonged dispute, and finally settled in Nepal's favour in 1839.[34]

These border questions were, in fact, settled without difficulty. Both the Governor General and Mukhtiyar Bhim Sen Thapa accepted the situation and worked with it even though there were certain areas in which neither were wholly satisfied. The idea of withdrawal of the Resident from the Kathmandu did not materialised. However, both of them agreed to respect the frontier and necessary instructions were given to their respective officials.[35]

While the relation between Nepal and British was just established a serious problem arose on the northern frontier of Nepal. Late in May 1816, Shee Chan Choon, the Chinese Emperor's special envoy, arrived in Lhasa with his army. He sent a letter, by way of Sikkim, to Capt. Latter, explaining that he had come to investigate the situation in the Himalayas and would shortly arrive at Tingri, a pass on the Nepal-Tibet border. It might be recalled that Nepal had political relations with China since 1792 when the latter had intervened in the Nepal-Tibet war. At the end of war, Nepal promised to send periodical mission with presents to Peking every fifth year. The Chinese on their part kept aloof from the internal affairs of Nepal. Since the commencement of the Anglo-Gorkha war, the Darbar was trying to entreat the Chinese Emperor against the British. In 1815, when the Gorkhas had lost Kumaon and Sikkim, the Amban at Lhasa was reportedly urged to forward their letter to Chinese Emperor at Peking.[36] The Darbar. in their letters, sought for aid in the form of money and weapons.[37] The request was politely refused. The Ambans not only refused to forward the letter to the Chinese Emperor, but the reply was curt:

> Your Highness (the Maharaja of Nepal) requested both cash and weapons from the Ambans and you requested that we write to the Emperor about this. The Emperor of China sits on the heads of all. Never has any king of this world been able to damage the wealth or weapon of China. But it is not China's custom to give money or weapons to other countries. Therefore, we Ambans cannot send your request to the Emperor.[38]

Mukhtiyar Bhim Sen Thapa was not detected with Amban's reply. Rather he variegated the case that the Anglo-Gorkha war was actually a direct threat to Tibet. The Darbar further fabricated false notion that the British had offered a huge amount of money provided the Darbar allow them to pass through their territory to Tibet and had ordered Kathmandu to pay the British the tribute formerly paid to China.[39] The Chinese Commander immediately sought explanation from the Governor General to ascertain the allegation, that

> such absurd measures (as those alluded to) appear quite

> inconsistent with the usual wisdom of the English. It is probably that they never made the declaration imputed to them. If they did, it will not be well... An answer should be sent as soon as possible to Tingaree (Tingri) stating whether or not the English really made the absurd propositions imputed to them...[40]

At the same time they dispatched a letter asking them (the Darbar) to be more specific on the matter.[41] While replying the letter, the Governor General explained the origin of the war with the Gorkha and explicitly blamed them for the attack on British territories, Butwal and others, killing several company officials. He further added that:

> it has been agreed that accredited agents shall be received by each government from the other and all the usual offices of amity between neighbouring and friendly states will be studiously performed. The British Government has no view of aggrandisement and only seeks to remain at peace with other states and no motives of ambition and interest prompt it to extend its influence and authority beyond those barriers which appear to have been placed by nature between the vast countries of India and China.[42]

The Darbar was not satisfied with the Ambans. They continuously pressed them to send the request to the Chinese Emperor for help or give permission to accept British overload and be exempted from the obligations of sending quinquennial mission. Persistent efforts of the Darbar finally induced the Ambans to dispatch along and exhaustive report to Peking. On the basis of the report, the Chinese Emperor ordered a small army of five thousand to proceed towards the border with an avowed object was "to investigate the cause of war and to ascertain who were in fault".[43] Further the Darbar was warned that if on investigation turn out 'fabricated falsehood' against them as suspected, they would receive punishment. In the same letter, the Darbar was directed to send deputation along with a letter asking forgiveness of its action and promise to continue the quinquennial mission.[44] It is difficult to ascertain with what object the force was dispatched. It may be due to the Gorkha allegation that the British demanded a free passage through Nepal to invade Tibet, or the Chinese were jealous of the recently concluded Anglo-Gorkha relations. It may also be possible that the force was dispatched because Nepal had not sent the usual periodical mission on the last occasion. However, it is clear that the Chinese could not have intervened effectively in the Anglo-Gorkha war on the basis of their own strength. The Ambans knew that the Nepalese and the British inhabit far distant lands to interest the Chinese Emperor.[45]

The Ambans knew the intention of Bhim Sen Thapa to bring the Chinese under its influences. He was warned that the Chinese forces that arrived in the border was not to protect or help Nepal against the British. The Darbar was flatly told that "not even one of your requests will be fulfilled". Rather, the letter ended with a treat to invade Nepal "with a mighty force and annihilate you", if the quinquennial mission to emperor was not dispatched in time.[46]

The arrival of the Chinese force had put Mukhtiyar Bhim Sen Thapa in awkward position. Since the war had been already over and Treaty of Sagauli had been signed, it would serve no purpose at all. The Gorkha had fought the war without the permission of the Emperor. Yet, Bhim Sen Thapa hoped to exploit Calcutta's apprehensions so long as the Chinese force was on the border to effect two basic objectives—the withdrawal of the British Resident at Kathmandu and the restoration of part or all of the territory lost in the Sagauli Treaty.[47]

Bhim Sen Thapa started giving exaggerated accounts of its intentions to the Resident that the discontinuation of the periodical mission and the arrival of the British Resident in Nepal were the main reason of the Chinese action. He further reported that the Chinese insisted that he should personally explain the reason for it discontinuance.[48] He even tried to win over the British support against the Chinese. On 30th August, 1816, the Resident was told that being situated between the two powerful states they could only be saved by throwing their lot with the British.[49] The Darbar envoys, Gajraj Misra and Chandra Sekhar Upadhaya explained to the Resident that China:

> was deeply offended considering Nepaul a tributary of the Emperor, at this Government's having entered into war and concluded peace with the English without his sanction or knowledge; and that the Chinese army had advanced

> for the express purpose of resenting this offence and entering Nepaul.[50]

The Gorkha had most frequently alleged that the recently concluded relations with the British had given rise to the Chinese action. The Resident reported that "it was necessary for them to throw themselves into the arms of one of the powerful neighbours and gave me clearly to understand that they (the Gorkhas) would prefer adhering to us".[51]

The British Government did not take the Chinese affairs seriously in the beginning and hoped they would retire immediately. But upon Resident's taking serious view of the situation, Lord Hastings formulate detailed policy statement. He did not like any permanent establishment of the Chinese influence in Nepal which would have given opportunity for dispute with that empire.[52] At one point the Governor General could not afford to estrange the Chinese, because the commercial interests of the British in China were of such great consequence, that small advantages arising out of the Treaty of Sagauli stood nowhere in comparison. He was ready to make major concession on the Nepal question if necessary to appease the Chinese Government. On 16th September, 1816, he observed that:

> the maintenance of peace and amity with the emperor of China as an object of such vast consequence to the commercial interest of the United Kingdom that no efforts ought to be spared on the part of this Government to prevent the present state of things from taking a turn which might occasion even any suspension of those relations. Therefore, exclusive of all consideration and convenience for this Government, the avoidance of any engagement with the Nepalese which may embroil us with or even give umbrage of the Chinese must be regarded as the basis of our whole proceedings.[53]

He was even ready to concede the withdrawal of the Residency from Kathmandu if unavoidable "to remove this source of jealousy entertained by the Chinese". He was compelled to take such step because of the brewing troubles with the Marathas and Pindaris. Meanwhile, the Chinese Commander in Tibet answered the

Governor General's letter of August confirming the ulterior motives of Bhim Sen Thapa and the allegations levelled against the British. It was ascertained that "the Gorkha's story has proved entirely false".[54] And the settlement between Nepal and the company was just and no blame was to be attached to the British. Assured now that the Chinese were not disturbed by the establishment of a Residency at Kathmandu the question of its withdrawal was dropped.

Having failed to secure British intervention, Bhim Sen Thapa eventually dispatched a mission consisting of Dalbhajan Pande, Ranbir Singh Thapa and Bhakta Bir Thapa on 10th September, 1816 to attend on the Chinese officers.[55] The delegates handed over a letter from the Maharaja of Nepal in which it was stated that "from the first, the Gorkha Raja has existed by the blessings of the Emperor and now under the auspices, he looks obtain relief and protection and in continuing his faithful tributary, to enjoy his favour to the day of judgment".[56] The Gorkha delegates tried to conceal the wrong done by the Darbar during the meeting. The Chinese officials who berated the Gorkhas for their untrustworthiness and stated, "you and the Feringhi (the English) concluded a gha (treaty). Both letters agree. When you already have a settlement why do you ask for more You must live in peace with others".[57] Further, they remarked that:

> You have told us that the English entered your country for the sole purpose of establishing there a warehouse and on what plea can I attempt to remove merchants for such people are not molested in any country whatsoever.[58]

The Gorkha deputies pressed the Chinese officials that even if they could not provide assistance to Nepal as requested, at least they should write to Calcutta asking the British to withdraw their Residency from Kathmandu. Dalbhajan Pande, one of the delegates, told them that "if they (British) were merely merchants it would be of no import but they are soldiers and commander and what connexion have troops with merchants". The Chinese Commander refused to agree their explanations rather rebuked the Gorkha delegates that:

> The English have written to us that they sent the Resident

> with your consent. Therefore, at what have you to complain. And as to what your Rajah wrote about the English having demanded of him the roads through Bhote with the intention of penetrating into Bhootan and China, it is false for if they had those views they were not likely to go by Nepaul when they have less circuitous routes.[60]

However, the Chinese wrote to the company requesting the withdrawal of its Resident from Nepal to maintain friendly relations. Lord Hastings, in his reply strongly affirmed that he would ready to withdraw the Residency from Kathmandu if China would appoint an agent in Kathmandu to prevent future confrontations like recent hostilities. But the Chinese official responded that there was no need to depute a Chinese agent to Kathmandu and thus accepted the British Residency there.[61]

During the period of clarification, it was clear that China strongly disliked Gorkha militarism. Indeed Peking's sovereignty over Kathmandu did not oblige it to ignore Nepalese jingoism far less encourage it. The Chinese Emperor clearly told the Nepalese King that the latter's entreaties for military or political assistance could not be entertained because "the sovereign authority of the Emperor of China does not extend over Nepal"[62], but had to pay respect to the Emperor and to send the quinquennial mission.[63] The Chinese recognised Nepal's right to wage war, sign treaties and maintain independent relations with other countries.[64]

The withdrawal of Chinese troops from Tibet in 1817 led to the improvement of Anglo-Gorkha relations. The Chinese episode hardly affected both of them. The Nepalese, British and the Chinese realised the limitations of their respectives positions and did not like to go beyond that. For the present the limited interests in Nepal cause China no apprehension, although China's position in Nepal did have a restraining effect on British ambitions in the country. The Governor General, for his part placed on record a clear statement that:

> The independence of the state of Nepaul had not been affected in any way by its treaty with the British Government which claimed no supremacy over it, exacted no services and Nepaul and China whatever they were before had consequently undergone no change in

> consequence of the affairs having become connected with those of Nepaul through recent events that any impression of this sort arising from the establishment of British residency at Catmandoo was entirely unfounded since the arrangement had no other object than to facilitate and adjustment of depending questions and to promote and improve the relations of friendship.[65]

All attempts made by Mukhtiyar Bhim Sen Thapa to the Chinese against the British during 1816-17 did not produced any results. Instead, he was merely instructed "to remain on good terms with his neighbours and attend to all matters with the utmost diligence". [66] Once he failed to gain assistance from the Chinese, he turned towards several Indian Native states. It may be recalled that during the Anglo-Gorkha war, the Darbar had sought support from disaffected Indian States against the British. And Bhim Sen Thapa even planned to form a confederation to drive away the British from the region. Secret letters and emissaries were dispatched to the Courts of Sikh, Marathas, Gwalior and other states. But the efforts were futile. An opportunity once again, set in to re-establish contacts with the Indian Native states in the context of Maratha war 1817-18.[67] It is true that Nepal had been in correspondence with the courts of Sindhia since the days of Rana Bahadur Shah's exile in Banaras. The Treaty of Sagauli, though restricted contacts between Nepal and the Native states of India, former had secretly continued.[68] Most historians write that till 1816 Bhim Sen Thapa was manoeuvring by conspiracies and intrigues with the Chinese and the disaffected Indian states. It cannot be denied that constant military activities and recruitment went on unabled after the war. Nor can it be challenged that the Gorkha emissaries were secretly involved in intrigues with the Indian states against the British. To any keen observer and certainly to one as shrewd as Bhim Sen Thapa, it was evident that nothing could come of such intercourse.

A close examination of the nature and extent of intrigues reveals that Bhim Sen Thapa did not intend to break the Treaty. Nor was there any doubt in his mind about the policy of keeping peace. He was indeed convinced that the maintenance of peace was the best policy for the independence of Nepal. It was argued that the motives behind the military preparation was to keep the army busy to whom he owed his own position in the Darbar. Even the Resident remarked on 19th August, 1816 that best disposition was felt by the existing Darbar administration. He further reported that the restoration of Tarai and the brief intervention of Chinese, the relations further improved. On his letter to the Government of India on 4th June, 1817, he wrote:

> It is worthy of remark that the nature of my official intercourse with the government has of late undergone an evident improvement. They are perceptibly becoming by degree less jealous and apprehensive of us and more reconcile to our connection...[69]

However, towards the early part of 1817, the occurrences in Central India gave a fillip to the Darbar activities and consequently reasons for the British to be suspicious. The problems with the Pindaris and Marathas was brewing since long time. The former were a powerful gang of robbers of Central India of the disbanded soldiers of the Maratha Chief. They used to plunder the neighbouring territories in Rajasthan, Bundelkhand. Their cruelties created a feeling of awe and terror. Every year they created devastations in the British provinces and were getting stronger due to pacific policy of the British and encouragement from the Maratha chiefs.[70] Sindhia and Holkar also invaded the Rajput states, exacted Chauth and always challenged the British authority. The Maratha Peshwa Baji Rao II was most restive under the subsidiary alliance and only awaited an opportunity to relinquish from the ignominious treat. The British reaction to the correspondence between the Maratha and Nepal Darbar was mild until trouble began to develop in early 1817. When the Peshwa appealed for support against the British was circulated, the British Government asked the Darbar for an official explanation.[71] The situation in Central India prompted Bhim Sen Thapa to renew the clandestine intrigues by sending Nepal's emissary Pandit Padma Mani to various disaffected Indian Native states with a view to recover their lost territory.[72]

On 3rd August, 1817, Gardner reported that "a correspondence of this nature has been mentioned since a long time through the agent of this state at Gwalior. It is certainly far from being of a friendly character".[73] Secret informations were exchanged between the Darbar and the court were found to be decidedly compromising. Some of these letters were intercepted by the British Officials.[74]

Matter reached its height in November 1817 when Peshwa Baji Rao II attacked the British Residency at Khadki. On the same day, the British succeeded in concluding a treaty with Daulat Rao Sindhia and the latter promised never to have any further contact with the Pindaris. At the same time, the army of Sindhia was placed at the disposal of the British Government. One by one the Marathas confederations submitted to the British. And incidentally, Nepal's emissary Padma Mani was apprehended by the British official with his hostile papers. The reverse suffered by the Marathas, the treaty with Sindhia and Gaekwad and the intercept of secret letters with Padma Mani dimmed any enthusiasm at Kathmandu for such a foolish venture. The Resident was informed to communicate the development to Bhim Sen Thapa. It had desired effect on the Darbar who alleged that Padma Mani had exceeded his power and would be removed and assured to maintain peace and friendship.[75]

While such development was going on, Bhim Sen Thapa ordered military preparations. Troops were alerted to prepare the defence. The army on the border were warned to be vigilant to the dangers of a surprise attack. A letter was sent to Bakhtabar Singh Thapa of Palpa on 24th November, 1817:

> We have been informed by you of the assembling of the English troops in the Teraee—you are directed to keep on the alert as the English are treacherous and be careful you are not surprised and destroyed by a night attack as Parsuram Thapa was. If the troops of the English are come with any other design, do you keep us informed of this intention in order that the necessary measures may be taken[76]

Such uproar in the Darbar was the result of Governor General who had undertaken a tour in the upper province with some military detachment. It was indeed Bhim Sen Thapa's policy. Being the Mukhtiyar of a defeated martial nation, he had always to keep the soldiery in a good humour by maintaining a war jingoism so as to secure his own position in the Darbar. It must be kept in mind that there always existed a permanent 'war party' in the

Darbar. "Levies of troops", reported Gardner that "continue to be made and the military force was gradually been increasing not only in the valley but as I am informed in other provinces".[77] With this final move Bhim Sen Thapa checkmated for the time his opposition in the Darbar. He had earlier turned to the army for support in his strauggle to control the Darbar. Now, he had the means to motivate and his position in government was once more secure. As a result of these stratagem, he assumed the burden of governing Nepal and made himself responsible for the welfare of its citizens and the security of the state both for the present and the future.[78] Recognition of Bhim Sen Thapa's skill in maneuvering the factions at the Darbar to achieve his purpose should not obscure a very basic truth. His elevation was the product of patience, a shrewd mind and a mastery of local politics.

As regard to recent upheaval, Bhim Sen Thapa himself observed that "all persons were not unanimous of the same way of thinking and that different times induce different conduct and ideas". He went on "that procedure of this Government had been in a great measure swayed by the violence party spirit here".[79] Whatever may be the outcome, it cannot be denied that he made some capital out of the British troubles. By 1820, the relations between the Darbar and the British relatively improved. The Resident expressed satisfaction that the routine business was attended to regularly and gradually every indication of hostility passed away. He wrote to the Government of India that:

> the feeling of distrust and suspicion, which was so long and generally indulged appear to have been dismissed from the mind of the administration.[80]

Notes

1. Rose, Leo E., *op. cit.,* pp. 88-89; Thompson, E., *op. cit.,* pp. 164-165.
2. Ramakant, *op. cit.,* 56-58: Nepali, C.R. *op. cit.,* p. 63.
3. *FSC,* 29th March, 1817, No. l.
4. Reisman, David, *et al., The Lonely Crowd,* New Haven, Conn.(1961) p. 211.

5. Stiller, F.L., *op. cit.*, p. 106.
6. Nepali, C.R., *op. cit.*, p. 118: Ramakant. *op. cit.*, p. 60. Stiller, F.L., *op. cit.*, p. 113.
7. Ramakant. *op. cit.*, pp. 58-60.
8. Stiller, F.L., *op. cit.*, pp. 102-105: Ramakant. *op. cit.*, pp. 46-49. Nepali, C.R. *op. cit.*, pp. 116-117.
9. Aitchison. *op. cit.*, Vol. II, pp. 173-75.
10. *FSC*, 4th May, 1816, No. 70.
11. Ramakant, *op. cit.*, pp. 51-55.
12. *FSC*, 24th August, 1816, No. 12.
13. Stiller, F.L. *op. cit.*, pp. 218-220.
14. *FSC*, 24th August, 1816 No. 11.
15. *FSC*, 2nd November, 1816. No. 29.
16. *Ibid.*, No. 34.
17. Appendix.
18. *FSC* 14th September, 1816. No. 4.
19. Memorandum presented to the Maharaja of Nepal dated 8th December, 1817; Aitchison, n. 22, Ch. I, pp. 113-115. Appendix.
20. *Ibid.*, Letter of Maharaja of Nepal, 11th December, 1816.
21. E. Thompson., *The History of the British Empire in India.* London, (1843) 4:344.
22. *FPC*, 28th December 1816, No. 50.
23. Princep, H.T., *op. cit.*, p. 207.
24. *FPC*, 8th August 1817, No. 57.
25. Stiller, F.L., *op. cit.*, pp. 220-221; Ramakant, *op. cit.*, p. 51.
26. *FPC*, 3rd April 1818, No. 41.
27. *Ibid.*, No. 51.
28. *FPC*, 8th April, 1819. No. 56.
29. *FPC*, 19th June, 1819, No. 10: Campbell's Sketch: 1819; The Government wrote to the Resident of Lucknow that "the construction of the Treaty now attempted by the Nepalis must ofcourse be resisted. Although it was not the intention of the Government to derive the Nepalis of the entire Terai west of the Kosi, yet the cession of the whole of it, quite to the foot of the hills, was distinctly exacted, and any part which might subsequently be left to the Nepalis was to be received by them as a gratuitous boon from this Government, admitting of no discussion. Our Resident in Nepal was directed (19th June, 1819) to address a formal demand to the Rajah for the immediate recall of the Gorkha troops now forcibly

occupying the disputed lands on the Oudh frontier, and continues the dispatch: 'in the event of your not meeting with sufficient attention to your demand, you will intimate the Darbar that continued contumacy will lead to the application of the strict principle of the Treaty to the whole eastern portion of the Terai, and you will be prepared to receive the Governor-General's orders for withdrawing from the Court'."

30. *Ibid.*, No. 11.
31. FPC. 10th April 1817, No. 55; *FPC*. 3rd May 1817, No. 16; *FPC*. 31st May, 1817, No. 83; *FPC*. 21. November 1817, No. 49. Also see *FPC*. 30th January 1818, No. 43.
32. Ramákant, *op. cit.*, p. 54. Campbell's Sketch.
33. *FPC*. 30th January 1818, No. 43; *FPC*, 13th March, 1818, No. 20.
34. Tickell's, *Events in Nepal*, 1839.
35. Stiller, *op. cit.*, pp. 224-225: Pemble, John., *op. cit.*, pp. 343-344.
36. Rose, Leo E., *op. cit.*, pp. 85-86; For further details see Poudel, Bishnu Prasad, *Nepals Relations with Tibet*, 1792-1856. (Ph.D. Dissertation, New Delhi, 1963).
37. *Ibid.*
38. Nepali, C.R., *op. cit.*, pp. 300-302; A letter of Chinese Ambans in Lhasa to Maharaja of Nepal (Translation).
39. *Ibid-* A letter form the Maharaja of Nepal to Chinese Amban.
40. *Ibid-* A letter from Chinese Amban to the Governor General.
41. *FSC*, 13th July 1816, No. 17, 20th May, 1816.
42. *Itihas Prakash*, *op. cit.*, Vol. I., p. 70.
43. *FSC*, 3 August, 1816, No. 16. Governor General, Lord Hastings to the Chinese Commander in Tibet, 3rd August, 1816.
44. *FSC*, 27 July 1816, No. 12, Chinese Commander to Nepal Darbar, 18th May 1816. Nepali, C.R., *op. cit.*, pp. 312-14. The Darbar was told by the Amban that "we have not asked whether you are fighting with the foreigners or whether you have made peace with them. We are not concerned. Nor will soldier be send to your aid...Think well and tell us who it was who said this. We have come for this sole purpose, to fight them and to burn them to cinders. We have not come to give your country the help that you requested. As soon as you receive this letter, write to us telling us truthfully whether the English told you this or someone in your own country invented this idea that you should leave the Tibet road and

not to send the emperor gifts. After we have considered your answer we will come with our army to turn them to cinders and completely destroy them".

45. Ramakant, *op. cit.*, pp. 66-67.
46. Nepali, C.R., *op. cit.*, Appendix, pp. 312-14 Chinese Commander to Nepal Darbar, 31 July 1816.
47. *FSC*, 10th August, 1816. No. 18. The Resident reported that the Chinese "were rather intended to create alarm in my mind so lend me to suppose that these Chinese were severely preparing to afford some military aid" and "thus induce as great latitude"
48. *FSC*, 14th September, 1816. Nos. 39 and 41; *FSC*, September 1816, No. 18.
49. *FSC*, 14th August, 1816, No. 42.
50. FSC, 14th August, 1816, Nos. 38-42.
51. *Ibid.*
52. *FSC*, 14th September, 1816, No. 19.
53. *FSC*, 14th September 1816, No. 43: He further stated that "the subjection of Nepal by the Chinese in the sense of establishment of the Chinese power in that country would indeed be a circumstance greatly to be deprecated by us, as bringing us more directly in contact with that Government and multiplying the chances of dispute and dissensions".
54. *FSC*, 11th January, 1817, No. 6, From Ambans to Government of India, 28th December, 1816.
55. *FSC*. 12th October, 1816. Letter from Maharaja of Nepal to Chinese Emperor, 7th September 1816.
56. *Ibid.*
57. Nepali, C.R. *op. cit.*, Appendix, p. 305. Letter from Ranbir Singh Thapa to Bhim Sen Thapa, 26th October, 1816.
58. *FSC*. 11th January, 1817, No. 3.; Pemble, John., *op. cit.*, pp. 344-345.
59. *Ibid.*
60. Nepali, C.R., *op. cit.*, pp. 300-302.
61. *FSC*. 11th January, 1817, No. 3.
62. Quoted in Majumdar, K. *op. cit.*, p. 104.
63. Dhanalaxmi, R., *op. cit.*, p. 31.
64. Nepali, C.R., *op. cit.*, pp. 312-314, Letter of Shee Chan Choon to the Darbar of Nepal.
65. *FSC*. 14th September 1816. No. 43, Letter of Governor General

The Council of Ministers consisting of four to five Ministers were formed to assist the king in daily administration. Chautara and Pramana were deputed as area officers. It can be assumed that there were Minister level authorities in charge of different districts, unit, provinces.[9] Similarly, the appointment of Chautara existed in the Gorkha and Sen rajyas. No mention of law could be seen during Malla period. As such, administration was carried out by the royal priest and designated officers on the basis of policy matters. The panchayati system evolved and developed during the Lichhavi period continued on even during the Malla period. The ultimate source of decision in the administration was the king. It has seen that different officers functioned on the basis of work distribution in administrative set up with different titles like—Taksali, Chem Mandal, Guthi Katak, Gana Nayak, Mahane, Desh Nayak.[10] Hence the main responsibilities of administration during the Malla period was to maintain peace, security, defence of kingdom from external aggression, collection of taxes, maintain cordial relations with the neighbouring countries, preserve religious traditions and customs etc.[11]

In the absence of historical evidence on administrative system of the scattered Baisi and Chaubisi rajyas, prior to the unification of Nepal, nothing can be said about it. However, in the kingdom of Gorkha, established by Dravya Shah (1559-1570), the influence of the administrative pattern as practised by the previous rulers; justice loving and reformist king Ram Shah (1606-1633) and the great warrior Prithvi Narayan Shah (1742-1774) continued even after the unification of Nepal. It is said that the unification of Nepal as a single kingdom became possible by the Gorkha kings.[12]

Before we discuss the administrative system during the Thapa hegemony, it is necessary to study about the system of administration immediately after the unification. In spite of changes in tenure of reign, it seems that the Gorkha rulers of Nepal tend to follow the administrative tradition of their predecessors. They considered it against the religion to break away the existing pattern and tradition. In such a manner, Nepal administrative system is solely influenced by religion. This religious feeling has also helped in protection of old Nepali traditions to some extent. The following sentences exemplify as to how Prithvi Narayan Shah viewed existing traditions and customs:

> I have seen the traditions and customs evolved and enforced but the king Ram Shah, Jayasthi Malla and Mahendra Malla. I also wished to evolve twelve thousands of such traditions and customs had god willed.[13]

He was unable to contribute much towards administrative system as he was busy waging and fighting wars most of the time. So the administrative tradition prevalent in the Gorkha continued on in toto in entire Nepal. The government's function was to collect taxes and revenue, maintain peace and security and to look after legal administration especially. It was believed that the supremacy of Government prevailed all over the kingdom. The peasants, cultivators submitted directly to the palace. During Shah rule, except for the conspiracies among the authorities, no example of government wanting to be involved in maintenance of peace and security is found.[14]

Petty cases were arbitrated in the courts of local panchayats. There was a provision for Bhara Panch (five Bharadars* with similar power) to arbitrate on the matter related with important palace affairs. Dhanabraja Brajacharya, complex of historical documents of Nepal has claimed the existence of Bhara Panch or Panch Pramana as a strong organ of the administrative system during Shah rule.[15] Evidence can be derived that popular opinion of the majority of the people received due respect and decisions were made on the basis of it, from the fact that Prithvi Narayan Shah appointed Kalu Pande as Minister because he was the choice of people, whereas he favoured Biraj Bhakheti. Legal matters, especially in the court of king were decided on the basis of religious and moral sanctions. People were not denied the right to present required evidence and witness in legal case. As such, the distance between the ruler and the rule seems not to be far and away. Big projects were carried out through social assistances. However, supremacy in administration was limited to few privileged section. So there was no participation of general public at all in the administration. But it does not indicate that the public were totally aloof from the problem of the nations. In the event of external aggression, they used to come out with whatever kind of weapons they possessed, in order to defend their territory. It is quite natural that it was beyond their capacity to take keen interest in the activities and affairs of kingdom due to their ignorance. Few sections of the privileged and high caste, who could win confidence of king, were able to collect and keep the written documents issued by the king granted to them during a king's tenure so that their descendants also could continue to enjoy it even after their retirement.[16] The subsequent rulers too followed the tradition evolved by Prithvi Narayan Shah. A piece from his 'Dibya Upadesh' clarify the fact that '....let the descendents of Kalu Kawardar not be denied of Kawardari; also Shiv Ram Basnet's descendents (who was in-charge of south); Kalu Pande's descendents (who was in charge of Bhot, Tibet). Let the Bharadari be given alternatively to the Pander, Basniats, Pants, Magars etc. They are loyal and trusted servants'.[17] Thus, the administration centred around family base. Those sections having part in the administration automatically got elevated in social strata and economically, better than ordinary people. They gradually grew more powerful and, sometimes, paralysed king's political and administrative machinery. Towards the later part of the eighteenth century, the Shah king promulgated the administrative system to be complemented throughout the kingdom.[18]

During pre-war, Bhim Sen Thapa had followed the administrative system laid down by his predecessors. However, efforts are being made to discuss the contemporary administration in separate headings.

In the central administration, the king was the supreme authority. As Hindu states, the sources of all royal power and prerogative were derived from the ideal embodied in 'dharma'.[19] It was the basis and the authority in society. The state must, therefore, function in accordance with the ideals of Dharma or at least aspire to do so. In theory, the king was above queries about his work and activities. He was looked upon with respect and veneration by all sections of people. Though the king was hereditary monarch yet was not the absolute despot. He has to rule over his subjects with the principle of justice and morality. He was a benevolent monarch and not a cruel administrator. His chief duty was to maintain peace and order, to protect the people from external aggressions, to punish the wrong-doers and work for the welfare of his subjects.[20] The main organs of the central administration was the committee of Bharadars consisting the Chautariya, Kazis, Sardars, Kharidars, Kapardars and Khazanchi.

The Chautariya was a member of the royal family but not in line of succession (a collateral) and usually the king's brother. The functions of Chautariya on the administration of the country:

> ... is to appoint and dismiss the Kazis. Whatever any Kazi shall transgress a treaty, arrangement, justice or the customs of our country, he shall be reported to the king and punished in accord with the king's command. After consulting with other officers, appoint men who are loyal, wise, cleaver, fearless and with good background. Inform the king and after receiving his answer, take them to see the king. If a Kazi proves disloyal, if his work begins to deteriorate, first make certain of the fact, then inform the king. On orders from king, punish him according to the nature of his offence. If the nation prospers, this also should be reported to the king. If the Kazis and nobles thrives, this too should be reported to the king.[21]

Its shows that the Chautariya occupied a high position in the administrative strata of the country. He served as the king's hand in the execution of royal orders. In spite of exalted position of Chautariya, in the Darbar, its function had considerably diminished from 1804 onwards since all of this work was taken over first by Rana Bahadur Shah and later by Mukhtiar Bhim Sen Thapa. Yet, Chautariyas continued to be appointed during the period under review as the king was being minor. It seems that the regent queen Tripura Sundari Devi appointed additional Chautariyas to appease the members of royal family although the administrative machinery was in the hands of Mukhtiar Bhim Sen Thapa. The presence of these Chautariyas however brought new complications to the administration.[22] In fact, their close and constant vigilance on both the minor king and the regent as well as in the administration had created problem for the Mukhtiar to manoeuvre. It was the presence of these persons in the administration that made the regent's patronage so valuable to Bhim Sen Thapa.

The main organ of the central administration was the committee of Bharadars. Important decisions on matter related to the administration were made by the Bharadari Sabha chaired by king. There were Kazis to discharge daily administrative duties.[23] Their appointment could be terminated or renewed annually on Panajani by the king. The Kazis and Sardars looked after the high level civil and military administrations. While the Kapardar was entrusted with royal household, the Khazanchi looked after the government properties, treasury and revenue of the state. The Kharidars were entrusted with the civil administration. It appears from the available records that expansion of Bharadars took place after Rana Bahadur Shah returned from Banaras in 1804.[24] The newly appointed Bharadars along with the old had to perform specific duties assigned to them under close control and supervision of the king. They not only discussed important matters pertaining to state but also matter relating to the palace. The role of Bhara Panch evolved during the Malla period continued in the Shah era as Bharadari Shabha whose decision was recognised as law. King used to deliver policies, directives and advises in the Shabha to be executed by official in such a manner, intra-relationship between palace and administrative structure developed through Bharadari Shabha. It further discussed the matter such as corruption in the government, declaration of wars, cancellation of renewal of appointment of Bharadars and other important matters like revenue collection and land reclaimation.[25]

Besides, there were Guru and priest called Dharmadhikar who functioned as the justice. The Brahmin's status being highest in the social strata, they were exempted from manual works and death penalty whatsoever be their crime.[26]

After Bhim Sen Thapa took over the Mukhtiarship in 1806, he seems to make efforts to become more organised and secured taking advantage of prevailing administrative condition. When Rana Bhaduar Shah was still alive, there was an ample opportunity for him to become chief Kazi while Panjani was held in 1804, but chose to remain as a mere Kazi, initiated his ambitious plan and later availed the opportunity to consolidate power in 1806 after the assassination of Rana Bahadur Shah and become Mukhtiar. It alleged that he immediately appointed his close relatives into the military hierarchy? But the close study of the period revealed that such steady infiltration were found. In fact, most of the Thapas who held jagirs were men who held the posts before the war.[27] Yet during the period under review few Thapas were elevated to the post of Kazis and some of them occupied high level posts in the administration. Within the central administrative organ, there were inner circle and outer circle Kazis. The former comprised those who were in the decision making level of the government and the later were on command of troops or were posted as Governor in the districts. It is true that no single family monopolised the inner circle of government. Thapas, Kanwars (Rana), Basnyats and Pandes all had shares in the prerogatives of the inner circle.[28] Indeed Bhim Sen Thapa tried to establish the balance required for any longer tenure of office by including representatives of the leading Kshatriya families in his very group. Both civil and military officials of high ranking sat together and discussed the various matters pertaining to administration, collection of taxes, expansion of military with a view to defend the country from external invasion as well as the development programme. However, in the absence of national planning and statistic, the administration could not provide proper and effective service. The government ran on decentralised-centralisation pattern, at least in theory.[29]

Bhim Sen Thapa's administration was sympathetic towards woes of the general public can be gauged from the various reforms he tried to bring uniformity in social and economic life of the people.[30] Conflicts can be traced in administrative system as the centre had decentralised some power to district authority in certain cases while the zilla administrators had to maintain direct contact with the centre even on triffle matters. Thus before him, the state's whole administrative power was with the centre and the areas outside its periphery were administered locally. Therefore, Bhim Sen Thapa, with a view to maintain balanced administration appointed experienced and able Chautariyas, Kazis, Bada Hakims as Governors to run the administration at various places.[31] Accordingly, Chautariya Bum Shah was appointed as Governor of Kumaon; Mathbar Singh Thapa in Salyan and Puithan; Amar Singh Thapa (father of Bhim Sen Thapa) in Palpa. They were given legal authority as well to perform their duties sincerely in accordance with the interest of the state.[32] To help them, specific numbers of soldiers were posted. Each Governor had a Kharidar to assist with the correspondences and whatever records had made. It is also observed that military administrators i.e. Sardars were given priority to administer newly acquired territories. Jumla, Doti, Palpa, Makwanpur, Chainpur and Vijayapur were recognised as administrative centres by the Government.[33] In the Tarai areas six subbas were appointed. The regional administration in many places emerged in the post-unification period, and then continued even after the war. However, the Shah rulers did not create new administrative units that would serve as regional centres apart from the already existed. Further, there was no simple and uniform imposition of administrative jurisdiction. The administrative centres became very important as executive units of government for the implementation and enforcement of law. Its main duty was security and protection of the government as well as the collection of taxes. Apart from the occasional teams that toured the country and the teams of judges deputed from Kathmandu, there is no way to describe the relationship between the regional administrators and the village people.[34] However, the village people were engaged in certain points as, defence, compulsory labour obligations as were preempted for service like hulak, work in arsenals and the supply of certain goods and materials to the governments. Further the villagers had accepted the arbitration of taxes and justice (major cases only). Thus there was very little interference of the centre or control of local affairs except on justice and protection. From the above explanation, one can conclude the main role of regional provincial administration was to assist the centre. But Bhim Sen Thapa's administration is termed as 'decentralised-centralisation' because the orders issued by the government were not addressed to the administrators of region/ province but to the public in general. It reveals that he was careful as they (Governors) might pose a threat to the centre on the basis of their territorial authority and support.[35]

In the district administrative set ups, there were Kharadars, ditthas, bicharis, chhemdel, chaudhuri, rajouta sipahi, etc below the administrators. The amalis at the village level were responsible to the district administrator under whom were the general public. According to this, the general public had to contribute their labour for public works.[36] As such the people seems to be isolated from the administrative process during Bhim Sen Thapa's rule. As no concrete contribution was forthcoming from the district administration to the society and the people except for the general construction works, they were left at the mercy of the amalis.

The administration of justice is another aspect which need to be pondered in the history of post-unification Nepal. For Ram Shah's initiation of judicial system is the long 209 year's rule under Shah dynasty from the establishment of Gorkha kingdom till the conquest of Kathmandu, only his rule could be viewed as the age of reform.[37] Prithvi Narayan Shah also had contemplated to establish a kingdom based on rule of law eulogizing Ram Shah's legal reforms. During early Shah rule, Bara Panch occupied an important place specially at central level as judicial organ while there were panchayats at zonal levels.

Nepal is a state influenced by religion since time immemorial where Hindu and Buddhist centre of knowledge scattered all-over the kingdom. Thus the administration of law was based on religious precepts and customs of various ethnic groups of Nepal. There were different ethnic groups and they were bound by customs that differentiated them from their neighbours. In spite of the cultural interactions which developed over the years, the society was marked by strong ethnic diversity. Apart from this, the cultural influences of Tibet who had migrated from north with Buddhists belief had profound impact on Nepali society on northern districts. Whereas in the south we can find the deep impact of Indian culture predominantly Hindu in nature.[38] It was the product of both Rajput and Brahmins migration from the plains.[39] Besides, there were areas where these two cultures failed to penetrate in the many parts of the hill regions of Nepal.[40] The hill societies that had developed in Nepal had grown up with narrow confines of the states that marked the pre-unification period. The assimilation of the cultural influences resulted the evolution of customs acceptable to the society and were perpetuated by them in law, ritual and in the common life of the society. The evolution of custom had the force of customary law in each society. Into this pattern of interacting influences and cultural developments the law of Gorkha, which was essentially Hindu law was introduced.[41] The law of the state was Hindu in a sense that it find its final authority in the Vedas. However, the Hindu law was not a body of law accepted by judicial system based on the concept of legality. The Dharmashastras and smritis expressed ideal in terms of meaningful to contemporary society.[42] Thus, Hindu law was the law of life individual expositions of that law provided 'rationalized and systematized body of customary law and observances'.[43]

The administration of justice in Nepal was a gradual evolution. Immediately after the conquest of the hill states, a Gorkhali Military Governor with widest possible powers in the local administration was introduced into the area. But they were directed to respect local religious practices and to ensure that these practices be continued with least interference. In fact, the Central Government intended to preserve and maintain peace and harmony in the newly annexed territory. Yet the dearth of reliable on codified law makes difficult to draw acceptable conclusion. C.R. Nepali has made an attempt to comment on administration of justice in Nepal. But he fails to provide the actual structure of judicial hierarchy.[44] Babu Ram Acharya provides a background from Prithvi Narayan Shah's *Dibya Udapesh* and his administrative order primarily based on the classic concept of Hindu law and polity.[45] Remgi provides a well documented data on the implication of economy on the administration of justice. He points out that the right to dispense justice was synonymous with the right enjoyed by the military officials, jagirdars and revenue collectors when the king's court of justice were non-existence over large areas of rapidly expanding kingdom. Thus it clearly reveals a weakness in the politico-economic organization of the country.[46]

The most important document on judicial administration in Nepal can be found from Mukhtiar Bhim Sen Thapa's time. He felt the need of proper laws and regulations to govern the country into the right direction.[47] However, the separation of executive and judiciary was not manifested. Thus Bhim Sen Thapa had issued a judicial regulation in the name of king to the judicial inspectors posted in various districts for strict compliance. It contained forty regulations. The preamble of it reads as:

> We issue these instructions to direct your work in the administration of law and justice in the area of our kingdom lying between the Kanak-Tessta river on the east and the Mahakali River on the west. Show no favouritism. Accept no bribes. Remain true to our salt, carry out your investigations in accord with these instructions. If any person—within this area of your jurisdiction, regardless of his rank—should file a complaint or a report against you, we shall not act until we heard from your side of the case, and then we will punish the one whose side we see the fault to lie. Carry out your investigation with full assurance.[48]

The nineteen regulations dealt with the subject matter of government revenues and properties; seven deal misappropriation of government or religious funds or property either directly or indirectly. Other four were on caste offences or obligations and four with personal rights. The three regulations on bribery and favouritism are treated in a manner to indicate that the government's primary concern was the falsification of its records in favour of an individual to the prejudice of government interests. The other remaining regulations dealt with the unjust eviction of a tenant from his household; slavery; excess on cash loan and finally with complaint against the amalis, the heads of village administrative councils.[49]

From the above regulations, one can conclude that Bhim Sen Thapa was more cautious in dealing with various aspects of evils that prevailed in Nepali society. He tried to bring social justice to the people of Nepal by imposing ban on gambling, intoxication, slavery. He was also concerned with prevailing system of land tenure as well as the tax collections. Through it, Bhim Sen Thapa had intended to increase the government revenue for maintenances of army.[50] In principle the regulations cover everything. However, a closer analysis of these regulations reveal three shortcomings especially on the condition of peasants, and its relations with the landholders. It also fail to empower the team of investigations to find out the unjust demand made by the jagirdars, amalis and birta owners or hear against them on excess imposing of rents. Thus, as a result of this, the farmers from Saptahari and Mahotari districts proceeded to Kathmandu in May 1809 with complaints of exorbitant rents and oppression from the landowners. In response to their submission, the darbar immediately deputed officials to investigate the matter on the spot and redress the grievances of the peasants.[51] The teams were further entrusted with a power to refund the excess amount of collection to the farmers and also to realise the outstanding payment due to him. In the following year, information reached Kathmandu that the farmers of Doti, Kumaon, Accham and Dullu-Dailekh were deserting their lands due to harassment by the landholders. In 1815 another complaint of excessive demands made by the military official on the farmers of Chainpur was reported.[52]

The legal system in Nepal developed gradually. The judicial powers of the local Governors were greatly curtailed. The specific duties to them showed the tendency to centralize judicial responsibility. The task of dispensing the cases were entrusted to the local officials like amali, jimmiwal. They arbitrated petty cases on the local level. During the post-war period, a new element entered the centre's administration of justice. The codification of local custom into the legal structure and an increased

Sanskritization of justice throughout the country emerged. Dhana Bajra Bajracharya and Tek Bahadur Shrestha remarks that Bhim Sen Thapa tried to set aside Praja Pancha (people's court) that existed for ages:

> ... the leaning of autocratic ruler like Bhim Sen Thapa was not much towards democracy. They were wary of even the hardly surviving organ like Praja Pancha.[53]

As the possibility of setting up of organization an eruption of dissenting voices if courts were allowed to be set up everywhere, Bhim Sen Thapa issued an order as 'let no court be held in house (at village level), if conduct, let it be intimated to us'.[54]Bhim Sen Thapa did not mean to undermine the status of village level court i.e. panchayat but to preserve its sanctity for impartial judgment. In his Lalmohar addressed to Dalbhajan Pande, the hakim at the royal court, he was instructed that:

> When guru, Purohit, chautariyas, kazis, sardars, subbhas, court officers of Kumarichok subedars, jamadars, amalis, ijadars, soldiers, on the roll mete out injustice and when all sections of society belonging to four races and thirty six castes come pleading, let justice be proved after proper investigation. If case is beyond your capability refer it to us and act according to our direction... etc.[55]

From above directives, it reveals his impartiality for running the judicial administration at the centre. At the same time, it also shows that before the law of land all are equal irrespective of ranks, caste and position. He tried to establish a centralised judiciary system in Nepal.[56]

The progress of judicial administration in Nepal during the period under review contained two types of documents. In the first set of documents, we can find that bicharis (judges) were appointed in the districts with detailed instructions for guidance while discharging their duties. This standard directives was issued on 9th April, 1828 and the contemporary British Resident Hodgson called it the 'Desh Achar'. The first type of document contained seventeen directives which dealt with economic offences; civil and criminal cases; and etc.[57] According to Hodgson, there were four committees of judges—Kotalinga, Ita Chapli, Taksar and Dhansar.[58] Some of the cases which fell under the jurisdiction of district, were arbitrated by the district administrators, while some of them were referred to centre directly which was again, sometimes, sent back to district administrators with authority of re-arbitration. There existed, in fact four judges for investigation and submission of summary of findings and also ditthas and government lawyers to assist them. In the process of investigation, necessary informations were gathered with the help of the people. Generally, a court under the chairmanship of the judge was formed in the district who heard the cases and when the respondent was not satisfied with the decision of amali at the village level court. If still not satisfied, one could move or appeal the case to higher court for redresses. So, even from modern outlook, the judicial system during the period appears to be people-centric, classified and practical.[59]

The second aspect of the document contains the local customs and traditions similar to Hindu law and ideals which were legalised accordingly. And those aspects which were at variance with Hindu law for which no exception can be made were set aside. It further deals with the ritual purity and inter-caste sexual offences. The government, in the process of administration of justice, passed strict regulations either at centre or at the local level, banned certain evil customs of common practices. However, traditional customs were recognised and approved by the government.[60] Gradually, the right of Central Government to intervene in local society in the matters other than land tenure was recognized. The article 12 of the Regulations clearly instructed to the judge that whenever cases were brought for decision "...consideration should be given not only to the Lalmohar in force for the area but also the regulations that after careful investigation have been established by the Bharadars according to the local caste differences and customs".[61] Quite possibly local Governors in the interests of peace and tranquility did allow at different times the continuance of practices that were not totally acceptable to orthodox Hindu. But this had no significance at all in the context of the tolerance built into legal structures. Such action, however, were officially unrecognised and arbitration that what one Governor permitted, another could forbid. It was the correspondence with Central Government the detailing of local practices for which exemption was sought and the government's grant permission under carefully spelled out conditions that established the legal structure that lasted. Mukhtiyar Bhim Sen Thapa's untiring efforts for Sanskrization of the administration of justice in Nepal finally materialized in 1854 when king Surendra Bikram Shah promulgated the first code of law—the Muluki Ain.[62]

The land tenure and revenue system under the Gorkha rulers prior to the war of 1814-16 has been briefly discussed in the preceding chapter. Here, an attempt is being made to study the various experiments undertaken by Bhim Sen Thapa. It is found that during the period under study, the land belonged to state. As holy scripture regarded the king the owner of land, geographical territories was considered as kingdom since the usage of term—'Bhupati' started.[63] However, for the assessment of land and revenue collections, the lands were divided into three categories;: (a) Raikar—land owned by the state, (b) Guthi—land granted for religious and philanthropist institutions or for similar purposes and (c) Kipat—a form of customary communal land tenure prevalent among Rais, Limbu, Sherpas etc. and other communities in the hill regions including Kathmandu valley.[64] Thus, the land belonged to the state and that only land granted to individual under certain categories of Birta would be available for sale and purchase.

Mukhtiyar Bhim Sen Thapa took more realistic measures to reform the land assessment and revenue collections from the prevailing system. He clearly understood that main source of state income was land revenue. Therefore, to check misappropriation of revenue derived from this source, he used scientific method for survey of land and carefully recorded them and assessed the tax to be deposited to the government treasury. Between 1817-1837, various schemes were undertaken in this field with dual objectives:(a) to ensure a stable revenue collection and deposit to government treasury, and (b) to protect the tenants from the high-handedness of the revenue officials.[65]

According to the available documents, there was no uniform system of revenue collection throughout the kingdom. One set of pattern was followed in the hills and the adjoining areas of Kathmandu and another set was practised in Tarai regions. In the former regions, settlements of land revenue collection were made directly in the name of individual on a contractual basis and provision was made for adjustments. And it is also noted that in other hill regions settlements were made between the government and Ijaradrs, who in turn deposited the revenue collection.[66]

The introduction of Kut system invariably changed the system of revenue collection. Although the arrangements were made with individual, most settlement were made with the village headmen who were for the entire village as one unit. In this regard, Regmi writes "the headmen then apportioned to each ryot a share of the total amount assessed in this manner, collected the stipulated amount from each ryot and handed the proceeds over to the chief administrative officer of the district. Since he belonged to the village, he could be expected to ensure that shares were based on the taxable capacity of each family. Thus the village headmen dealt directly with the government representative at the district level and enjoyed enhanced status and authority. At the same time,he was held personally liable for the full payment of the stipulated amount".[67] But the system had serious recession as the headmen was responsible for the remission of the revenue assessed to the government even if there were natural calamity like landslide, drought etc. It also weakened the regional administration because the headmen had established direct communication with the Central Government. Under such arrangement, the regional administrative authority had no direct role in the collection of revenue for he was more than responsible for the proceeds of collections. He did not have any authority to appoint or dismiss the local revenue functionaries who enjoyed a statutory status. There was no strict regulations authorising the district or zonal officials to make necessary supervision of revenue collection or to punish the defaulters in payment or misappropriations of the proceeds.[68]

Under the Kut system, the jagirdars demanded high rent, in proportion to the land could produce, from the tenants. In many cases tenants complained that the level of Kut rent was too high and demanded reintroduction of the 'adhiya' system. The government instead of reverting to 'adhiya' system made minor reduction in Kut rent. However, the jagirdars insisted that Kut rents assessed on the jagir-land were too low and demanded high rent.[69] The government issued an order in favour of jagirdars and were authorised to evict those tenants who failed to pay the enhanced rents and allowed to engage cultivators from outside the village. The government order of 1818 reads—

> Since Kut rents on the lands assigned to you as jagir bear no relationship to (productivity); you are hereby authorised to inspect your lands and prescribe rents according to (productivity). Tenants on their part shall agree to pay rents so determined on the basis of (productivity of) the land. In case they do not so agree, evict them and allot the lands to other people belonging to the same district who agree to pay (the increased rent). Existing tenants shall not be evicted if they agree to pay Kut rent. [70]

The order further cancelled all existing Kut allotments on jagir holdings thereby terminating the tenancy right of the cultivators. In 1827-1828 officials were deputed to different districts in both eastern and western hill regions whether the order was strictly followed. By this order, lands were now allotted to the person who offered to pay highest amount of rent, irrespective of where he actually lived. The custom that only local inhabitants should be allotted lands for cultivation lapsed. The jagirdars were given unrestricted rights to evict their tenants in case they failed to pay the higher rent. They were deprived of security and tenancy right. Initially, the new system worked as there was no other alternative but to cultivate the land with higher rent. But many farmers were compelled to leave their lands and search for some other means of livelihood. The abandonment of land holdings and eviction compelled the central administration to reconsider this policy.[71] In 1833, Mukhtiyar Bhim Sen Thapa cancelled Kut allotment to non- residents on certain categories of jagir lands assigned to the army and reallocated them to residents.[72] Each allotment was made to the cultivators who cultivated the lands with his family and subletting was prohibited. In April 1833, an order was issued by the government that:

> Tenants who obtain jagir and Raikar land on kut tenure obtain remissions every year on account of floods and washout, as well as in consideration of the lands being waste. They do not repair or reclaim such lands even when this is possible. Remissions, therefore, had to be granted on large areas of land.[73]

The revenue collection system adopted in Tarai regions had certain problems. The restoration of Tarai in December 1816 necessitated the compilation of fresh records of lands revenue. Before the war, revenue collection had been entrusted to Chaudhuris and ijaradars. During the immediate post-war period, the government had to rely on its own revenue officials and ensure that revenue did not go below the pre-war figure. But apparently no one was willing to assume Ijaras in that chaotic situation, the government was compelled to introduce Amanat system for the time being.[74] It was in 1820, the ijaras system was restored once the land records were completed. The system worked with the fair amount of efficiency. But the local revenue functionaries found their position insecure because the ijaradars dismissed them whenever they liked.[75] Therefore, in 1828, local revenue functionaries from entire Tarai districts approached Kathmandu with the request that they should be appointed as sub-contractors for five years at a time and promised to yield higher payments, reclaim wastelands and keep ryots happy if their demand was conceded. Bhim Sen Thapa accordingly sanctioned arrangement for the appointment of such functionaries for five years.[76] This system satisfied the government who found that they were able to dispense entirely with the district level ijaradars. Separate contractual arrangements were made directly with the local Chaudhuris for the collection of revenues in areas under their jurisdiction. The same arrangement was made again in 1834 for another five years.[77]

Bhim Sen Thapa realised the importance of maintenance of a strong and well-organised standing army at the very outset of his Mukhtiyarship. He knew it very well that a kingdom could not prosper or defend the state on the basis of his other administrative reforms only. Hence the military administration was the need of the day. He augmented to strengthen the existing army as early as in 1805 when he advised Rana Bahadur Shah to confiscate the birta grants for military purpose and to great extent modernised the soldiers. Further, in the pre-war period forts were constructed on the important places and old ones repaired. Troops were stationed in all the forts and maintained strict discipline. In 1811, he was appointed as the general of the Gorkha army.[78] In 1814-16, he led the Gorkha soldiers in war with the English and suffered a defeat with loss of considerable portion of territories. The humiliating defeat, however, did not demoralised him as well as the chiefs. In the post-war period the army was searching for a role to play, that he knew very well. He adopted an appeasement policy towards the Gorkha soldiery and chiefs on whose support his own tenure of office depended. To keep his hold on the army, he followed a policy of keeping the war fever at its high pitch. Throughout the kingdom, new recruitment was made, military stores were accumulated, ammunitions were manufactured and parade were held regularly. He ordered the troops to move to various places in the capital. Such movement of troops tends to keep the men of the line alert and help to maintain discipline.[79] When resident Gardner reached Kathmandu in 1816, he found the soldiers jealous, proud and insolent. However, due to lack of upward mobility of the army, the soldiers feared the reduction of rank after the treaty of Sagauli. It was reported that there was some talk of reduction in the ranks of the army but such measure would be a dangerous and impolitic one for Bhim Sen Thapa.[80] Thus, Mukhtiyar did not reduce the existing military personnel for fear of unrest.

Nepal had a peculiar system of recruitment of army. It was this short term enlistment as a real factor for the growth of Gorkha militarism. Under this system enlistment into the ranks was annual. After year of service a soldier became a Dhakareah. That is put off the roll. Three years after his discharge, he could be re-enrolled into the service for another period of one year, repeating the process so long as he was able to bear arms. Although military service was not compulsory, the short term system made it practically universal and ensured that the number of men trained in arms was far larger than the actual standing army. Not unnaturally, war and conflict were to their interest for it gave them an opportunity to re-enlist before time.[81]

The British Resident in 1816 estimated the standing regular army of 10,000 men which was more than the state required to maintain law and order. After three years the number rose to 12,000 men and by 1831 it was estimated of 15,000 regular army with 30,000 men off the roll. The increase of army was possible because of the restoration of Tarai by the British Government.[82]

The increased number of army required proper place to be accommodated. In 1822, Bhim Sen Thapa acquired two square kilometers of land at Mala tar (Chauni) for Sri Nath Regiment for construction of barracks to accommodate the army. Again, in 1824 more land was requisitioned and by the end of the following year, the new barracks was ready for the Sri Nath regiments.[83] It clearly shows the manner in which Bhim Sen Thapa felt himself obliged to conciliate the army in order to ensure their continued support while at the same time trying to increase his hold over them. Further, he ordered to establish commercial complex nearby for soldier's convenience. Necessary infrastructures were provided to the army according to the ranks. In the meantime, Kazi Bakhtawar Singh, Mukhtiar's brother was posted as Governor of Palpa in place of Uzir Singh who was summoned to Kathmandu. His nephew Mathbar Singh who held the post of commander of Sri Nath Regiment and Uzir Singh who were important army officials, enjoyed the respect of the soldiers. The presence of his close relatives in the capital gave an ample opportunity to discipline and impose his policies on the army without alienating the support he drew from the military class.[84]

For better and smooth running of the administration of the army, different persons with ranks were appointed. For example, the Kazis looked after both civil and military administration in the regions where he was posted. They commanded troops in time of war or act as a Governor in the district in time of peace. At the level of Sardar, the next lower rank in government, the pattern that emerged was one of constant change and regular turnover. In Gorkha army the captains were more fortunate and tended to hold their posts longer, these men, few in number, were central figures in the corps of the army because they exercised field command and therefore, appeared to have enjoyed greater permanence. In the same category were subedars, or commanders of military companies. There were more changes in the rank of Subedar than in that of Captain, but Subedars enjoyed much more stability than those holding the rank of Sardar.[85]

In spite of all their efforts, Bhim Sen Tahpa faced certain problems from the troops. Discontent among the lower and middle level officers stemmed up from the restriction of promotions to mere handful of men and the insecurity that dogged them. Dismissals from service were frequent. But under the Panjani system that called for automatic dismissal and re-appointment of all personal each year, the blow of final dismissal was always a distinct possibility. Apart from this, the most important cause of military discontent was irregularity in pay. These military Sardars, Subedars, or officials were given jagir instead of cash since the time of Prithvi Narayan Shah. It worked well for the time being only. But the army moved from one place to another which created problem of collection of the rents. The jagirs system was thus modified as the top officials were given individual jagirs and the rest of the men received their payment from company and regimental jagirs.[86]

In short, it should be agreed upon the fact that the use of military organisation as the only means of safeguard of national and nationalism was a timely and farsighted interpretation of the prevalent situation. For the above study, we may point out the following distinctiveness in Bhim Sen Thapa's administration:

1. Though it appears decentralised, Bhim Sen Thapa's administrative system, in fact, was centre-oriented.
2. Though he had appointed Thapa clan in the administrative organ, it is clear that he had tried to be an autocrat.
3. We may conclude that he had tried to grab all administrative powers and rights only for himself because Lal Mohars he used to get were different from those received by other Kazis, Sardars or any other officials.
4. The royal power is overshadowed due to his autocratic home policy.
5. He even overshadowed the Bharadari Sabha. It appears that he wanted to monopolise administration as these matters of his own interests without any consultation with the Bara Panch Sabha.
6. He abolished social panchayat system. So no participation of people in any field could be found in the contemporary Nepal.

Apart from the negative characteristics cited above, we find some positive measures followed by Bhim Sen Thapa to reform the administrative system of Nepal during his Mukhtiyarship. He did whatever he could for the people and country. In fact, he had given a new dimension.

Notes

1. Baid, Ratna Kamal, *Sarbajanik Prasasan Sidhanta.* Kathmandu,

2. Pande, A.R., *op. cit.*, p. 56.
3. Upadhaya, Syam Prasad, *Nepal ko Prasasnik Byabastha,* Kathmandu, (2029 BS),p.15
4. Bajracharya, D. and Shrestha, T.B. *op. cit.*, p. 21.
5. *Ibid.*, pp. 27 and 51-58.
6. Pande, A.R., *op. cit.*, pp. 59-60.
7. Bajracharya, D., *Madyakalin Nepal,* (n.d), n. 65, p. 102.
8. Upadhaya, S.P., *op. cit.*, p. 18.
9. Bajracharya, D., *op. cit.*, p. 102.
10. *Ibid.*, pp. 22-24.
11. Pande, A.R., *op. cit.*, p. 60.
12. Pant Nayaraj, and others, *op. cit.*, p. 323.
13. *Ibid.*
14. Pant, N., and others, *op. cit.*, p. 323.
15. Bajracharya, D. and Shrestha, T.B., *op. cit.*, p. 209.
16. Pande, A.R., *op. cit.*, pp. 62-63.
17. Yogi, N. Nath., *Itihas Prakashma Sandhi-Patra Sangrah,* Vol. I., (2022 BS), p. 314.
18. *Ibid.*
19. Lingat, Robert, *The Classical Law of India,* Berkeley (1973), pp. 202-204. Gajendragadkar, P.B., *The Historical Background and Theoretic Basis of Hindu Law,* Calcutta. (1962), p. 2.
20. Stiller, L.F., *op. cit.*, p. 89.
21. Shah, R., *op. cit.*, p. 18; Nepali C.R., *op. cit.*, p. 124.
22. Nepal, C.R., *Ran Bahadur Shah,* Kathmandu (2020 BS), pp. 72-73.
23. Shah, *op. cit.*, p. 19.
24. Ramakant, *op. cit.*, pp. 16-18. Rose, Leo E., *op. cit.*, p. 79.
25. Kumar Satish, *Rana Polity in Nepal,* New Delhi, (1967), pp. 93-95.
26. Pande, A.R., *op. cit.*, p. 67.; Gyanu, D., *op. cit.*, p. 49.
27. Shrestha, S., *op. cit.*, p.
28. Hamilton, *op. cit.*, p. 108.
29. Stiller, F.L., *op. cit,* p. 197; Pande, A.R., *op. cit,* p. 67.
30. *Ibid.*
31. Pant, N.R., *op. cit., Purnima,* Vol. 24, (2026 BS).
32. Regmi, M.C., *op. cit.*, p. 127.
33. Stiller, F.L., *op. cit.*, p. 133.
34. Hodgson, H.B., *op. cit.*, p. 124.: M.C. Regme, *Land Tenure and Taxation in Nepal,* pp. 40-41 and 70-71.

35. *Ibid.*, Also see Shrestha, B.P., *An introduction to the Nepalese Economy, Kathmandu* (1974).
36. Shrestha, M.K., *op. cit.*, pp. 2-3.
37. Upadhaya, S.P., *op. cit.*, p. 31.
38. Stiller, F.L., *op. cit.*, pp. 165-167.
39. Rose, Leo E., and Seholz, T., *op. cit.*, p. 22.
40. *Ibid.*
41. *Prithvi Narayan Shah's, Dibye Upadesh:* Duncun, M. and Derett, J., *Introduction of Modern Hindu Law,* Oxford (1963), pp. 2-3; Lingat, R., *The Classical Law of India,* Berkeley (1973). pp. 230-231.
42. *Ibid.*
43. Stiller, F.L., *op. cit.*, p. 165.
44. Nepali, C.R., *op. cit.*, pp. 224-248.
45. *Prithvi Narayan Dibye Upadesh;* Radha Krishnan's, *The Heart of Hinduism,* Madras (1936), pp. 17-18; Duncun, M. and Darett, J. *op. cit.*, pp. 1-2.
46. Regmi, *op. cit.*, pp. 6-7, 40-41, 70-71.
47. Regmi Research Series 4 (December 1972), pp. 239-240. *Prithvi Narayan Shah's Dibye Upadesh.*
48. Regmi Research Series 3 (June 1971) 128-137: Translated for Dinesh Raj Pant, *Swami Maharaja Ran Bahadur Shah ko BS1862 ko Bandobest;* Purnima No. 24: 238-267. See Appendix.
49. *Ibid.*
50. Bhim Sen Thapa's Documents, 1A/77/40.
51. Bhim Sen Thapa's Documents, 7/967/183.
52. *Ibid.*, 3/137/320.
53. Bajracharya and Shrestha, *op. cit.*, p. 230.
54. *Ibid.*, p. 231.
55. Nepali, C.R., *op. cit.*, pp. 225-226.
56. Pande, A.R., *op. cit.*, p. 74; Yogi, N. *op. cit.*, Vol. I. p. 99.
57. See Appendix.
58. Hodgson, B.H., *"On the Administration of Justice in Nepal with some Accounts of the Several Courts, Extent of their Jurisdiction and Modes of Procedure"*, Asiatic Researches, 20 (1836) 94-134.
59. Stiller, F.L., *op. cit.*, p. 171.
60. Bhim Sen Thapa's Documents, 28/265/372-380; Regmi Research Series 3 (January 1971).
61. *Ibid.* 6/544/201-203; (July 1810); Regmi Research Series (February 1971), 3.

62. *Mulki Ain of Surendra Bikram Shah Deva,* published by H.M.G. Nepal (2023 BS).
63. Pande, A.R., *op. cit.,* p. 75: Yogi, N.N. *op. cit.,* Vol. 1, p. 100.
64. Regmi, M.C, *op. cit.,* p. 37: Also see his book, *Land Tenure and Taxation in Nepal,* Berkeley, 4 Vols.
65. *Ibid.,* p. 173.
66. Bhim Sen Thapa's Documents: May 1827, 43/207; 1836-1837, 35/154-257; 1838, 38/74.
67. *Ibid.,* May 1834, No. 35/478.
68. *Ibid.,* March 1854, 27/301
69. Regmi, M.C., *op. cit.,* pp. 178-179.
70. Bhim Sen Thapa's Documents, January 1828, No. 27/70.
71. *Ibid.,* January 1828, Nos. 43/161, 43/244, and 43/275.
72. *Ibid.,* December 1833, No. 20/445.
73. Bhim Sen Thapa's Documents, January 1828, Nos. 27/70-90, December 1833 No. 26/445, March 1833, 26/338; April, 1833, 26/286.
74. Regmi, M.C., *op. cit.,* pp. 174-175.
75. *Ibid.*
76. *Ibid.,* November 1818, No. 43/140.
77. Bhim Sen Thapa's Documents: October 1835, Nos. 26/377, 426-427.
78. Nepali, C.R., *op. cit.,* pp. 245-249: The Lai Mohan reads "His Majesty, My father was very pleased with the trustworthy work you performed. He ordered you to do the work of the Mukhtiyar in the administration, saying he would agree to whatever you chose to do. In order to set you above the Kazis, since the Kazi were all equal in rank and there was no special honour in the title, he gave you the rank of General".
79. Ramakant, *op. cit.,* pp. 57-58.
80. Campbell's Sketchs: On 14 May 1817, Resident Gardner wrote that "there has been some talks of a reduction in the ranks of the officers of the army; but such a measure, must, I think, be dangerous and impolitic one for the Minister to touch upon in the present feeling of that body, the members of which are naturally much dissatisfied and discontented with their fallen condition; and this temper not unfrequently breaks out, though it has not hitherto shown itself in any very serious way. I suspect, the Government is, not a little embarrassed on this account; for it must be sensible that the military force

is greater than the state now requires, or can conveniently maintain, at the same time, from the nature of its constitution, the Minister have not the hardihood, perhaps, to attend effect the requisite reduction".

81. Hodgson, H.B., *"Origin and Gasification of the Military Tribes of Nepal". JASB,* Vol. H (1833). Later published under 'Selections'; MacMunn, George, *The Martial Races of India,* New Delhi (Reprint, 1972), pp. 184-200.
82. Campbell's Sketches: Pradhan, K.L., *op. cit.,* p. 17.
83. Nepal, C.R., *op. cit.,* pp. 89-91: Bhim Sen Thapa's Documents, 34/234-421/196.
84. *Ibid.,* Stiller, F.L., *op. cit.,* pp. 206-207.
85. *Ibid.,* p. 195.
86. Regmi, M.C., *Land Ownership in Nepal* (1976), 2:6 and 3:10.

VI

Bhim Sen Thapa and the Residency: 1816-1834

The Anglo-Gorkha war of 1814-16 came to an end on 1st March, 1816 when the Treaty of Sagauli was formally ratified by the Maharaja and a permanent political relation between Nepal and the British was established. At that time Maharaja Girwan Juddha Vikram Shah was on the throne and Bhim Sen Thapa as Mukhtiyar[1] since 1806. The Maharaja being minor, the latter had all powers in his hands and was the guiding spirit of the Darbar for all practical purposes. He can easily be called one of the greatest statesmen of Nepal since the unification of the kingdom. He was the man who accompanied the Maharaja Rana Bahadur Shah in exile in Banaras. On his return, Damodar Pande was executed and Maharaja Rana Bahadur Shah took over the administration in his hands as Mukhtiyar. Bhim Sen Thapa was appointed as the second Kazi. During his Mukhtiyarship, Rana Bahadur Shah greatly strengthened the Gorkha army through the confiscation of Birta. This made him unpopular among the Bharadars particularly with the Brahmins and in 1806 he was assassinated by his own half-brother Sher Bahadur Shah. In the crisis that followed, Bhim Sen Thapa acted quickly and effectively to remove the opposition and raised the third queen Tripura Sundari Devi as Regent of the minor king. He became Mukhtiyar in 1806. From 1806 to 1813, with the help of Gorkha soldiery, Bhim Sen Thapa had considerably extended the territories of the kingdom in all directions. However, the policy of slow and steady encroachment on the plains, forcible occupation of twenty two villages in Butwal and Seoraj finally led to war with the East India Company. Bhim Sen Thapa maneuvered to avail assistance from China and the disaffected Indian Native states against the British proved futile. Nepal had to face eventuality alone. The result was the defeat of Gorkha at the hands of the British. The Treaty of Sagauli ended the days of the Gorkha military expansion.[2]

With the establishment of the British Residency at the court of Kathmandu, Bhim Sen Thapa adopted a policy to restrict the Resident's sphere of activities. His policy was peaceful but not friendly; nor was it free from deep laid distrust. The Resident was boycotted and treated with indifference. He even determined to follow the letters of Treaty literally as a result of which the Resident was reduced to the position of an honoured prisoner. He kept his hold strong enough on the soldiery and engaged to show that peace was not so dishonourable. Recruitment was made and military parades were held regularly just to engage the army.[3] The Resident and his staff were not allowed to go about the country at will. They could only ride towards certain fixed places in the morning and evening, more or less confined to the four walls of the Residency. Every precaution was taken to keep them away from the people and the Bharadars. Diplomatic-privileges were denied to the Resident and his personal baggages were also regularly searched. Foreign visitors were strictly prohibited.[4] Further, the Gorkhas were very much apprehensive of the traders from British India. There was an oft-quoted saying that 'the tradesmen bring the Bible and the Bible brings the bayonet'. They had seen that the English came to India as traders and became her master. Bhim Sen Thapa had imposed restrictions in the free commercial intercourse with the inhabitants. The direct access of the traders to the Resident was debarred and they had practically no legal means to redress their grievance.[5] It is also a fact that religious sentiments also contributed a lot to it. They were told that if the foreigners got a hold in the country, their religion would be extinct. Bhim Sen Thapa saw that within sixty to seventy years since the battle of Plassey, the English built up their colonial empire in India. He was the first Gorkha statesmen who grasped Lord Wellesley's Subsidiary Alliance system. He witness one native state after another trapped within the net of the system and his policy was steadily directed to save Nepal from similar fate.[6]

The policy of keeping the English totally aloof from the internal politics of the kingdom became the core policy of the Mukhtiyar.

He developed a genuine sentiment among the Bharadars that the treaty restricted all contacts with the Resident except officially and that he alone was capable to deal with the English.[7] The opposition factions were also debarred from meeting the Resident and told that intercourse with him would ultimately lead to the formation of discontent faction in the state. He ably induced the Bharadars and people till the Maharaja Rajendra attain the majority and Regent queen's death in 1832.[8]

With the establishment of the British Residency, Lt. Boileau took the charge of the Residency till the arrival of Sir Edward Gardner. He found the Darbar and particularly Mukhtiyar Bhim Sen Thapa haughty and uncourteous.[9] During the presentation of his credential, he saw Bhim Sen Thapa was the centre of real authority. He described the personal trait of the Mukhtiyar as 'at thirty-seven he was tall, his figure spare, his countenance animated. His eyes revealed a quick intelligence'. In spite of the lost of major war, Bhim Sen Thapa stood in full Darbar under the gaze of the king, talking animatedly with the representative of the victorious country and not one of his rivals knew where to apply that sudden push or find the right leverage to oust him.[10]

As already discussed, Bhim Sen Thapa's policy towards the British and its representative was based on the principle of isolation. In fact, the concept of isolating the resident dates back from Anglo-Nepal Treaty of 1801. The article IX clearly states that:

> It is incumbent upon the Vakeels of both states that exclusive of the supreme authorities and officers of Government, they hold no meetings with any subjects or inhabitants of the country without the concurrence of the aforesaid authority, neither should carry on any correspondence with them nor, in the event of their receiving any letter or writing from any such persons should they return an answer, but they ought to disclose the particulars of such letter or writing to the aforesaid authorities by which means as all apprehension and doubt will be removed and the sincerity of friendship clearly manifested.

On April, 1816, the officiating Resident reported to the Government that "a company of sipahees have been ordered by Bhim Sen Thapa to be dispersed between my house and the city during all hours, and to apprehend any person who may be thought to hold communication with me; and it has been given out in the city that any one so offending shall be punished".[12] The Darbar also imposed restriction to collect data or information about the country and present any intrigue between the Resident and the disaffected elements. The restrictions that banned on the Resident arose as much from this distrust and it did from fear of what the resident might do if he were free to roam at will and contact whomsoever he pleased.

Sir Edward Gardner[13] joined as Resident in May 1816. He was clearly instructed to ensure that Nepal was conciliated and she acquiesced in the losses and culminate good relations with the Mukhtiyar. While issuing such directions to the Resident, the Governor General clearly understood the situation in Nepal and wrote that he,

> prepared to expect frequent indication of this spirit in the early stage of our intercourse with Gorkha as well as much irregularity and evasion in the execution of the Treaty and in transactions immediately arising out of the renewal of peace....[14]

He was further asked to adopt a friendly attitude and to show every practicable degree of favour and avoid any kind of confrontation with the Darbar. The first and foremost task of the Resident was to implement the Treaty and maintain the relation with Nepal with a view to the security of the frontiers when Bhim Sen Thapa pressed for the return of Tarai lands, Gardner immediately recommended to the government the retrocession.[15] During the negotiation, which lasted for six months from July to December, finally settled with the restoration of the Tarai land except the twenty two villages. Further, demarcations of boundary were also undertaken accordingly.[16]

While the issue of the restoration of Tarai lands was going on, the appearance of Chinese troops in Tibet placed both Bhim Sen Thapa and the British Government in an awkward position. It was true that during the Anglo-Gorkha war, the Darbar sought assistance from the Chinese emperor through the Ambans in Tibet. Taking advantage of the Chinese arrival in Tibet, Bhim Sen Thapa tried to create in the British a fear that the Treaty having been made without the approval of China, the latter would strongly disapprove it. The Resident was accordingly informed that the Chinese has assumed a threatening posture of Peking's displeasure with Nepal's new political relationship with the British.[17] Further, Bhim Sen Thapa wanted to play upon Calcutta's apprehension over the recent development in Tibet to effect the objectives of the withdrawal of British Residency from Kathmandu and retrocession of Tarai lands. The Chinese Commander Shee Chanchoon, at the request of the Darbar politely wrote to Lord Hastings to withdraw the Residency in consideration of ties of friendship between China and India.[18] However, the report that the Chinese had not been influenced by the Nepalese entreaties soon relieved the British. At the same time, the Chinese Commander had rejected the Gorkha version of the late war as absolutely perfidious and did not press for the withdrawal of its representative from Kathmandu, when Governor General assured that the Resident would not interfere in the internal affairs of Nepal.[19] Thus Bhim Sen Thapa failed to achieve anything. Rather, he was warned to maintain good relations with the British and fulfil the treaty obligation to dispatch periodic mission to China.[20]

Yet, Bhim Sen Thapa was not entirely disillusioned. He was not a man who easily surrenders his objectives. The intrigues with the disaffected Indian native states resumed with much vigour when the English were fully occupied with the problems of the Pindaris and the Marathas in 1817-18.[21] However, before the situation became unmanageable, Gardner informed the Mukhtiyar the arrest of Darbar's representative with secret letters addressed to Indian Native rulers and sought immediate explanations. The defeat of the Marathas, suppression of Pindaris and signing of the treaty with Sindhia, 1817 finally cooled down Bhim Sen Thapa's temper. Gardner held the opinion that the late intrigues were positively hostile and were intended to break the treaty at the first favourable opportunity. The Resident remarked that:

> the intrigues this government has been engaged in were of nature decidedly inimical to our interests and it seems pretty certain that it had been resolved to commence hostilities against the British Government in this quarter as soon as it was ascertained that war had actually occurred with Sindhia.[22]

Yet, a closer study of the situation and the available records show that Bhim Sen Thapa was manipulating to keep the soldiery busy maintaining a war atmosphere so as to secure his own position. He had earlier turned to the army for support in his struggle to control the Darbar. Now, he had the means to motivate and control the army. It must be remembered that there always existed a strong opposition faction in the Darbar who had threatened his position. On recent intrigues, Bhim Sen Thapa remarked that 'all persons were not unanimous in the same ways of thinking and that different conduct and ideas and that the procedure of this government had been in a great measure swayed by the violence of party spirit here'.[23] His control of the Darbar was not re-established on the basis of the solution he offered. Rather his victory was the outcome of patience, a shrewd mind, and mastery of local politics. And in order to make that the support of the soldiery more effective while at the same time rendering it subservient to his own interests he capitalised on a situation of confusion and fear to orchestrate a deep suspicion of further British intervention in Nepali politics. He was thereby able to portray himself not as the one who led the nation to defeat, but as the champion of the independence of Nepal.[24]

In spite of these developments, Resident Gardner reported to the Government the prevailing tranquility and a wish of Mukhtiyar Bhim Sen Thapa too maintain friendly relations. The official business transactions was carried on regularly and slowly the indication of hostility towards the British passed away. On 12th August, 1820, he was happy to inform the Government that:

> the feeling of distrust and suspicion, which was so long and generally indulged appear to have been dismissed from the mind of the administration. Government is daily reconciling itself more and more to actual circumstances and has become sensible from the conviction of the policy of attempting to alter them.[25]

From 1820 onwards, the relations between the Resident and Bhim Sen Thapa was relatively friendly and peaceful. But in 1824, opportunity once again set in for the Darbar to forge an alliance with Burma (presently Myanmar) against the British imperialism. The Burmese representative at Calcutta met Chandra Shekhar Updhaya and offered the willingness of his government to make friendship with Nepal. The disclosure was communicated to the Darbar for its response. In 1824 just before the outbreak of Anglo-Burmese war, a Nepal envoy was sent to Burma to study the political condition, attitude towards the British and the legal system.[26] While the effort of forging alliance with Burma was developing gradually, in 1825, a complaint of border incursions had been lodged against Nepal. The area where the incident took place came under the jurisdiction of Uzir Singh Thapa *m* Palpa.[27] Stiller is of the opinion that there is a clear connection between the border incursions, Uzir Singh's disagreement with Bhim Sen Thapa on policy, the unrest among the military. The more restless army officers wanted to capitalize on the British involvement in Burma. Uzir Singh who sided the army was a man of importance and known for his boldness in opposing the Mukhtiyar when it suited his purposes.[28] A recent historian has pointed out that at this very moment, Bhim Sen Thapa proffered military support to the Governor General's Burma campaign. The offer was indeed an effort to siphon off some of the army's militant spirit while retaining a firm hand on the situation.[29] In 1824, Gardner wrote the Government giving the information about prevailing condition in the Darbar:

> I hear rather unpleasant of dissensions among the chiefs here have late appeared. The fact, I imagines., is that a party has for a length of time witnessed with dissatisfaction and bad nature the assumption by the Minister Bhim Sen of the sole power to the exclusion of most of the Sardars from any participation in public affairs and the seclusion of the young Raja, who seldom or never appears in public and that this feeling is showing itself in the form of an opposition to the measures of the Minister even by some subordinate of his own family.[30]

The Darbar's overture to forge an alliance with Burma ended with the defeat of Burmese at the hands of the British in 1826 when the treaty of Yandaboo was signed. Further, the English would never allow to have such friendship which pose danger for her colonial design.[31]

The relations between Bhim Sen Thapa and the Resident relatively became peaceful from 1826 onwards. Meanwhile, Sir Edward Gardner retired from the Residency in 1829. Till the arrival of new Resident, Hodgson was asked to officiate the post.[32] He was alarmed at the Gorkha military system created by Bhim Sen Thapa. In his Memorandum Relative to the Nepal Army, he tried to draw the attention of the Government to the short term enrolment system in the Nepal army as a real factor for the growth of Gorkha militarism. Under this system, a soldier become off the roll after one year of service. After three years he could be re-employed into the service for another one year and continued the process so long as he was able to bear arm. Hodgson found the system extremely dangerous to the security of the British frontier. He strongly advocated to absorb off the roll soldiers into the Indian army as a 'safety valve'.[33] In support of his proposal, he urged the Government that:

> If he could draw off the surplus soldiers of Nepal into our army, we might do her immense service, enabling her to adopt the institution to her circumstances, at the same time we provide ourselves with the best material in Asia for making soldiers out of it.[34]

He thought that such measure would certainly lessen the burden of Bhim Sen Thapa to maintain the system and at the same time secure the strategically important frontier.

The next important issue that Hodgson took up was the problem of border settlement. He found that the Treaty of Sagauli had broadly defined the boundary between Nepal and Oudh but the border remained largely undemarcated. On the entire stretch of more than three hundred fifty miles there were only six boundary pillars and most of them were beyond repair. Since the border was to be settled for pretext of any future aggression, Hodgson drew the attention of Government for immediate solution. Accordingly survey and demarcation of Indo-Nepal boundary was done in 1829-30. By April 1830, old pillars were restored and new ones were erected where necessary by mutual agreement between Nepal and Oudh.[35]

Closely connected with the settlement of the border was the question of extradition. In April 1831, the Darbar informed

Hodgson that 12 Nepali timber agents had taken refuge in the Company's territories. Of the 12 individuals, nine were accused of being revenue defaulters and the remaining three were charged with fraudulence and breach of public trust. These accused, it was said, to owe a large sum of money to Nepal Government, and the Darbar had always and promptly attended to the similar demands of the Company although the latter seldom handed over Nepali criminals and fugitives. Since the Treaty of Sagauli was entirely silent of the whole question of extradition, Hodgson felt the necessity of a formal agreement on this issue. He had hoped that Government of India would take advantage of these problems to formulate general rule for the future guidance of both states. But the Government had no such intention and when the subject was placed before it, it directed that no departure be made from the existing system.[37] Hodgson was not happy with the remark of the Government. In May he wrote to the Government that unless formal agreement on the issue was done, the advantages secured by the recent border settlement would be futile. Crimes on the border would increase and Tarai would soon become the home of criminals and fugitives from justice.[38] He indeed admitted that the Nepalese code of law was primitive, backward and judicial administration cruel, yet law in Tarai were less severe and as such enforcing new regulations would not be too difficult.

The Government of India was not inclined to such a formal agreement for the establishment of special courts. It considered the Nepalese judicial system and its penal code too cruel, as for example, minor crimes were awarded the punishment of mutilation or even death. Hodgson was accordingly informed that the 'Governor General is far from desiring':

> To enter into any stipulation that shall bind the Government under all circumstances to surrender debtors and defaulter to any bordering native state that may demand refugees as such a plea. It will be far preferable....to keep the matter on its present footing so as to allow the Government to judge each individual's case that may occur according to its own particular merit.[39]

Just as the extradition was being attended to, Hodgson was informed of the arrest of Ahmed Ali, a Kashmiri merchant of Patna, by the Chinese authority at Lhasa on the charge of being employed by the British Government to collect secret informations of the country. He was asked to get Bhim Sen Thapa's help for the release of the merchant. At the Darbar's request the Kashmiri Merchant was released by the Chinese authority, but confiscated all his properties.[40]

Nepal offered tremendous opportunity for the development of trade with Tibet and China. However, the restrictions imposed by the Darbar on free trade entirely relegated the British commercial objective to the background. As early as in March 1830, Hodgson submitted a very lengthy report to the Government explaining the attitude of the Darbar's on trade as:

> the Gorkha Government is ignorant of the value of foreign commerce and has been heretofore too jealous of us to allow of our broaching the subject or seeking through it any privileges in regards to direct participation of the commerce of Nepaul or Bhote...[41].

In his report, he further added that it was the Gorkha who conquered the Kathmandu valley sixty years ago by their turbulent habit and spirit of the universe aggression that put an end to all commerce of Nepal—both north and south. Through the native traders Hodgson wanted to revive the commerce with Nepal and China.[42]

Towards the end of 1831, Hodgson again submitted a lengthy and elaborate accounts of the commercial routes from Kathmandu to Tibet. The report contained a detailed account of the trade routes from India to Nepal and Tibet; The Tibetan frontier marts and trade with central Asia. Appended to the report were several pages of tables and statements showing the manner and expense of conveying goods; amount and nature of duty levied by the Nepal Government at different places; the distance between Kathmandu and the frontier markets; rough estimate of cost of goods in India and its selling price at Kathmandu the total annual and imports to and from Nepal.[43]

The report further spoke of other advantages. If Nepal's trade was allowed to develop, it would result in the displacement of the old feudal classes by the emergence of new social groups. The new social elite would naturally pursue different political ideas and would play a subservient role to the British. On the other hand, the increased trade with and through Nepal with Tibet and China would further give the British an exclusive command on Nepal's wants which would ultimately lead the Government of India to control her and her policies.[44]

The new year 1832 showed a sign of improvement of relations between the Darbar and the Resident. The latter was invited to attend the royal function held on the birth of Maharaja's second son. On this very occasion, Hodgson saw a sign of change in Bhim Sen Thapa's attitude towards the royal family who had "a few days back left Kathmandu on a visit to Gorkha" he reported:

> ostensibly and I believe also really to endow a temple. But this being the first occasion for 20 years on which the Minister has quitted the Raja's side, the vulgar do not fail to seize on it for speculation after the manner the more specially as the Minister and his powerful relatives have been more or less a feud during the past six months.[45]

The family feud arising out of the posting of the military command stationed at the capital was settled by equal distributions among the Thapa families.[46]

Hubert Maddock who was appointed to succeed Sir Edward Gardner in January 1832, arrived in Kathmandu sometime following March. Within a week of his arrival, the queen Regent Tripura Sundari Devi died. The death coincided with the attainment of majority by the Maharaja Rajendra. With the kingdom in mourning, no indication of change was immediately apparent. Observing the political situation in Nepal, the Resident informed the Government that:

> the first indication of the line of conduct which he (Bhim Sen) may pursue in what to him and to the States must be considered an important crisis. The suspension of all public business during the period of mourning for the late Ranee has prevented the manifestation of his (Rajendra) intentions and of the party spirit of those who are looking for a change and...the state of feelings among the Sirdars of the court to form any probable conjuncture of the influence by which the Raja will be guided.[47]

It is in fact true that the history of Nepal since the beginning of the nineteenth century was that the minor kings gave the Mukhtiyar Bhim Sen Thapa an opportunity to consolidate his power and position in the Darbar. But the death of Regent and the attainment of Rajendra's majority seems to be detrimental to the Mukhtiyar. Even though the Maharaja professed keen interest in the state affairs, he lacked experience and resolution in handling the matters. Inexperience accompanied by irresolution was likely to prove disastrous in the struggle for power. Therefore, the inevitable consequences were bound to be conspiracy, revolution and counter-revolution, foreign intrigues, murders and massacres.[48] Even at this favourable opportunity to assert his authority, Maharaja Rajendra could do nothing but simply reinstate Bhim Sen Thapa, endorsing full civil and military power at the annual panjani of 1832. Bhim Sen Thapa immediately took all precautionary measures to keep away the Maharaja from the Bharadars whose advices and counsels might be prejudicial to his position in the Darbar.[49]

Meanwhile, the Mukhtiyar's policy of isolating the Residency continued. Communications with the Darbar was carried on through the Munshi. The Resident's personal contact with the Maharaja was confined to two occasions, annually—Holi and Dussera. The movement of Resident's staffs were continued to be restricted and the general public were also debarred to meet the Resident. Maddock in his displeasure of the state affairs wrote to the Government of India that:

> the peculiar circumstances under which the Residency was established probably deterred the Resident from adopting the usual mode of keeping himself informed of the ordinary proceedings of the court.[50]

The immediate reaction of the Government of India towards Bhim Sen Thapa after the death of Regent was of sympathy. He was regarded as a 'great and able' man whose internal administration had been admirable and whose talent and energy constituted perhaps the best support of the British India. The approbation shown by the British to the Mukhtiyar hardly brought any change in their relations.[51]

In September 1832, the question of Resident's jurisdiction over Company's subject in Nepal cropped up. The problem had its origin in the case of a sweeper belonging to the Residency was alleged to have had illicit relations with a Nepalese women. This under the existing custodies of Nepal constituted a serious crime entailing a very severe punishment. The aggrieved husband had right to revenge if the crime was proved and to carry out the sentence. The event aroused a lot of indignation among the Bharadars and those opposed to Bhim Sen Thapa sought to make capital out of it. The problem was ultimately resolved when the Darbar agreed to the Resident's right to try and punish his own subjects according to the Company's laws. The sweeper was ultimately convicted and sentenced to five years rigorous imprisonment and sent to India to undergo punishment.[52]

Meanwhile, Maddock found the climate of Nepal unsuitable to his health and left the Residency on three months leave on 2nd December, 1832. On the same day, he informed the Government of India, on present Ministry under the Mukhtiyar:

> subversion of Bhim Sen's power would be an event greatly to deplored though its was possible to effect it without tumult or insurrection. We can hardly expect to see the present Ministry succeeded by one equally efficient and it is to the strength and vigour of his administration to which has prevailed in Nepal and for the maintenance of its friendly relations with British Government for the last sixteen years.[53]

Ever since the death of the Regent Maharani Tripura Sundari Devi in April 1832, the chief supporter to Bhim Sen Thapa's career, the political scene in Nepal underwent a visible change. The death coincided with the attainment of majority by Maharaja Rajendra and his hold on the state could no longer remain unchallenged.[34] The immediate cause for worry was however not the return of Pandes to power but the fate of his relations with the British. In the Darbar politics, the control of the relations with the Resident was regarded an important function of state. And to be able to keep the British representative within bounds was to earn the respect of the Darbar. If the Maharaja had chosen to deal directly with the Resident it would have been a clear indication of the diminution of Bhim Sen Thapa's authority. In his letter to Macnaghten Hodgson summed up Bhim Sen Thapa's worries:

> during the past year there has been degree of shyness towards the Residency originating in the Premier's anomalous situation in respect of his sovereign and in an apprehension on his part that Mr. Maddock's appointment was the prelude to some material change in the style of our intercourse with the Darbar under the decent pretext of suitableness to the Rajah's new state of majority.

He further pointed out that nothing of the sort having been attempted the Minister's fear seems to have subsided.[55]

Following the resignation of Sir Maddock in February 1833, the Governor General of India, Lord William Bentinck recommended Hodgson to the post of Resident. He placed before the council for consideration on the basis of his experiences he had as assistant to Resident, and

> he is a gentleman of very considerable merit and attainment, his conduct when reasonably in charge of the Residency has given great satisfaction to the Government and in addition to the adventure of intimate acquaintance with the feeling and institutions at all times earned a degree of prudence and conciliation which makes me confident that this important charge may be advantageously confined to his hand, the report that has from time to time transmitted upon laws and usages of the Nepalese with other statistical information do him much credit.[56]

In his appointment letter, Lord Bentinck assured him that 'I shall vest you in full power to that effect of declaring that I will confirm whatever you may transact with the Rajas in my name and on my behalf according to the instructions with which I shall have furnished you for that purpose'.[57]

When Hodgson joined the Residency, Bhim Sen Thapa congratulated him on his appointment and arranged a formal meeting with the Maharaja Rajendra. A week later, Hodgson was invited to attend a review of troops by the Maharaja. Reporting the event, he said:

> I am happy in being able to report to you that the reserve

> I am happy in being able to report to you that the reserve characterising of our intercourse with the Darbar for the past year seems fast emerging into a better and more cordial spirit.[58]

Ever since the establishment of Residency at Kathmandu, the British Government's policy towards Nepal was one of the strict non-interference in the internal politics.[59] The residents were clearly instructed to maintain a friendly relation. In their efforts, it has been said that the Mukhtiyar who was in-charge of the administration had greatly helped them to maintain such relations. The Government of India, on the other hand, hoped to gain confidence to change her traditional, social and political institution.[60] However, the hopes entertained by the British were futile and Nepal continued to follow the same old policy.

Hodgson, in his letter to the Government described in great detail how during Rajendra's minority the Mukhtiyar consolidated his power. Even after attaining majority, the Maharaja was placed under strict vigilance. When he desired to make an excursion into the lower hill resort, the Maharaja was prevented by all sorts of idle tales and obstruction. Hodgson reported:

> the Raja is hemmed into his palace which he cannot stir unaccompanied by the Minister, and then only to the extent of a ride or drive. Even within the walls of his palace the Minister and his brother reside, the later in the capacity of 'dry nurse' to His Highness.[61]

Thus, Bhim Sen Thapa's policy of non-intervention had its advantages and disadvantages. It certainly diminished the chance of collision with the Bharadars which narrowed the means of observing the British Government and shut out some scope to the prevailing party to misrepresent the British Government when necessary.[62]

Of the three Residents who served in Kathmandu, Gardner (1816-1829), Maddock (1831-1833) and Hodgson (1833-1843), it was with Hodgson that Bhim Sen Thapa had the greatest difficulty. Immediately after taking the charge of Residency, Hodgson demanded of the Darbar that the British representative in Nepal should at least receive all marks of respect and honour he was entitled to. He went to the extent that Resident and the Mukhtiyar were considered to be of equal rank and the mark of respect given to the Mukhtiyar by the sipahis should be extended to the Resident.[63] While agreeing to Hodgson's demand, the Government of India cautioned him that:

> Yet as the discontinuance of act of courtesies which has been usual to grant might be construe into International indignity. His Lordship-in-Council is of the opinion that it would be better to avoid a course which probably be the course of 'unnecessary irritation'.[64]

In the beginning of new year 1834, Hodgson told Bhim Sen Thapa that he had been expecting a change in the form of communication between him and the Nepal Government in view of the Maharaja's attaining majority. The Mukhtiyar politely agreed and the following day sent his Munshi to enquire from Hodgson the 'nature and extent' of the changes he desired. The latter told the Munshi:

> My friend, I am the Maharaja's guest and it is not for me to say I am ill-served as placed at his table...All I can observe is that most gradual change will please me best and the least one consistent propriety.[65]

He further elaborated his points that on one occasion Bhim Sen Thapa would pretend to be powerless declaring he was no longer in control of the state. Yet on the question of the Resident's direct access to the Maharaja he would not admit the latter's minority. He demanded to know whether the Maharaja was still minor or not. It is true that the Maharaja had recently assumed the responsibilities in all matters of ceremony and business including relations with the Chinese. He therefore demanded that the Resident and his official Munshi and Chobar should be granted the privileges of direct access to the Maharaja as this had already been done in the case of the other Bharadars.

The following day, Bhim Sen Thapa sent information through Mathbar Singh Thapa and Raj Guru that the "Maharaja will be most happy to see him (Hodgson) as often as he choose to come to Darbar". But his Munshi had to observe the existing system of official business to avoid inconvenience. Now, Hodgson came to know that the main obstacle in the closer relations between the Maharaja and the Resident was the Mukhtiyar Bhim Sen Thapa. A section of influential Bharadars headed by Raj Guru expressed willingness to support the British to deal with the Maharaja.[66]

Fort William was disappointed in Hodgson's action. He was reprimanded that:

> It is not the wish or desire of his Honour-in-Council that you should use the name of the British Government in any such discussion on the subject of the nature of the intercourse to be observed between the Resident and the Court of Nepal and it is directed that you will not make any demands even in your own name, from which if they were not acquired in, you could not possibly recede.[67]

He was further informed that since the question of direct access to the Maharaja had been already conceded to the Resident and his Munshi, there was no reason to pressurise the issue further. The Governor-General in Council correctly perceived that the situation in the Darbar was clearly borne by subsequent events. The Resident and his followers were granted free access to the Maharaja. Bhim Sen Thapa voluntarily waived the right to search the Residency's goods by Nepal's customs. At the same time restriction on the Resident's movement within the city was relaxed.[68]

The direct access to the Maharaja with the Residency did not last long. The problems and trade and frontier once again relegated to the old footing. Hodgson feared that "if this system be left in *status quo* with his (Bhim Sen) death or retirement, a crisis will occur, whether in a civil war or an aggression on us: but in both cases it would affect our interests". He argued that there was no man like Bhim Sen Thapa. He would be persuaded to change the system to be handled by less intelligent person.[69]

By September 1834, Bhim Sen Thapa became more powerful than before. He appointed his brother Ranbir Singh Thapa as the Governor of Palpa with exclusive civil and military powers. He revived the same old policy towards the Resident. He even informed the Bharadars with the false rumours of encroachment of the British subject to serve his own ambition and purposes. Such was the condition in Nepal. Hodgson considered it necessary to demand direct intercourse with the Maharaja openly. He emphasised that his demand was a "distinct right", a privilege given to all ambassadors. As regards the Mukhtiyar's attitude, he wrote that:

> The Minister (Bhim Sen Thapa) has hitherto in delivering his countrymen and by nourishing in them a feeling of deep and hostile attitude towards us has rendered them ripe for whatever acts of violence and aggression he may at any time propose.[70]

Three days later, the Resident reported to the Government of India on Rajendra's position in the Kingdom that "the Rajah is surrounded by the Minister's creature and is at present helpless", and

> Bhim Sen has all the powers in his hands…The Rajah is so uncomfortable in his honorary confinement that the probability is the Minister may work on him with success to make voluntary retirement of his throne in favour of his infant son and in the highest conformity with sacred code of the Hindu, to which His Highness is proved.[71]

Hodgson's anxiety and eagerness for diminution of Bhim Sen Thapa from power rather than to have direct intercourse with the Maharaja received sharp rebuke from the government:

> Whether the Raja rules the Minister or the Minister rules the Raja. Your business is with the Government as you find it… Your duty is strict neutrality and conciliatory in offensive conduct towards all.[72]

By the end of 1834, an important political development took place in Nepal's history which tremendously affected Bhim Sen Thapa's position. It was the Kala Pande, under the leadership of Ranjung Pande, who were nearly extinct in 1804, came into limelight. He had been trying to avenge the treatment that had been meted out to his father, Damodar Pande; to recover the family lands, honours and the family tradition position in the China's affairs. Ranjung Pande was however a man without principle. He was unstable whom few could rely on. It is a fact that the subsequent events proved that he had no love for his country. In spite of his shortcoming he was supported by the senior Maharani who had similar idea to remove Bhim Sen Thapa from power.[73] Having support from the palace, Ranjung Pande immediately petitioned to the Maharaja in November 1834 to restore the family honours and properties. The petition was received in favourable manner. In fact the Maharaja was in search of some decisive force to counteract the influence of Mukhtiyar Bhim Sen Thapa. The sudden revival of the Pande, well received by the palace surprised the Bharadars, and Bhim Sen Thapa's authority no longer remain unchallenged. From December 1834, it can be reckoned the commencement of a counter revolution and intrigues by the Kala Pande faction.[74]

Notes

1. Nepali, C.R., Lalmohar appointing Bhim Sen Thapa as Mukhtiyar, vide Appendices, 3 and 4.
2. For details see Ch. IV.
3. Ramakant, *op.cit.*, p. 58.
4. *FSC*, 15 June 1816, No. 16 of 2 June 1816.
5. Sen, J., *Indo-Nepal Trade in the Nineteenth Century*, Calcutta (1977), pp. 13-39.
6. Landon, P., *op. cit.*, Vol. I, p. 82 : Hunter, W.W., *op. cit.*, pp. 98-99.
7. Campbell's Sketches. He observes that the policy adopted by Bhim Sen Thapa towards the English was not to allow the later to interfere in Nepal's internal affairs. He further writes "so that to the independent principles, or suspicious temper of her own rulers does Nepal in some degree save the fortunate circumstances of our being without any influence in her internal administration... In short Nepal is free and independent of the British power".
8. P.T. Para, 55.
9. *Ibid. FSC*, 11 May 1816, No. 30.
10. Stiller, F.L., *op. cit.*, p. 88.
11. Aitchison, C.U., *op. cit.*, Vol. II.
12. Campbell's Sketches.

13. Hasrat, B.J., *op. cit.*, p. 221.
14. Hunter, W.W., *op. cit.*, Ch. I, footnote on p. 58.
15. Stiller,F.L., *op. cit.*, pp. 216-220.
16. Yogi, N.N., *op. cit.*, p.93.
17. Rose, Leo E., *op. cit.*, p. 211.
18. Lamb, Alister, *Britain and Chinese Central Asia: The Road to Lhasa,* London 1960), pp. 45-46.
19. *Ibid*, p. 58; Pemberton, *op. cit.*, pp. 88-99 and 343.
20. Rose, Leo E., *op. cit.*, p. 94.
21. *Ibid.*, p. 96.
22. FSC,16 December 1817, No. 87; Resident to Government of India, 2 December 1817.
23. *FSC*, 27 March 1819, No. 31.
24. Dungel, G., *op. cit.*, p. 27: Bhandari, D., *op. cit.* p. 429: Gyawali, M., *Nepal ko Sangchhipta Itihas,* Kathmandu (2043 BS): Yadav, Pitambarlal, *Nepal ko Rajnaitik Itihas,* Nepal (2040 BS), p. 141.
25. *FSC*, 2 September 1820, No. 11: Resident to the Government of India 12 August 1820.
26. Nepali, C.R., *op.cit.*, pp. 129-133.
27. Thapa, Dumbar S., Reminiscences (Unpublished) p. 8, says that "A Darbar was held to discuss the expediency or otherwise of signing the Treaty of Sagauli, and when Bhim Sen Thapa declared for peace, Colonel Uzir Singh Thapa, a young man... flushed with his recent victory over General Wood in addition to his other success against the British while he himself was yet in his teens, is said to have snappily twitted his uncle and electrified the assembly with the remarks—'You should be ashamed of yourself to propose this action. You had better go into a lady's gown'. The obvious implication was that Bhim Sen Thapa should retire and leave the administration in more capable hands". C.F. Stiller, p. 226.
28. *Ibid.*
29. Ramakant, *op. cit.*, p. 95.
30. *FSC*, 16 December 1824, No. 8: Resident to the Government of India, 20 November 1824.
31. Nepali, C.R., *op. cit.*, p. 132: Nepali has lucidly explained the manner in which friendly relations with Burma be concluded. An instruction containing nine questionnaires of political system, relations between king and the members of council and with other countries was handed over to the Nepali envoy.

32. Buckland, C.E., *Dictionary of Indian Biography*, London, (1906) p. 203.
33. Pradhan, K.L., *op. cit.*, p. 18.
34. *FMPR*, Vol. 125.
35. *FPC*, 28 May 1830, Nos. 19-21.
36. Ramakant, *op. cit.*, pp. 119-121.
37. *FMPR*, Vol. 127.
38. *FPC*, 18 May 1831, No. 23.
39. *FPC*, 10 June 1831, No. 24: Princep to Hodgson, 10 June 1831.
40. *FMPR*, Vol. 127: Tickell, J.R., Excerpts from the letters of the Residents at Kathmandu to Government, from 1830-1840. (*vide* Bikramjit Hasrat, *History of Nepal*, Punjab (1971) refers as Tickell.
41. *FPC*, 26 March 1830, No. 24: Hodgson to the Government of India, 8 March 1830.
42. *Ibid.*
43. *FPC*, 23 January 1832, Nos. 57-62: Hodgson to Princep, 31 December 1831.
44. *Ibid.*
45. Campbell's Sketches-1832.
46. FPC 12 March 1832, No. 45: Hodgson to the Political Secretary to the Government of India, 24 January 1832.
47. FPC 28 May 1832. No. 52. Maddock to the Government of India, 6 April 1832.
48. Jain, M.S., *op. cit.*, pp. 7-8; Old field, *op. cit.*, Vol. 1, p. 293; Ramakant, *op. cit.*, p. 98. Hunter, W.W., *op. cit.*, pp. 64-65, 124-125 and 126.
49. Campbell's Sketches-1832.
50. *FPC*, 27 August 1832, No. 18; Maddock to the Government of India, 20 June 1832. He further reported that 'While the jealousy of the Nepal Government and its original aversion to the establishment of our mission here are still undiminished the narrow bounds within which it studies limit (of) its intercourse with the Resident and the strict interdict placed upon its subjects who might otherwise seek our society have conduced to render our situation more isolated with reference to the Court and to the people".
51. Hunter, W.W., *op. cit.*, p. 99. Also *FPC*, 28 May 1832 No. 53; Maddock to the Government of India, 1 May 1832.
52. Tickell's *Events in Nepal, 1830-1940.*

53. *FPC*, 19 February 1833, No. 160; Maddock to the Government of India, 2 December 1832.
54. Pradhan, K.L., *op. cit.*, p. 36.
55. *FPC*, 19 March 1833, No. 26: Resident to Government of India, 8 March 1833.
56. *FPC*, 4 February 1833; No 56; Lord William Bentinck to the Chief Secretary to the Government of India, 4 February 1833.
57. 12 February 1833; No. 48. Lord William Bentinck to Hodgson, 12 February 1833: Also A. Kharita from Governor General of India to Maharaja of Nepal, 5 February 1833.
58. *FPC*, 5 March 1833, No. 19: Hodgson to the Secretary Government of India, 18 February 1833.
59. Sanwal, B.D., *op. cit.*, p. 215; Ramakant, *op. cit.*, p. 101.
60. Pradhan, K.L., *op. cit.*, p. 37.
61. FPC 5 March 1833, No. 19, Hodgson to the Secretary to the Government of India, 18 February.
62. *FPC*, 25 July 1833, No. 26. Hodgson to the Government of India, 11 July 1833.
63. *Ibid.*
64. *Ibid.*, No. 27.; Government of India to the Resident, 25 July 1833.
65. *FPC*, 13 February 1834: Nos. 6-7: Hodgson to the Government of India, 28 January 1834.
66. *Ibid.*
67. *Ibid.*, No. 8; Government of India to Hodgson, 13 February 1834.
68. *FPC*, 22 May 1834, No. 46: Hodgson to Government of India 10 May 1834; and No. 47; Government of India to Hodgson, 22 May 1834.
69. *FPC*, 10 July 1834, No. 144: Hodgson to Government of India, 19 May 1934; Also, Campbell's Sketches, 1834.
70. *FPC*, 9 October 1834, No. 17, Hodgson to Travelyèn, 20 September 1834 and No. 18; Travelyen to Hodgson, 9 October 1834.
71. *Ibid.*
72. *Ibid.*
73. Nepali, C.R., *op. cit.*, pp. 38-83.
74. *Ibid.*, pp. 204-206.

VII

Bhim Sen Thapa, Hodgson and Darbar Politics — 1834-1836

In this chapter an attempt has been made to study the relations between Bhim Sen Thapa and Hodgson and the politics of Nepal from 1834 onwards. In the preceding chapter we have discussed in details the policy of Bhim Sen Thapa towards the British Government in India and particularly with the Residents at Kathmandu since 1816. The Resident manoeuvred to acquire direct access to the Maharaja and the various obstacles posed by the Mukhtiyar have also been explained.

From the very beginning, Hodgson took a very aggressive stance on several major aspects where he felt relations between the two governments could be improved. The areas of importance according to him, apart from the direct access to the Maharaja, were trade, frontier problems and the Nepal standing army.[1] As regards trade he had three distinct complaints with the Mukhtiyar's policy on the development of trade and commerce; higher custom duties on Indian goods entering into Nepal; the restriction of entry of Indian merchants into Nepal and the discrimination against the Indian merchants.[2]

With a view to solve the problems, Hodgson took up the issue of trade and commerce in May 1834 which he had left off three years ago. In his memorandum to the Government of India he explained the British's endeavour to open the trade routes from various corners to Tibet and China and under the costly mission of Turner, Bogle, Kirkpatrick and Knox.[3] He further elaborated the reports on the native people engaged in trades and hoped to change the material life of the Nepalese people and bind them to the Company notwithstanding the anti-British policy of Nepal whoever was in power. The higher ranks in Nepal became solely dependent on the plain for their luxuries and convenience. If Nepal could be bound to the British of "many beneficial ties that severance of the connections will no longer be subjected to the Darbars caprices, animosities or ambitions".[4] For him the development of trade in Nepal seemed to a political than from an economic viewpoint. He pointed out that:

> I am the last person who would propose political aids to commerce, the very soul of which liberty, I would only by quite explanation: assay the removal of obstacle to its natural course which were thrown in its way by the Darbar.[5]

In another dispatch of 31st May, he confessed that "my reasons for desiring to see extended commercial intercourse between Nepal and plains rather political than economic". He emphasized that the martial propensities of the Gorkhas remained *status quo* even after the decade of friendships and this would continue unless some material change was brought to bear upon their habits. He cautioned the Government that "she (Nepal) is now formidable as ever. Mere chance may certainly dissipate without harm to us…From their present suicidal course and gradually to dispose them to shut their institution and habits to their circumstances".[6] Any other measures would be rejected by the Darbar except the commerce. It would certainly bind the people. He, thus suggested:

> I would reach the Government through the people, commerce would be my instrument. Nor would I interfere further than merely to procure commerce an unrestricted course, conformable to the spirit and even better of those commercial engagements by which Nepal was bound to us.[7]

Hodgson's complaints that the biggest hurdle was the system of custom duties based on the Commercial Treaty of 1792. According to the terms of the treaty, custom duties be charged reciprocally of 2½ per cent *ad valorem* on the goods imported into Nepal from India and *vice versa*. Since 1792, the company had regularly levied the duties as high as six to ten per cent of the duties on goods that enter into Nepal.[8] This was the matter which Hodgson wanted to correct. He found that the problem lay not with the treaty, but in the administration under Bhim Sen Thapa, who refused to accept it. From the beginning, the Treaty was never implemented by the Darbar and finally the Mukhtiyar repudiated it in 1834.

The opportunity came in 1834, when the Magistrate of Murshidabad reported the Resident of timber being accidentally omitted from the list of Nepali goods subject to only 2½ per cent duty on import into India.[9] Bhim Sen Thapa immediately preferred the claim and demanded to the Resident to know why customs charges on Nepalese timber had suddenly been raised above the regular duty. To Hodgson this was an obvious recognition of the Treaty by the Mukhtiyar and it deprived Nepal of her only plausible pretext for violating it. He wanted to know why Bhim Sen Thapa had consistently demanded, more than 2½ per cent on all Indian goods imported into India. Thus he wrote to the Government of India urging him to press this advantage. He declared that "we have hold on Darbar in case of need" and

> Shall we (He asked) at once and unconditionally rectify the casual omission of the timber as produce of Nepal in our custom duty schedule or shall we hold back the rectification a while, avow the omission as a fortunate accident and use it to point our argument in favour of the gradual and voluntary reforming by the Darbar itself of its past ommission and comission which alone at present we profess to seek.[11]

Hodgson further clarified that it was Bhim Sen Thapa who deliberately violated the Treaty of 1792. The Company had been strictly observing all the provisions of the Treaty. It was the Darbar who levied higher duties on goods from India and was in violation of it. It was, therefore, the responsibility of Bhim Sen Thapa to clarify the Nepal 'Government's position *vis-à-vis* the Treaty.[12] To solve the problem, Hodgson suggested to deal directly with the Maharaja, the nominal chief of Nepal. The maintenance of direct relations with him now had become an object of some importance.[13] Hodgson informed the Government of India of his having meeting with Bhim

Sen Thapa and the Maharaja desired to maintain *status quo* in respect of the Treaty and allowed to continue it for five to six years. However, he proposed for one year's period of grace. In reply to Hodgson's proposal, the Governor General asked him to ascertain whether Darbar did or did not recognise the Treaty. He was curtly told that "the Treaty must be binding on both parties or on neither". It was not the intention of the British to weaken the ruling faction and whether the Mukhtiyar had exercised too much power or not was the Maharaja and the people to decide.[14] The Governor General, instead, permitted Bhim Sen Thapa to repudiate the old Treaty which he did in November.[15] Hodgson was however, informed by the Darbar through Mathbar Singh that his Government decline to recognise the Treaty but they wished to continue its trade relations with the Company. The non-recognition of the Treaty by Nepal was a bitter disappointment to Hodgson. All his efforts to implement the Treaty seemed wasted. On 2nd December Hodgson remarked that "the blustering attitude of this Darbar cannot deceive me, but I know too well its false position and bias to do or even anything calculated to bring about disturbances."[16]

To the surprise of Hodgson, Bhim Sen Thapa brought in a message from the Maharaja offering a new agreement in corporating the "sum and substance" of the Treaty of 1792 and 1801 in so far trade was concerned . Hodgson thankfully accepted the offer and in March 1835 he sent a completed draft of this treaty to Fort William for comments and suggestions. In the proposed treaty uniform and moderate custom duties of 4 per cent Khuldar and 5 per cent Mahendra Mulli would be levied on the respective goods of India and Nepal. It also provided a list of specific custom houses, speedy justice to the merchants of either countries residing on other. The new agreement, if applied would check the illegal infiltration of goods. It had been Hodgson's complaints that Indian traders residing in Nepal experienced real difficulty in having their case tried and getting justice in Nepali courts. However, in certain respect, the proposed treaty fell short of the Resident's expectations. In the new proposed agreement, the right to search was nowhere mentioned. Earlier the Nepalese traders complained of indiscriminate search of their goods even after the duty was paid. Hodgson assured that such harassment would no longer be permitted once the duty was paid. On the question of adult-restrictions to the entry of British coins into Nepal. The proposed treaty thus went a long way toward easing relations between Bhim Sen Thapa and Hodgson.[17] The Government of India while considering the draft proposal, observed that the important provisions were omitted and the 4 per cent *ad valorem* duty on Nepalese goods that entered into Indian territories was too low to be accepted.

Yet the proposal was placed before the Board of Control for consideration.[18]

Closely connected with the trade was the problem of means of transactions-coinage of which Hodgson complained very often. He felt that the trade and commerce could not be developed unless there was an adequate and acceptable coinage. Nepal collected considerable amount of money through taxes on Tarai land and sale proceeds of rice in Indian rupees. Nepal also acquired Indian rupees from the trade with India. Thus it felicitated increase in trade. However, it was the policy of Nepal Government to melt down all the accumulated Indian rupees and remint them as Nepal coins.[19] As a result of this practice Indian rupees were removed from the circulation. Apart from this, the rules were strict. Indian rupees could legally be exchanged only at the mint. No Indian rupees could be taken out of Kathmandu valley. The Indian trader further lost on the rupees exchanged , and trade suffered for want of a readily acceptable medium of exchange. Hodgson felt it as a gross injustice and wanted the restraint on the export of Indian rupees from Nepal lifted. This was the very issue which Hodgson raised during the preparation of trade agreement.[20]

To solve the coinage problem, Hodgson took initiative of his own. The Residency was, as per his new innovation, authorised to issue bills of exchange in payment for various goods purchased from local traders for the maintenance of the Residency.[21] Since the bills of exchange were readily redeemable in India. Hodgson saw no reason why they could not be used as a substitute for a freely convertible coinage. He started to issue bills of exchange also for cash. The system in fact, provided security to the traders. In course of time, Hodgson accumulated huge amount of rupees for the bills of exchange, with no way of getting them off his hands. He was forced to ship them to India.[22] When the Board of Control learnt about this, he was sharply rebuked and was directed to furnish explanation of the proceedings by which he had accumulated the sum of sixty thousand rupees in his Residency. It appeared from his letter to the Accountant General and sub-treasurer that he had convoked his privilege of drawing bills, granted to him solely for the purpose of providing the wants of the Residency to the purpose of humouring the Darbar and the merchants of Nepal and that he had engaged in some scheme for promoting trade.[23]

Other areas of problem as seen by Hodgson were the Nepal-Sikkim boundary and the extradition of criminals. The boundary between India and Nepal remained comparatively quiet since the completion of the demarcation in 1829-1830.[24] The Sikkim frontier thus remained the only source of inconvenience. Resident Gardner did not take up the issue, fearing that would create new problems for him to satisfy the Darbar. Thus the boundary between Nepal and Sikkim remained unadjusted till 1833 when it came to the forefront and gave prolonged dispute.[25]

The real bone of contention was the tract between the old and new beds of the Mechi river below the bifurcation i.e. Kopilashi. Earlier, the old Mechi river was fixed as boundary line between Nepal and Sikkim whereby Kopilashi fell in the latter's share and remained in its possession for seventeen years. The Darbar also did not raised any objection on the arbitration of the Government of India. But in October 1833, the Mukhtiyar Bhim Sen Thapa informed Hodgson that the real Mechi in 1817 was the new stream and claimed the tract—Kopilashi. The Raja of Sikkim immediately protested to the Indian Government against the Darbar's intention. Hodgson, after thorough investigation of the record, hoped to settle the problem as

> the Maharaja is bound by the Treaty and is ready and willing to accept our mediation in the settlement of this dispute.[26]

In the same letter to the Government of India he suggested to appoint an European Officer to investigate the issue. But the Governor General took the matter rather lightly and informed the Resident that "he is not in the least to account for the proceeding complained by the Nepal authority. It is possible that it may have originated in a petition instituted to the Government on behalf of the Sikkim Rajah of aggression on the part of Nepal.[27]

On 17th November, Hodgson proposed to the Government of India to appoint a European Officer to investigate the boundary. He also pointed out that Bhim Sen Thapa professed willingness to aid the investigation team. According to him, it was an opportune moment to solve the boundary problem, otherwise, he feared that

> these folks (Gorkhas) are fierce... and one day the want of a frontier may lead us the Empire into trouble. We should take this occasion to survey and build pillars at least as high as the point of bifurcation... we must be content to "wait on providence" with this abled but hostile Minister (Bhim Sen Thapa).[28]

However, the Governor General was not in a hurry to appoint any European Officer to arbitrate the dispute at the moment, but approved his demands for a summary of Darbar claims on Kopilashi. Similarly, the Magistrate of Rangpur was directed to procure a statement from the Rajah of Sikkim.[29]

On the basis of the Darbar's statement and the map furnished by the Magistrate of Rangpur, it appears that the object of dispute between were never aware of the subject matter at the time when survey was undertaken in 1820. Bhim Sen Thapa informed Hodgson that since the Darbar did not have any valid claim over the said disputed tract the matter maybe settled without further delay.[30] Hodgson was, however, cautioned by the Government of India that:

> His Lordship-in-Council does not deem it necessary to act upon the suggestion 'that the whole boundary of Sikkim and Nepal should be carefully inspected. 'Such a measure would probably give rise to a variety of interest and absolute claim on either side which might otherwise never have been revived.[31]

In April, Bhim Sen Thapa proposed to Hodgson erecting saul pillars among the border of Sarun, Gorakhpur, Tirhut and Purnea. In the meantime, the Resident received a report of the Rajah of Sikkim regarding the Gorkha transgression across the Mechi river and harassed the Lepchas and urged the Government of India to establish a frontier police chowki. Hodgson feared that unless the boundary was properly surveyed and demarcated such incident would continue unabated. He recalled that the Darbar had waved its claim over the Kopilashi tract but left out to survey the boundary up to the hill—Dhoopgachi. Accordingly, Major Lloyd was appointed as the Commissioner to survey and demarcate the boundary.[32]

In July, Bhim Sen Thapa deputed Sardar Daryan Singh and Lachmi Das to Hodgson with a statement from Rajah of Sikkim who charged that the Gorkha continued to retain the lands north of Kalkazhar or the extreme north of Kopilashi, Siddhi Khola. The Subba of Illamguri claimed that the land belonged to Nepal and the Sikkimise refugees forcibly occupied it by constructing houses.[33] On the basis of the report, it is found that prior to 1828 there were no inhabitants in the present disputed lands. Survey were conducted in the winter of 1834-1835. During the survey. Major Lloyd was accompanied by the Nepalese agents up to the foot of the hills. Demarcation of boundary at Jhilimili, Chatyabari, Kalkaghar and the south end of Ramanagar were completed. As regard to Siddhi Khola, it was left to be settled after the malaria season ended. The Governor General was satisfied with the manner the Kopilashi dispute was settled.[34]

The partial settlement of Nepal-Sikkim boundary did not relieve Hodgson of other problems. On 15th July, 1834, the Magistrate of Purnea informed him of numerous daring robberies occur along the Indo-Nepal border. The request for the arrests was often turned down by the Nepalese local officials unless they received order from the Maharaja. He complained,

> as these dacoits are of frequent occurrence along the border of Nepal (Morung)...The Nepalese Government will send strict injunction to their local officers to afford any legitimate aid when requested to do so, instead of throwing obstacle in the way and thus facilitating the escape of the criminals...[35]

He also suggested to deploy police personnels along the border to apprehend and suppress the dacoits and requested Hodgson to press the Nepal Government to issue instructions to local functionaries.[36]

Hodgson was aware of the forest tract between the Tarai hills and the plains which afforded utmost facilities to the criminals for hiding. Unless bilateral agreement on rules and regulations on the issue had been prepared, he feared that it would continue unabated. He, therefore, suggested to the Government of India;

1. "to surrender all criminals whether one's own subjects or those of demanding party or else;"

2. "never to surrender one's own subject charged with criminal offences but secure them at the requisition of the demanding party and try and punish oneself upon proof furnished by the demand who is to prosecute before the court and according to the laws of the accused national"....[37]

The Government of India accordingly instructed Hodgson that "the most equitable and convenient general rules to follow in such cases is to surrender the presumed criminal to stand trial". If the Darbar accept it, it must be implemented under strict precaution with regards to the possibilities of the accused being guilty. It should be applicable equally to the refugees and other foreigners residing under the protection of any state. Bhim Sen Thapa agreed to the proposal of the Resident to the general principle of surrender as directed on both sides in case of dacoits and criminals.[38]

Yet, the Indo-Nepal borders remained open to the dacoit, criminals and thug to carry on their clandestine activities, Hodgson who saw it a problem that was real. Whenever there is long, open border there are those who commit crimes on one side of the border and seek refuse on the other side.[39] It indeed happened along the Nepal-India border and a realistic process of cooperation and extradition was needed. To get such an engagement, Hodgson would have to convince Bhim Sen Thapa. It was in 1835, that the latter could convince the Darbar to come into agreement. The Government of Nepal instructed its local officials posted on the border that:

> whereas in the month of Kartik of last year an agreement was entered into the Honourable Company's Government to effect that, in future, dacoity should invariably be punished where perpetrated, and that no objection to the surrender of dacoit should be raised...surrender the accused so often as a valid presumption was established.

The Nepal local officers were further warned that failure to comply with the agreement would be severely punished.[40]

One of the subjects of great interest to Hodgson was the military system of Nepal. In fact, he turned his attention to this almost immediately he took over as Assistant Resident at Kathmandu. Within five years, he collected sufficient data on the organisation and composition of the Nepal army. The document entitled: 'Memorandum Relative to the Nepal Army' drew the attention of the authorities at Fort William on Nepal army as a real factor for the growth of Gorkha militarism.[41] The late war with the British had by no means annihilated the army of Nepal. Rather the revenue reforms and re-investment of Birta holding shortly after the conclusion of peace, made rapid expansion possible and several new regiments were created. He found the army of Nepal much larger and more efficient than the one that had given the British anxious moments a decade back. Hodgson perceived that in a country like Nepal without trade outlets and other constructive programmes, the natural preoccupation of the martial people would be war. Nepal had accordingly concentrated all her resources on raising an efficient standing army through rotation system.[42]. Under this system, enlistment was annual. After one year's service a soldier was put off the rolls. After two years he could be enrolled again in service for one year. Once discharged, the soldiers lived in a very precarious condition, they got no pay and loathed any other job except soldiery. These soldiers desired nothing but wars, so that they could come up on the rolls, such a system not only posed immediate danger to the British Government on a strategically important frontier but also tended to adversely effect the hopes for the extension of trade through Nepal to Tibet and China. Although he found the Gorkha individually proud, overbearing and extremely suspicious, he was quite convinced that in service he would prove "as docile and steady and peaceable body of troops as any other in the world."[43]

Thus by relieving Nepal of substantial amount of trained soldiers Hodgson hoped that Nepal would be a peaceful neighbour and British objects in the Himalayan region could be achieved without much hindrance. These views quickly attracted the attention of Lt. General Sir Edward Paget, the Commander in Chief in Bengal. Sir. Paget at once suggested to the Governor General-in-Council not only to augment the existing Gorkha Battalions but also formation of new in the manner advocated by Hodgson.[44] Gardner, then the Resident, agreed to the martial qualities of Gorkhas but was concern that:

> even on entering our service, the Gorkhas would not separate themselves entirely from their native country as

> they could not remove their families from Nepal (in the Nepal Government's strong disapproval of it) and...that however faithfully they might conduct themselves on general occasions in the event of any rupture with Nepal, they possessed the feelings of patriotism which would induce the greater part of them to adhere decidedly to their national allegiance.[45]

Instead, he favoured the policy of using the Gorkha occasionally as mercenaries. Nothing came out of the proposal. Apart from the distaste for mercenaries, the Government of India felt it would be difficult to replenish or supplement with bodies of recruits from Nepal proper when necessary. Besides, the shortage of European officers made an increase of the native ranks undesirable.[46]

The growing military resources of Nepal under Bhim Sen Thapa led Hodgson to reopen the subject once again. "This was a nation of warriors and conqueror", he reminded the authorities in Calcutta:

> whose vision glory we first observe, stripped them into two campaign of the half territories and left them the future as blank as the present...The more I consider the martial enthusiasm of the Government. I am amazed that a standing army and incessant military display have not hurried the country into war. Troops are more than 14 years ago, with daily preparation...Truth is that the warlike affairs are the habits and passions of the people.[47]

The number of men trained in arms was constantly growing under the singular method of recruitment by rotation. The number of men would soon have been over 14 thousand. A steady army of such disproportionate size and in constant state preparedness was unsafe for the British. For internal security and to maintain law and order in the state Nepal hardly required a force of three thousand men on the rolls.[48] He drew the attention of Fort William to the accumulation of huge military stores and construction of forts at Makwanpur in eastern Nepal under the order of Bhim Sen Thapa. Hodgson's own conclusion was that Bhim Sen Thapa was augmenting the strength of army not only to invigorate his position as Mukhtiyar, but also in preparation for war with the company at a favourable opportunity.[49] In these circumstances, there was only two alternatives for the Government of India: "either to look indifferently on as heretofore with the knowledge that a perseverance by Nepal in her present plan of supporting a large and useless army will lead her to renew contact with the British after or during Bhim Sen Thapa's administration, or, by an indirect means to try to induce a change of Bhim Sen's policy from one of exclusively warlike and hostile to one of peace.[50] It would serve the purpose for security of India. It was further felt politically and militarily wise to enlist the Gorkhas in large number for "the more Gorkhas we have in our service, the safer we should be".[51]

In his Memorandum of October 1833 to the Government of India, Hodgson calculated that no less than 30,000 of the roll of soldier belonged to Khas, Magars and Gurung tribes. He spoke highly of the character, love of enterprise freedom from the caste prejudices, military habits and their amenability to discipline which would make them in the company's service "most highly prized".[52] Hodgson already saw the weakness in the Indian Native army. On several occasions the sepoy refused to embark for foreign service. Between 1782-1784 four native regiments had to be disbanded due to misconducts. The native army refused to proceed to Ava in 1824-1826 on the pretext of caste and religious prejudice.[53] Therefore, he believed that the physical and moral qualities of the Gorkhas would serve a salutary example for the sepoy mostly of orthodox high caste Hindu. While comparing the Gorkhas with the native sepoys, Hodgson observed:

> these highland soldiers, who dispatch their meal in half an hour and satisfy the ceremonial law by merely washing their hands and face and taking off their turbans before cooking, laugh at the pharisaical vigour of our sipahis, who must bathe from head to foot and make puja ere they begin to dress their dinner, must eat nearly naked in the coldest weather, and cannot be in marching trim again in less than three hours.[54]

All these move that Hodgson took must be considered as a step to the fulfilment of his policy of inducing Bhim Sen Thapa to change. His effort of the recruitment of the Gorkha soldiers was infact designed to siphon off revenue that might otherwise go into the military establishment and to give an outlet to the military spirit of the hill tribes.[55] However, the Governor General seldom took Hodgson seriously. The standing army of Nepal and the rotation system did not impress him neither. He was certain that Bhim Sen Thapa did not plan an invasion of either India or China. The one experience he had with both the countries was enough to convince anyone with the intelligence that Bhim Sen Thapa possessed that such an effort could be counter-productive.[56]

Hodgson was, however influenced by Nepal army. He was concerned about its size, the use of rotation system, increased number of trained military personnel at Bhim Sen's disposal and the possible uses of the army against the British. He clearly perceived the army was a creation of the Mukhtiyar, that had to be controlled. He apprehended that with the beginning to age and to lose his hold on the administration, this creation would become irresponsible and, therefore, a danger to peace and stability. According to this, the Mukhtiyar be pressed to change his stand to defused the situation and maintain good relations with the Company. The failure to appease the Governor General to his appeal, he forced Bhim Sen to change his view. In spite of his least influence on Darbar's politics he put increasing pressure on the Mukhtiyar at a time when Bhim Sen Thapa was least able to counter this.[57] There is no doubt that he was trying to bring about a real change in Bhim Sen Thapa's attitude before it was too late. Many changes were required in the attitudes of the men who made up the administration of Bhim Sen Thapa. Hodgson's meddlesome instinct merely aggravated the already tense situation prevailing in the Darbar. He was obsessed with the dangers he saw in Nepal's overlarge army.

The beginning of 1835 saw a sign of change in Bhim Sen Thapa's position in the Darbar. It seems that the Maharaja who attained majority in the later part of 1831* would sooner or later wish to assume the administration of the state. This was Bhim Sen's main worry. In fact he lost his principal supporter, Queen Regent, Maharani Tripura Sundari Devi in 1832. Similarly, the attainment of Rajendra's majority deprived him of the only excuse for absolute rule. In June 1834, the powder magazine at Kathmandu exploded, killing thirteen workmen and wounded fifteen persons. The earthquake of the previous year, was considered as portent predicting dire consequences for the state. The Brahmin community who always blamed Bhim Sen Thapa for the confiscation of Birta lands way back in 1805 by Rana Bahadur Shah despite clear evidence to the contrary, could not allow such event to pass unnoticed. In fact they exploited the situation in the days ahead.[58]

The political situation then developing in Nepal was summarised in detail by W.W. Hunter, as:

> By the beginning of 1835, seven factions had developed at the Court of Nepal, all requiring to be carefully watched by the Resident from time to time coquetting for his support and from time to time making appeals to the popular war-like sentiment in Nepal against the presence of a foreign representative at their capital. Hodgson had the delicate task of maintaining an attitude of dignified non-interference towards them all, which should not improperly pledge his Government on the one hand, nor give offence on the other. The principal *dramatis personae* in the series of tragedies that followed may be briefly enumerated.

First, the minor king ambitious of becoming actual ruler, at first with the help of Ranbir Singh, the brother and rival of the Prime Minister, subsequently with the aid of Pande faction hostile to the Prime Minister's whole clan. After suffering many degradations, the poor king was finally deposed in 1847 and died a state prisoner.

Secondly, the king's chief wife, known as the Senior Queen, who tried to assert her authority by the help of the Pandes. After furious outburst in which she more than once quitted the palace in a rage, she died on her way to exile, as rumoured at the time, from poison, but apparently from the jungle fever caught on her flight towards the Indian plains in 1841.

Third, the king's second wife known as the Junior Queen hoped to assert her authority by supporting the Thapa's (the clan of the Prime Minister Bhim Sen Thapa) and by opposing the Pandes. After a long struggle, she obtained her full political rights as queen in January 1843 restored the Thapas with the gallant Mathbar as Prime Minister, but lost her power on his assassination in 1845 and was thence, exiled to the Indian plains.

Fourth, the Chautariyas or collateral branches of the royal race, with hereditary claims to high office, kept down during the long supremacy of Bhim Sen reasserted their rights as his (Bhim Sen) power waned and secured the Prime Ministership for their clan more than once after his (Bhim Sen) fall, but lost their leaders by exile and assassination and finally went down in the great massacre of 1846.

Fifth, the Thapa family headed by the Prime Minister Bhim Sen, who, after a six year struggle to maintain his power ever since the death of the old queen Regent, was degraded in 1837, and cut his throat in prison to avoid torture in 1839. His rival brother Ranbir became a fakir (wandering mendicant) to save his life. His gallant nephew Mathbar, after a long exile obtained the Prime Ministership through the influence of the junior queen in December 1843 and was murdered in 1845.

Sixth, the rival family of the Pande family had been crushed for thirty years by Bhim Sen. Headed by Ranjung, the son of the Prime Minister murdered at the beginning of the century, they began to reclaim their right in 1834. By the palace intrigues of the senior queen, Ranjung obtained more than once the Prime Ministership and after many murders, perished himself in the general slaughter and exile of the Pandes in 1843. His principal kinsmen were beheaded. The aged Ranjung was brought to the place of execution but being in a dying state, he was merely shown to the people and removed to his own house, where he died naturally a few hours afterwards.

Finally, the Brahmin party, in turn allied and opposed to all foregoing factions of the military caste. Unjustly kept out of their hereditary appointments, the Brahmins emerged with Rangnath Pandit as their leader on the downfall of Bhim Sen Thapa. During the confusion which followed, the hostile factions allowed Rangnath Pandit to obtain the Prime Ministership till each could gather its own force. The Brahmin, however, discovered the time to be too perilous for a man of peace, and finding himself unsupported even by the Maharaja soon resigned the Primership. He reappeared from time to time especially as chief of a Coalition Ministry in 1840; always keeping out of harms way and content to retire to the safe seclusion of a religious life whenever danger threatened.

All these factors came in their turn to the front amid palace intrigues and massacres one after another. Each did its best to establish its power by destroying its rivals with the exception of the Brahmin party, each when its time arrived shared the common fate of slaughter and ruin.[59]

Thus was the situation in Nepal politics. It appears that Bhim Sen Thapa's position/influence in the Darbar was visibly declining. His relations with the British Resident was not friendly. The proposed Commercial Treaty submitted by Hodgson was rejected by the Governor General. He extended unilaterally to Nepal complete immunity from Indian custom charges, and hoped that Bhim Sen Thapa would return the favour by removing the custom duties on imports into Nepal from India. Nepal did not comply. It was indeed a setback for the Resident and a victory for the Mukhtiyar.[60]

Meanwhile military discontent was becoming more and more apparent. In 1835, the reduction of military emoluments in the form of birta became an issue of serious investigation. Way back in 1817-18, Bhim Sen Thapa had used the army to strengthen his position in the Darbar. The army officers supported him, but in return, they expected their interests.

But the sudden cutback of their emoluments and privileges could only mean that Bhim Sen Thapa was no longer in a position to defend the interests of military officers. A year earlier, Mathbar Singh Thapa had suggested that land grants made to Khas military officers should be revoked. In fact, the proposition was a sound measure to increase nation's economy. But it was against the military interests. Accordingly, Maharaja Rajendra appointed Rangnath Pandit to investigate the issue of military emoluments.[61]

Within the Thapa family, discontent prevailed. Ranbir Singh Thapa, younger brother of Mukhtiyar Bhim Sen Thapa, soon won the confidence of Maharani Samrajya Laxmi Devi, the moment she took possession of the royal seat. In fact she tried to assume the powers of the Regent[62] with the help of Ranbir Singh Thapa. When Mathbar Singh Thapa discovered this shift in loyalties, he quarrelled with Ranbir Singh and then resigned from the post of commander on the Sri Nath Regiment. When Bhim Sen Thapa came to know the incident, Ranbir Singh Thapa was removed from the palace immediately. The latter then went to his home at Sipa, outside Kathmandu. Mathbar Singh Thapa was sent there to bring him back but his effort failed. Then, Bhim Sen Thapa himself went to Sipa and brought Ranbir Singh to Kathmandu[63] and determined not to put him back into the palace rather he was appointed as the Governor of Palpa and promoted to the rank of Lieutenant General.[64]

To counteract the growing opposition in the Darbar, Bhim Sen Thapa appointed Kazi Surat Singh, a grandson of Kazi Amar Singh Thapa to a very high post in the central administration. Surat Singh was the first young man to break into the 'inner circle' of the old guard and his appointment must be considered as very important development. Orders from centre were jointly signed by Bhim Sen Thapa and Surat Singh Thapa thereafter.[65]

Meanwhile, an incident in the eastern Nepal under Kazi Elka Thop further worsened the Mukhtiyar relations with the British Resident. It was reported that a police action against the inhalants, mostly Sikkimese, flared up. On the basis of the Rajah of Sikkim's report, Hodgson lodged complaint to the Darbar. Bhim Sen Thapa immediately removed Kazi Elka Thop from his command. In his place, Mathbar Singh Thapa was posted to the command of eastern Nepal with promotion to the rank of Lieutenant General.[66]

Samrajya Laxmi, had tried to capitalise the situation for herself. She found a willing ally in Ranjung Pande and with him was determined to remove Bhim Sen Thapa from power. The situation that the Maharani exploited was not of her making. It had been prepared through thirty years of Bhim Sen Thapa's administration. She manoeuvred for Rajendra's abdication in favour of her son. It began way back in 1832 when the queen Regent died, she tried to control the administration of state. The plan was thwarted when her close aid Ranbir Singh was removed from palace.[67] She saw more and more clearly that Rajendra was moving to accommodate Bhim Sen Thapa. When the king chose to support Bhim Sen rather than Ranbir Singh, she had to search for an ally to help her to manage the transfer of power. It was Ranjung Pande, who came forward to the senior queen's aid. She required to establish Ranjung Pande as a credible alternative to Bhim Sen Thapa.

Meanwhile, Bhim Sen Thapa was secretly trying to prevent Maharaja from assuming control of the affairs of state so as to continue his rule. He was even said to have attempted to lead the youthful prince astray into debauchery so that he did not develop any ambition of government.[68] When it failed, the Maharaja was surrounded by Brahmins and priests to impress upon him the importance of religious matter over the temporal matters. When his effort failed, Bhim Sen Thapa hatched a plan for Rajendra's abdication. The Maharaja was confined to the palace. Every opportunity was taken to exhibit his son, Surendra to the public. Dr. Campbell writes of the incident:

> for some days past the little prince has been having lessons in riding from the old Minister; yesterday he was mounted on a pony and led out of the palace and attended by all the Sirdars; the Minister barefooted holding him, on and running alongside the urchin's horse traversed the principal streets of the city.[69]

Meanwhile, the army unrest was becoming more and more apparent. To counteract this development, King Rajendra appointed Bhim Sen Thapa the Commander-in-Chief of the armed force.[70] The Maharaja highly appreciated Bhim Sen Thapa's long and uninterrupted service to the nation as Mukhtiyar. It was sharply reacted to by the senior queen who had been working for the removal of Bhim Sen Thapa from the Darbar politics. She feared that the inability of Rajendra to assert the power would deprive her and her children of their rightful position in the kingdom. She publicly arraigned her husband: "You are an independent Raja indeed".

> You are a slave of Bhim Sen Thapa... a sheep led to the slaughter. Has he bewitch you or has he poured lead into your ears rendering you deaf. Let me and my children depart and leave you to the fate your imbecility deserve, or...you become religious and go to Benaras to bath and pray and leave me without eldest boy to rule the country and try if a women can succeed where a man has failed in annihilating the Thapas and asserting the lawful rights of sovereignty among her own people.[71]

The political situation became so complex that neither the Maharaja and the senior queen nor the Mukhtiyar could solve the problems.

Taking advantage of the political turmoil, in April 1835 Bhim Sen Thapa expressed his desire to the Resident to visit England and to see the scientific development there. Two weeks later a proposal was sent to Hodgson in the name of Maharaja that he had chosen Mathbar Singh Thapa to proceed to England.[72] The proposed mission, yet unrevealed, was welcomed by Hodgson, hoping that it was to prepare Mathbar Singh as his successor. The latter, he observed "is in the prime of life... his probable successor in the Ministry, frank, intelligent, wellbred, and free from all discreditable personal habits". Hodgson accordingly recommended the proposal to the Governor General.[73] No sooner had the Government of India assented, than rumours spread in Nepal that the main objective of the proposed mission was the removal of the Residency and the restoration of Kumaon. However. Bhim Sen Thapa denied the charge that there was any grain of truth in the rumours. Whatever his ultimate motive might have been, Hodgson intervened and wrote to the Governor General that the Mukhtiyar entertained the hope of negotiating directly with the King of England.[74] He recommended that the mission be allowed to proceed to England but only in private capacity. The Government of India accepted his proposal and decided accordingly.[75]

The matter was not disclosed to Bhim Sen Thapa. He made elaborate plans for the mission and on 26th November, Mathbar Singh Thapa left Kathmandu with an escort of six hundred and fifty men. In Calcutta he learnt that the mission to England had been scaled down to a private visit. Yet, the mission was well received and Mathbar Singh Thapa was given full military honours. Mathbar Singh did not proceed to England. He remained in Calcutta until March 1836. It was said that during his stay in Calcutta he had spent a hundred and fifty thousand rupees on this 'pointless mission'.[76] The mission was considered an expensive fiasco in Kathmandu. The mission, therefore, brought neither personal gains for Mathbar Singh nor for the Thapas single piece of evidence of achievement which they could cash upon at the domestic front. The Mukhtiyar showed his pique at the reversal of fortune immediately. The Darbar refused to accept the report on the Nepal-Sikkim boundary and revive the claims to Kopilashi.[77] He discontinued all discussions of a Commercial Treaty; he dropped the matter of extradition of criminal. This was followed by a refusal to allow the British official to follow-up the Thugee operation into frontiers where these criminals had taken refuge.[78] And finally he renewed his petty harassment of the Residency.

The mounting opposition to Bhim Sen Thapa was noticed. The Pandes openly defied the Mukhtiyar during the Dushera festival turning it "more like an overt strife of parties than we have been accustomed to under Bhim Sen". At one stage it was even thought that Ranjung Pande would succeed in fully reducing the Mukhtiyar's power and authority.

Notes

1. Stiller, F.L., *op. cit.,* pp. 227-251; Pradhan, K.L., *op. cit.,* pp. 42-63. Regmi, M.C., *op. cit.,* pp. 167-199.
2. ______, *A Note on Himalayan Trade,* JTU. 7 (November 1972) 18-19. Ramakant, *op. cit.,* pp. 119-121.
3. Pemble, *op. cit.,* pp. 54-89.
4. *FPC,* 10 July 1834, Nos. 141-151.
5. *Ibid.*
6. *FPC,* 12 June 1834, No. 140. Hodgson to C.E. Travelyen, 11 May 1834: Campbell Sketches-1834.
7. *Ibid.*
8. Campbell's Sketches-1834.
9. Tickell's, *Events in Nepal,* 1834.
10. *Ibid.*
11. *FPC,* 19 July 1834, No. 90: Hodgson to Travelyen, 6 July 1834.
12. *FPC,* 21 August 1834. Nos. 37-38: Hodgson to Travelyen. 2 August 1834.
13. *FPC,* 9 October 1834, No. 17: Hodgson to Travelyen. 20 September 1834.
14. *FPC,* 9 October 1834, No. 19: Travelyen to Hodgson. 9 October 1834.
15. Tickell's, *Events in Nepal,* 1834.
16. *FPC,* 15 January 1835, No. 43: Hodgson to Travelyen.
17. *FPC,* 20 July 1835, No. 18: Hodgson to Macnaghten, 25 March 1835.
18. *FPC,* 20 July 1835, Nos. 20-21: An Extract from the proceeding of the Governor General-in-Council, 1 July 1835.
19. Stiller, F.L., *op. cit.,* p. 235.
20. Pradhan, K.L., *op. cit.,* 62.
21. Campbell's Sketches 1835.
22. Ramakant, *op. cit.,* pp. 121-123.

23. *FPC*, 6 April 1835, No. 14: Government to Hodgson, 6 April 1835.
24. Tickell's, *Events in Nepal*, 1835.
25. Campbell's Sketches-1835.
26. *FPC*, 7 November 1835, No. 32-35; Hodgson to Magistrate of Rangpur, 18 October 1835.
27. *Ibid.*, No. 35. Macnaghten to Hodgson, 7 November 1835.
28. *FPC*, 5 December 1833, No. 55; Hodgson to Macnaughten, 17 November 1833.
29. *FPC*, 12 December 1833, No. 41: Macnaghten to Hodgson, 12 December 1833.
30. *FPC*, 10 January 1834, No. 28: Hodgson to Political Secretary to Government of India, 27 December 1834.
31. *IPD* and *COP* of 1834 and *FPC* 10 January 1834, No. 30. Macnaghten to Hodgson, 10 January 1834.
32. *FPC*, 12 June 1834, No. 138, C.E. Travelyen to Hodgson, 12 June 1834.
33. *FPC*, 31 July 1834, No. 15, "Note by the Resident Submitted to the Maharaja of Nepal".
34. *FPC*, 3 August 1835, No. 120: Government to Hodgson, 3 August 1835.
35. *FPC*, 21 August 1834, No. 35, Magistrate of Purnea to Hodgson, 15 July 1834.
36. *Ibid.*
37. *FPC*, 21 August 1834, No. 32, Hodgson to C.E. Travelyen. 29 July 1834.
38. *FPC*, 16 October 1834, No. 24 Hodgson to C.E. Travelyen. 24 September 1834.
39. Pradhan, K.L., *op. cit.*, pp. 21-23; Stiller, F.L., *op. cit.*, pp. 237-239.
40. *FPC*, 3 August 1835. No. 44.
41. *FMPR*, Vols. 125 and 127.
42. Oldfield, *op. cit.*, p. 175; Nepali, C.R., *op. cit.*, pp. 64-72.
43. FMPR, Vol. 125, 24 February 1825.
44. Bandenach, W., *An Enquiry with the Indian Army*, London (1826). Pradhan, K.L., *op. cit.*, pp. 16-18.
45. Campbell's Sketches-1834.
46. Hunter, WW., *op. cit.*, 107; Pemble, John, *op. cit.*, p. 353.
47. *FPC*, 14 October 1829, Hodgson to Political Secretary to the Government of India, 24 September 1829.

48. *FPC*, 26 March 1830, No. 24, Hodgson to Government, 6 March 1830.
49. Campbell's Sketches-1830.
50. *Ibid.*
51. MacMunn, *op. cit.*, p. 65.
52. *Ibid.*
53. Bharat, Amitya., *op. cit.*, pp. 90-124.
54. Hodgson, *JASB*, Vol. II (1833). He goes on to say, "in the war the former readily carry several days provisions on their backs: the latter would deem such an act intolerably degrading…In masses, the former have all that indomitable confidence, each in all which grows out of national integrity and success: the latter can have no idea of the sentiment, which at maintain the union and resolution of multitude in peril, better than all other human bonds whatever; and, once thoroughly acquired, is by no means inseparable from service under the national standard".
55. *Ibid.*
56. Stiller, F.L., *op. cit.*, p. 248.
57. *FPC*, 12 February 1833, No. 160.
58. Bhandari, D., *op. cit.*, p. 431; Pande, Sardar Bhim Bahadur, *op. cit.*, 147; Dungel, G., *op. cit.*, pp. 30-31.
59. Hunter, W.W., *op. cit.*, pp. 140-143.
60. Stiller, F.L., *op. cit.*, p. 266.
61. Tickell's, *Events in Nepal*, 1833-34.
62. Acharya, B., *Bhim Sen Thapa ko Pattarn,* Pragati. No. 10. pp. 117-118.
63. Dungel, G., *op. cit.*, p. 33.
64. Acharya, B., *op. cit.*, p. 118: Bhim Sen Thapa Documents, 43/373/1, (1890 BS).
65. Stiller, F.L., *op. cit.*, p. 262.
66. Acharya, *B., op. cit.*, p. 119; Pradhan, K.L., *op. cit.*, p. 74.
67. Dungel, G., *op. cit.*, p. 34.
68. Pradhan, K.L., *op. cit.*, p. 65.
69. Campbell's Sketches, 1834-1835.
70. Nepali, C.R., *op. cit.*, pp. 245-249.
71. Campbell's Sketches, 1835; Tickell, 1835.
72. *FPC*, 25 May 1935, No. 34. Hodgson to Government of India. 10 May 1835.
73. *Ibid.*

74. *FPC*, 21 December 1835, No. 29 and others.
75. Campbell's Sketches, 1835: Hasrat, B.J., *op. cit.*, p. 239.
76. Acharya, B., *op. cit.*, p. 119.
77. *FPC*, 16 October 1835, Nos. 89-92.
78. *FPC*, 6 June 1836, Nos. 88-92: Hodgson to Government of India, 10 May 1836. Also Tickel's, *Events in Nepal*, 1836.

VIII

Fall of Bhim Sen Thapa: 1837-1839

The anti-incumbency factor in the Nepali power politics can be traced way back to 1832 when the Regent Maharani Tripura Sundari died. and the subsequent events that followed were the main reason for the downfall of Bhim Sen Thapa. In the other words, the death of the Regent portended the struggle for power in the Darbar. The young King Rajendra, who by now attained the majority aspired to rule the country by himself. He could have easily extricated monarchy out of morass into which it had failed during his and his father's minority but he lacked strong determination, resolution and will to carry it through.[1] He proved to be a weakling before his two queens who were determined to control the state administration with the support of opposition. He called for various groups of Bharadars to organise common platform themselves in opposition of Bhim Sen Thapa. The political struggle which began as an attempt to revive the powers of the monarch very soon assumed the shape of struggle between the different groups of aristocracy to acquire controlling authority. In spite of the opportunity before him, Rajendra could do nothing but simply reinstated Bhim Sen Thapa as the Mukhtiyar with greater power in the Panjani. He feared that the Mukhtiyar and the Thapa faction who represented the military interests "a race of men who for the last fifty-five years have dragged the country and its princes at the wheels of military car".[2] The army had been, in fact, the sole means of power and its consistent patronage by the Mukhtiyar. The strength of Gorkha army was visibly increased and in 1836 the numbers swelled to seventeen thousand. It was difficult on the part of the King Rajendra to support Bhim Sen Thapa singularly as he was disliked by all. Thus it was not unusual on the part of the Bharadars to try to rise with the help of young king who had been living cautiously and submissively for the last two decades. Therefore, the Maharaja dictum was appreciated by the opposition Bharadars. The Maharaja was amiable, prudent and well disposed towards pacific policy rather than martial propensity followed by the Mukhtiyar since 1806. Thus the opposition was a reaction to the infringement by Bhim Sen Thapa upon the rights and privileges of the sovereign and the old aristocracy. The opposition consisted of almost all the ancient families of state and founder of her greatness in the past time. These were the men who suffered most at the hands of the Thapa faction. The prevailing political turmoil in the state compelled Rajendra to side with the Maharani and the Pandes reluctantly. "The Raja and his friends" remarked Hodgson,

> are now natural allies; and the general tendency of event is daily adding something to their influence by throwing into deeper shade the splendour of the military profession.[3]

Immediately after the death of Regent Maharani, the senior queen Samrajya Laxmi Devi who desired to emulate the example of the former Rani, was anxious to establish her own rights of regency. But Bhim Sen Thapa thwarted her move to control the official seal and the administration. Her failure led to removal of Ranbir Singh Thapa from the palace. There was then no one whom she knew well enough to trust in her effort to obtain a wider measure of actual power for King Rajendra and thereby for herself In fact, she was apprehensive of Maharaja's inability to assert might deprived her and her children of their rightful position in the kingdom.[4] She constantly pressurised Rajendra to remove Mukhtiyar Bhim Sen Thapa from power or abdicate the throne in Surendra's (eldest son) favour and rule the country as she desired. But Rajendra had moved steadily towards an accommodation with Bhim Sen Thapa and was unlikely to change this direction without substantial change in the situation in Kathmandu. Thus unwilling to surrender to her demand frustrated Maharani left royal palace with her children on the midnight of 8th November, 1835 creating an uproar in the Darbar. In fact she had been disgusted at Rajendra's inability to resist Bhim Sen Thapa's demand for special power for mission to Calcutta or England to negotiate the retrocession of Kumaon or the withdrawal of the British Residency from Kathmandu. Indeed, she decided to strengthen the hands of Rajendra. She felt that it was the Maharaja, the head of the state who should take up the matters with the Governor General in India for solution than the Mukhtiyar.[5]

In the meantime, she urged him to augment a new regiment under his close supervision, and direction to be used in time of need. But when he failed to obtain necessary financial allocation for the Mukhtiyar, she shouted angrily at him that:

> You have given him a sunnad making once for all everything to the Minister, who with his family and creatures eat up all so that neither have we any right nor even means to provide for our children.[6]

She went on saying that "you are no Raja, other rule and spend, you have your mere Gaddi and mouthful to eat. Such too is my share and your children". She strongly demanded that if fund for a new regiment was not available, let fifty thousand rupees from Tarai revenues be given to the children. Otherwise she warned that she would not take active part in the state affairs. In spite of her efforts to induce the Maharaja, she failed to achieve anything.[7]

From 1833 to 1835, she saw that the king was assaying towards an accommodation with Bhim Sen Thapa that would mean a very slow transfer of power. When Bhim Sen Thapa was made the Commander-in-chief, Samrajya Laxmi Devi had to search for an ally to establish her own authority once she evolved into an independent entity, without the help of Rajendra. It provided much needed opportunity to the Pande faction for the power struggle. Had she favoured Bhim Sen Thapa for her objective, the Pande would not have been able to vent their anger and jealousy towards the Thapas and her immediate ambition might have fulfilled. Had the senior Maharaja not desire to live with Rajendra to become regent Queen like Tripura Sundari Devi after making prince Surendra as king immediately as possible, to conspire against the Thapa was virtually impossible.[8]

Ranjung Pande was grandson of Kalu Pande who helped Prithvi Narayan Shah during the conquest and unification of Nepal, wanted to take revenge on Bhim Sen Thapa. He never forgot the treatment that had been meted out to his father, Damodar Pande and family.[9] In 1804, when Rana Bahadur Shah returned to Kathmandu he was blamed for the political upheaval in the country. Damodar Pande was executed and the family lands were confiscated and Ranjung Pande and his brothers were exiled to India. Thus to avenge, Ranjung Pande secretly maintained relations with the Dware, friends of king Rajendra kept them in good humour and had attracted them towards him. Through them, he criticised Bhim Sen Thapa's folly to the king.[10] The Pandes wanted to end Mukhtiyar's monopoly in administration by instigating the Maharaja against Thapa saying that Nepal was forced to accept the Treaty of Sagauli in 1816 after humiliating defeat in the Anglo-Gorkha war due to Bhim Sen Thapa's carelessness and that the territories lost to the East India Company could be reclaimed if the Pandes were appointed Mukhtiyar. However, Ranjung Pande was a man without strong support in the army and the Bharadars. He failed to cultivate friendship with the military leaders either. The subsequent events projected him as unstable man whom the people could trust. It was proved that he had no great love for either the nation or the military.[11] In spite of the shortcoming of Ranjung Pande, the senior Maharani chose him as an ally to topple Bhim Sen Thapa from power.

In November, 1834, Ranjung Pande petitioned the Maharaja for the return of his family's properties and honours. To the surprise of many, the king received this request favourably which clearly indicated that the Pandes had already gained considerable ground. "From that date may be reckoned", remarked J.R. Tickell, "the commencement of a counter-revolution and of those intrigues of the Kala Pandes which eventually succeeded so well in overthrow of their rivals and in repaying the cruelties they themselves suffered at his (Bhim Sen) hands".[12] The king, however, took no immediate action on it. Blessed with royal support Ranjung Pande immediately sent a letter to the Chinese Amban in Lhasa urging to restore the family's traditional ties with Tibet[13] through the Kathmandu Darbar. In the same letter he levelled false accusation that Bhim Sen Thapa had turned his coat supporting the British which had become enemy of China. The Amban communicated the request of Ranjung Pande to the Maharaja of Nepal urging him to depute Pande in the next quinquennial mission to Peking. The king did indeed take this task to himself* (for the last two dsecades the mission was decided by Bhim Sen Thapa but he appointed Pushkar Shah for the assignment.[14]

Hodgson, who was also eager to see the change in the administration of Nepal was disillusioned. Relations between the Resident and the Mukhtiyar became stern. The Darbar evaded all the proposals like Sikkim-Nepal boundary; refusal to allow the British officials to follow-up the Thugee operation into Nepal and the refusal to accept the proposed commercial treaty. In spite of these, Hodgson adopted a conciliatory attitude towards the Mukhtiyar. He observed that:

> Power is wholly on one side, right on the other but endurance has nearly gone to length amongst proud and patriotic people and the sole stay of the stronger party is an old man of 65 whose health and even sickness will be instant signal for a struggle between the several grown members of his family, during which struggle the amiable intelligent young prince can scarcely fail to redeem his own with the voice and aid of nobles.[15]

The Darbar politics acquired new importance. The probability of violence in the kingdom splitting over the frontier and the difficulty of fixing on the Darbar, the responsibility for action of its local officials were always a matter of concern. Further, within the inner circle, Hodgson found that "as all the personal interests of one are now promoted and all the personal interests of the other now crossed by an exclusive and absorbing patronage of army..."[16] In the opposition to the Thapas, the Resident saw the likelihood of change in the very near future which would be honourable and advantageous to the British. However, so long as Bhim Sen Thapa maintained his authority "by military means" this transformation could not be anticipated. Nor he was in favour of interfering the internal politics of the Darbar to produce turbulence in the kingdom. He hoped that after the retirement of the Mukhtiyar, the opposition would come to power and the Maharaja would be able to influence the Darbar into adopting a pacific policy towards the British with the later's active co-operation.[17] The Government of India considered it rather premature to take active interest in the prevalent situation in Nepal, but instructed the Resident to keep close vigil and report the political development regularly to the Government.[18]

The beginning of 1837 showed a sign of change in the Nepali political scenario. In February, at the annual Panjani, the Maharaja made most noteworthy changes in the administration. Mathbar Singh Thapa, Umakant the Darbar treasurer and several Thapas were relinquished from the office and the Pandes were appointed in their places. Ranjung Pande was also made one of the Kazi. Even the post of judicial administration was assigned to the Brahmin with legal knowledge, Ranbir Singh Thapa was the only one from the Thapa faction who retained the office. With Ranjung Pande's entry into the inner circle, it became more difficult for Bhim Sen Thapa to maintain his influence inside the Darbar.[19]

The declining position, compelled Bhim Sen Thapa to adopt a pacific towards the Company Government. The Darbar had finally agreed to surrender of the fugitives though on a reciprocal basis from the Thugee operation in India. The Mukhtiyar's proposal of deduction and pay cuts of the army earlier approved by Rajendra was implemented and a new regiment was raised. However, the Mukhtiyar and his adopted son were exempted from the reduction of pay. The Maharaja neither dared to remove Bhim Sen from office nor opposed the augmentation of the army.[20]

The stripping of Bhim Sen Thapa's authority by the Maharaja was seemed to be well planned. In June, the king ordered an inquiry into the Mukhtiyar's administration of the courts of justice, state mint and jagir lands assigned to the soldiers. It was believed to avoid discriminate the Mukhtiyar but to induce him to resign from the post out of humiliation so that change in the administration would be materialised. Meanwhile, the opposition under Rangnath Pandit emerged as major contender for the Mukhtiyarship. But it was not likely that the next Mukhtiyar would be given the unlimited powers which Bhim Sen Thapa had enjoyed and exercised. It also appears that the Maharaja intended to maintain overall control of the Government so that no one could exercise influence to others.[21]

In July 1837, Maharaja Rajendra announced a second Panjani, a complete break with the practices of the last thirty years. Normally, the Maharaja personally appointed only the Mukhtiyar and Kazis, and they in turn continued the Panjani through the ranks of the army and administration. But it was not in the second Panjani. He personally appointed all the officers of army and other administrations. Ranjung Pande was made a Kazi. At the general parade of army, the Maharaja ordered that in future new officers should not attend upon the senior officers. Its objective was to reassert a royal prerogative. This change sealed the fate of Bhim Sen Thapa. The patronage of the army from which the Mukhtiyar derived his power now passed into the hands of the Maharaja.[22]

Eleven days after the second Panjani, the youngest son of senior Maharani, Debendra suddenly died. The sad news that was circulated throughout the country confirmed that the young prince was died due to illness and there was no hands behind it.[23] However a week later, the Maharani informed her parents that Debendra was administered a poison and Bhim Sen Thapa was accused of being responsible for it in connivance with court Physician Ek Dev Baid. Almost immediately Bhim Sen Thapa was stripped of his office and put in chains. His lands and properties were confiscated as were Mathbar Singh and Sher Jung Thapa. The rest of the Thapa families were placed under strict vigil arrest. Ranjung Pande was made the Mukhtiyar[24] in his place. Tickell describes the incident:

> On 24th July, the Raja's youngest son died suddenly and a rumour quickly circulated through the palace that the child had been fallen victim of poison intended for its mother, the Maharani. This was followed by a report that the instigator of this was Bhim Sen or some of his party. The alarm soon spread from palace through the city, and in confusion that issued Ranjung was suddenly appointed the Minister of State and Bhim Sen seized, ironed and thrown into prison, while the whole of his family were placed under close arrest.[25]

Thus the Maharaja Rajendra, the senior Maharani Samrajya Laxmi Devi and the Pandes had successfully conspired to remove Bhim Sen Thapa from the Nepali politics. Almost all historians are unanimous that Ranbir Singh Thapa, the youngest brother of the Mukhtiyar was one of the conspirators in bringing down Bhim Sen Thapa from power.[26] The former was projected as main contender for the post of the Mukhtiyar and had lately visited the palace regularly. It is also alleged that if he was not against his brother, there was no reason to send him to Palpa as Governor of that province. How far the allegation is true, it is pertinent to analyse the political condition and the subsequent events that followed after the arrest of Bhim Sen Thapa.

The reason behind sending Ranbir Singh Thapa to Palpa had two main objectives. At the time, he had converted most of his landed properties into Guthi. Out of five, two Guthi were granted by the Maharaja. Not content with this, he urged his brother, Bhim Sen Thapa to approach Maharaja to grant him more Guthi. When Bhim Sen Thapa refused to concede the demand, he proceeded to Sipa in rage. Bhim Sen Thapa personally went there to appease him and finally brought him back to Kathmandu.[27] Later, he was made General of the Nepalese army and posted to Palpa as administrator. Palpa was one of the most important and prestigious provinces in western Nepal since the unification of Nepal. And from 1806, the Mukhtiyar appointed his own relatives as administrator there. Therefore, sending of Ranbir Singh Thapa to Palpa did not have any connection politically with the downfall of Bhim Sen Thapa. It was, rather a personal and family matter.

The other allegation was Ranbir Singh Thapa's regular visit to the palace. In fact, as a high ranking official in the Government, it was not usual for him to pay regular visit as official or private in the royal palace. It is true that his visit there was not of political nature, but to take part in the religious deliberation with the leaders of Joshmani sant.[28] At that time, the political development in the state had witnessed dramatic changes. Senior Maharani's influence prevailed in the Darbar. She intended to rule the country as Regent of her son with connivance of the opposition faction, similarly, the junior Maharani also aspired to control the administration through her Thapa coterie. Yet, the senior Maharani and her associate the Pandes did not have strong resolution to confront Bhim Sen Thapa openly. They had to reach someone within the Thapa family who could manipulate the situation for their design and play a subversive role against Bhim Sen Thapa's downfall.[29] They found Ranbir Singh Thapa to play the role. Most writers assume wrong concept of it. Among them, P. Landon writes that Ranbir Singh was jealous of his elder brother's accomplishments, who too wanted to become the Commander-in-chief of the army and gradually the Mukhtiyar, therefore, established friendship with the conspirators.[30] Even if we agree that he was deeply involved in hatching conspiracy with the senior Maharani and the Pandes against his brother and claim to be main contender for Mukhtiyarship, what actually did happen after Bhim Sen Thapa was put behind the prison. Instead, of awarding him the post of

Mukhtiyar, his properties were confiscated and was put in jail along with his brother Bhim Sen Thapa. Not a single member of the conspirators came forward to defend Ranbir Singh Thapa nor extended any moral support against the Maharaja's action. The wrong interpretation of the situation tarnished the personal life of Ranbir Singh Thapa. After release from the prison, he went to Kasi (Banaras) in India and ultimately became religious mendicant and was called Abhaynand.[31]

The appointment of Ranjung Pande as the Mukhtiyar ensued a dramatic change in the internal and external affairs. In the domestic front, the Pandes emerged as the strongest faction in the Darbar. They received active support from the royal families, and as a result, they professed a sentiment of war fever. They went to extent that "they must be a war Minister at all, for their long exiled and stripped them of all legitimate weight among their fellow nobles".[32] They were bitterly hostile to the English and this sentiment became their core policy towards the British Government. The anti-British sentiments flared up and intrigue with Lahore and protected states of the Company commenced with much vigour. As early as in 1837, secret Nepalese missions were dispatched to Lahore to forge an alliance between Kathmandu and Lahore against the British. They were reported to have received a warm welcome from Maharaja Ranjit Singh. Yet, nothing came of the Darbar overtures at that time. Ranjit Singh had more realistic view of the British power in India to entertain such alliance. Failing to forge an alliance with Lahore, the Darbar turned towards Gulab Singh, the Dogra Raja, who was more interested on cementing an alliance with Nepal. It was felt that a direct intercourse with Nepal not only promote commerce between Lhasa and Ladakh but also "would establish a direct intercourse with a power which he (Gulab Singh) thinks will not only tend greatly to augment his present influence but lead to an alliance which may at some time future period of reciprocal importance".[33] Hodgson, who was very much concerned of this development reported to the Government that:

> ...all circumstances of their (Pandes) character and position conspired to make the Kala Pandes determined opponents of responsible intercourse of our Government (Resident) at Kathmandu.[34]

The opposition factions immediately began to urge the Maharaja to remove Ranjung Pande from Mukhtiyarship. They felt the policy pursued by the Mukhtiyar towards the British would be detrimental for Nepal's survival. Maharani Samrajya Laxmi Devi also realised it and proposed Chautariya Jyan Shah to replace Ranjung Pande.[35] This group of the Chautariyas and the Bharadars strongly urged the Maharaja to release Bhim Sen Thapa from prison. The mounting opposition to Ranjung Pande, compelled Maharaja Rajendra to remove him from the office and in his place Rangnath Pandit's Ministry was installed.[36] One of the first acts of the new Ministry was to arrange the release of Bhim Sen Thapa. On 16th December, 1837, Rangnath Pandit secured an audience for the old man. Bhim Sen Thapa, in defence of his innocence, told the packed court that had he desired he could have assassinated the Maharaja long back when the latter was a minor. What was the benefit for him in killing the minor prince, Debendra? He argued that all allegations were fabricated to tarnish his image and remove from the post he held.[37] Maharaja Rajendra and both of his Maharani pardoned and sent him home with honour.[38] Soldiers of different ranks and files followed him home in felicitation. Mathbar Singh Thapa and Sher Jung Thapa were given similar treatment at the Darbar and huge crowd of soldiers accompanied them to their respective homes. The Maharaja issued a Lal Mohar restoring Bhim Sen Thapa's Tudikhel residence and garden and fraction of his farmer lands were returned.[39] In spite of his acquittal, Bhim Sen was not awarded any office. In fact no mention was made of the fact that there had been no basis for the charge on which he had been removed from office and imprisoned. Later on, he went to Borling and stayed there till he was recalled by the Maharaja in early 1829.[40]

The sudden reversal of the events stunned Ranjung Pande. For a moment, it seemed that he had achieved the success, he ambitioned. But now, it appeared that this had all been a cruel play. The short tenure of the Mukhtiyarship had, perhaps, hurt his feelings more than it helped him. Neither his own fortune had been improved. On the contrary, Bhim Sen Thapa's prestige gradually increased within the Palace.[41] Dr. Allen Campbell, the assistant Resident remarked that "Ranjung Pande was quite, thoughtful and apparently in low spirit".[42] Thereafter, Ranjung Pande immediately approached Maharaja Rajendra for permission to leave Kathmandu for Tarai. But the Maharaja persuaded him to remain in Kathmandu and held out to him some hope of present remunerasion and future employment in the administration.[43] The reason behind Rajendra's persuastion was to have someone like Ranjung Pande close at hands as a counter-balance to the Thapa in the administration.

The political situation in the Darbar did not serve anything to Bhim Sen Thapa to save himself either from present condition or future persecution. Meanwhile, Ranjung Pande was constantly putting preasure on Maharani Samrajya Laxmi Devi to use her influence on Maharaja Rajendra. Accordingly, in January 1838 Panjani, Ranjung Pande was rewarded the post of the Commander in the armed force.[44] Similarly, his brother, Kabir Pande was appointed Kapardar and made an intimate of the royal palace. At about this time almost one hundred officers and men of the Singh Nath Battalion resigned.[45] They openly called themselves private followers of Mathbar Singh Thapa and constantly showed allegiance to him. Many Dakhareah also followed the steps of the army. It clearly showed Mathbar Singh Thapa's hold and popularity with the military.

Mukhtiyar Rangnath Pandit, on the other hand, was steadily losing his popularity. His suggested reform and the correctly identified Mukhtiyar with this very unpopular policy[46]. His days as Mukhtiyar were obviously numbered and it only remained to be seen how long he would be able to hold his office.

Rangnath Pandit, thus turned his attention towards anti-British intrigues with various Indian states and foreign countries. A recent scholar sums up that "envoys were sent in all directions; in November 1837 to Nagpur; in January 1838 to Banaras, Rewa, Burma, Afghanistan; the following month to Allahabad, Bharatpur and Udaipur (Rajasthan), Hyderabad, Lahore and Kutch Bihar (Assam); in March to Rewa, Banaras, Mathura, Lahore and Kota; in April to Hardwar, Bhutan, Gwalior, Scindia and Lahore again".[47] The replies to the letter carried by the envoys were usually formal in tone and indicative of the extreme caution with which all rulers in the plains regarded anti-British conspiracies. Taking the advantages of the North west crisis, the Darbar tried to exploit the relations between British India and the Burmese. The situation became so tense that the Resident sought the Government of India's intervention.[48]

On the basis of the resolution passed by the Supreme Council,

Calcutta, an army observation to be posted in Gorakhpur under General-Oglander as "a measure of preparation and activity, if necessary". The Residents and political agents in Indian states were instructed regarding hostile dispositions of the princely states. The latter were to be warned against entertaining any Nepalese agents. The movements of the Nepalese envoys were to be strictly watched.[49] During the confusion, Mathbar Singh Thapa asked for and received permission to go to Tarai on hunt.[50] Once free from Kathmandu, he continued on through Tarai to India and further intended to proceed to Lahore to join Ranjit Singh. He was intercepted by the Company's forces and for a while intended. But by the end of 1838, he was released.[51] Meanwhile, the rumours of British troops movements in the northern India persisted throughout the autumn of 1838, and these tended to keep alive the suspicions that agitated the Darbar. Nepalese troops were sent out of the valley to reinforce the border outposts and in the process Bhim Sen's military support in the valley was weakened.[52]

The Maharaja was extremely divided between his fear and ambitions. He was worried that the recent intrigues carried on by the Darbar had been detected and-British might retaliate. The Indian Government had already directed the military authorities to acquire military intelligence of the frontiers and to be prepared for further instructions, should hostility between the two states become inevitable.[53]

In Nepal, the condition did not improve. Ranjung Pande had initiated to uplift the economy of the state by surrendering the Jagirs. In January 1839, he relinquished his lands, which had recently restored to him and urged all of the Bharadars to do the same.[54] Earlier in 1836, the resources saved from the retrenchment of payrolls had been used to expand the military by establishment of the Hanuman Dal Battalion. The Government tried to root out the corruptions that prevailed among the Bharadars. Ranjung Pande had found a sure political weapon in this measure, but a dangerous one. Action taken against the offenders were arbitrary. which constituted a direct threat to the Bharadars sense of security.[55] In fact his actions were politically motivated. His activity did not solve the problem as a whole, rather created fear, tension, insecurity and profound distrust among the Bharadars.[56]

The new year saw a change in the Darbar politics. Since, August 1838, power was concentrated in the hands of the Maharaja following the resignation of Rangnath Pandit. He had resigned having failed to gain effective control over the Government and because of constant opposition from senior Maharani and her Pande followers. Maharaja Rajendra clearly perceived that if the Pandes come to power backed by the senior Maharani, they would undermine his authority. Thus, he did not appoint any Mukhtiyar during the Panjani.[57]However, in 1839 urged by the senior Maharani, Ranjung Pande was appointed as Mukhtiyar but without substantial power which he, in fact, had to share with Chautariya Pushkar Shah.[58] The Pandes believed that if they were to remain in power, it could only be as a "war party". He understood that the Maharaja could only be won over by promising wars and conquests. To achieve his objective, he started grasping money, irrespective of the mode of consequences of accumulations.[59] Public expenditure was drastically curtailed and the Bharadars were to pay heavy taxes. Despite of knowing Maharani's aims and that of Ranjung's motive, Rajendra co-operated with their schemes of conquest and war preparations. In January 1839, the anti-British intrigues to various disaffected Indian states were resumed.[60]

Meanwhile, in March 1839, the charges against Bhim Sen Thapa were revived. He had to face the accusation that he had ordered the poisoning of the young prince. In April 1839, Ranjung Pande was made Mukhtiyar. He had been trying to set aside Bhim Sen Thapa permanently from Nepali Politics. On 18th May, Bhim Sen Thapa was charged for the alleged crime.[61] Spurious papers of evidence were produced. He was once again placed under close confinement for interrogation. The charges levelled against him were based on one evidence paper signed by Ek Dev Baidya, the royal physician, which claimed that back in 1816, Bhim Sen Thapa had administered poison to late Maharaja Girwan Juddha's wife who died instantly. Another set of evidence was from the widow of Bakhtawar Singh Thapa, accusing Bhim Sen Thapa of poisoning Girwan Juddha himself who was known by all to have died of small-pox. While defending his stand, Bhim Sen Thapa asked that "where was the proof of the crime for which he had been arraigned? Why had these accusations and statements not been brought forward when he had been dismissed from the office and imprisoned?[62] No one, except Ranjung spoke against him. And silence reigned. Tickell observed that "not a voice was raised in his (Bhim Sen) behalf throughout the Darbar, the chiefs sat by in dejected silence."[63]

Maharaja Rajendra was deeply moved by the sight of what was happening to Bhim Sen Thapa. He was totally convinced of the danger of the situation. The court was packed with disturbed Bharadars, united in their disgust at the situation but divided into isolated unit of fear and insecurity by their suspicion and distrust. Finally, Rajendra denounced Bhim Sen Thapa and ordered him out of the room in chains.[64] He remained in prison where he was treated brutally, which is almost beyond the power of words to describe. Ranjung Pande dared not have recourse to actual assassination, but he gave the strict orders that Bhim Sen Thapa was to be treated with careful calculated savagery which would in no long time drive him to suicide.[65] False rumours were spread every day the way the old Mukhtiyar would be punished. But the most unseemly rumours was that his eldest wife Bhakti Kumari had been compelled by Ranjung Pande to parade the street of Kathmandu without clothes.[66] Unable to tolerate, he became more and more dejected. The Old Mukhtiyar then gave the struggle and slashed his own throat with a blunt "khukri" in an attempt to take his life and end it all. Though the wound was mortal, the end was not quick release as he had hoped for. With no proper medical assistance, he lingered for nine days, later put an end to as tragic a life as even the history of Asia can provide. At last he died on 28th July, 1839.[67]

The events after the death of Bhim Sen Thapa was more pathetic. His corpse was refused funeral rites according to Hindu religion, but dismembered and exposed about the city. The mangled remains were thrown away on the overside, where none but the dog and vulture dared further heed them.[68] Further, womenfolk of Bhim Sen Thapa family were ordered to march to and fro Kathmandu to Borling on bare foot (*Ibid.*) Senior Maharani and Ranjung were not content with this nefarious scheme to destroy Bhim Sen Thapa permanently. The subsequent history of Nepal deserves to be remembered. Bhim Sen Thapa and his family's landed properties were confiscated. All the lands grant made by late Regent Maharani Tripura Sundari for the last thirty-five years were annulled. The Maharaja further declared the whole clan of Thapa excluded from public offices or state employment for seven generations.[69]

The inhumane treatment and the tragic death of Bhim Sen Thapa had impact on the then Resident Hodgson. The latter, in his various correspondence with the Government of India, expressed his desire to change the political system in Nepal, removing the old Mukhtiyar from Nepali politics, but not to the extent of such action. In his obituary statement, Hodgson wrote to the Governor-General of India on 30th July, the day after Bhim Sen Thapa's death:

> Thus has perished the great and able statesman who for more than thirty years had ruled this kingdom with more than regal sway; just two years after his sudden fall from power in 1837 prior to which even the uniform success of nearly all his measures had been no less remarkable that the energy and sagacity which so much promoted that success. He was, indeed a man born to exercise dominion over his fellows, alike by means of command and of persuasion. Nor am I aware of any native statement of recent times, except Ranjit Singh, who is, all things considered, worthy to be compared with the late General Bhim Sen of Nepal.[70]

The Government of India had expressed its views with feeling of extreme disgust and abhorrence, "the measures of indignity, insult and cruelty which the Government of Nepal had adopted towards the late and able Minister of the state".[71]

The overall situation in Nepal remained unsettled even after the death of Bhim Sen Thapa. Although Maharaja was the supreme authority of the country, he could not control the senior Maharani and the Pande faction who had been hatching a conspiracy to force the former to abdicate the throne in his son's favour and also to appoint Ranjung Pande as the sole Mukhtiyar of the state. A close study of the subsequent events that followed in the kingdom clearly testify the political instability and uncertainty. The Bharadars were completely confused of the prevailing situation and from 1839 onwards, it became more and more complicated. Rajendra could not appoint a competent person to run the state administration. In fact, he never recovered from the effect of the moment. More than anyone else, he seems to have been aware of the forces that had been unleashed. He also understood the situation that was no one who he could rely on. Unable to control the events, he became their victim.[72]

The mounting pressure of the senior Maharani compelled Rajendra to appoint Ranjung Pande as Mukhtiyar in February, 1840. Both Samrajya Laxmi and Ranjung Pande immediately worked at cross purpose against the Maharaja to make him unpopular among the people so that he might be forced to abdicate the throne in Surendra's favour and rule the country as a Regent of her son. To fulfil their objectives, they began to harass the public and create an atmosphere of rebellion against the Maharaja.[73]

The first incident was the announcement made by King Rajendra to reduce the pay of the soldiers at the instance of senior Maharani. The news spreaded like a wildfire. On 21st June, 1840, around eight thousand army personnels gathered at Tudikhel and demanded the restoration of their pay. When no proper response or commitment was coming either from the Maharaja or the Mukhtiyar, they dispersed with anger and burnt the houses of Pushkar Shah Chautariya and Rangnath Pandit. They also destroyed important documents. This was the first military uprising against the king in the history of Nepal. The Maharaja immediately issued a Lalmohar restoring the pay of the soldiers and ordered them to return to their respective places. The unrest was indeed a conspiracy deliberately aired at to undermine the position of Rajendra and the pro-Thapa Bharadars.[74]

The other incident was the clash with the British. A Gorkha Suba and his soldiers had forcibly occupied Ramanagar, a British territory on the border. The matter was finally settled when the British Government showed a mild remonstration backed by military. The Bharadars, supported by the British Resident, strongly opposed Ranjung Pande's policies. He was dismissed and in his place, a pro-British Bharadar, Fateh Jung Chautariya was appointed, in November 1840. Thus by the turn of new year, 1841 Rajendra had successfully reduced the influences of the Thapas and the Pandes from the Darbar politics.[75] The removal of Rangjung Pande from the Mukhtiyar post affected Samrajya Laxmi's dream to become Regent for her son. She had decided to leave Nepal and proceeded towards Kasi. However, on 6th October, 1841, she died and paved the way for junior Maharani to involve actively in the state politics. During October 1841 to April 1842, Rajendra and his son had harassed the Bharadars by avoiding to accept responsibility for the actions of each other. The maltreatment of the Bharadars by the king and the heir led to an attempt to install the junior Maharani as a superior influence in the palace, with the unanimous support of the entire Bharadars.[76] Consequently, king conferred the power to the Junior Maharani. It was hoped that she would be able to control both Rajendra and Surendra. But the Bharadars complained that king had established a diarchy wherein no one was safe irrespective of the fact whether he obeyed the ruler or the heir. Meanwhile, the political setting changed. The Maharaja was left with no other alternative but to invite Mathbar Singh Thapa to Nepal to assume the power of Mukhtiyarship.

Although the latter accepted the invitation, he doubted the Rajendra's creditability. Before he actually assume the power Mathbar Singh Thapa had decided to settle the score against the Pandes. Those involved in the poison case were punished by the king. He was also abled to get royal order restoring the status in the society which was annulled in 1839. However, Mathbar Singh Thapa could not rule the country much longer as the first Prime Minister of Nepal as he was assassinated in 1846 at tne massacre of Kot.[77]

Notes

1. Jain, M.S., *op. cit.,* p. 11.
2. *FPC,* 12 December 1836; Nos. 36-37.
3. *Ibid.*
4. Pradhan, K.L., *op. cit.,* p. 66.
5. *Ibid.,* p. 72.
6. *FPC,* 23 November 1835, No. 27: Hodgson to Macnaghten, 14 November 1835.
7. *Ibid.,* No. 28. As the Maharani left the palace, Rajendra approached Pushkar Shah the Raj Guru for passing ill amenity in the Darbar called him "a traitor to the family" for not opposing the Mukhtiyarships excess.
8. Stiller, F.L., *op. cit.,* p. 270.
9. Pande, Bhim Bahadur, *op. cit.,* pp. 135.
10. Lama, Budhabir, *Rajnik Sanskriti Antargat Mukhtiyar Bhim Sen Thapa-ko Pattan* (unpublished) (2044 BS), pp. 31-32: Acharya, Yagyanath, *Nepal ko Itihas,* Pokhara (2039 BS), p. 90.
11. Stiller, F.L., *op. cit.,* p. 273.
12. Tickell, *Events in Nepal,* 1834.

13. This letter is published in C.R. Nepali, *Bhim Sen Thapa,* pp. 206-207. For the last two decades, the mission was decided by Bhim Sen Thapa.
   * Nepali, C.R., *op. cit.,* p. 181, Lalmohar appointing Bhim Sen Thapa Commander-in-Chief.
14. Tickell, *Events in Nepal,* 1835.
15. *FPC,* 26 November 1835, Nos. 25-28: Hodgson to Macnaghten, 10 November 1835.
16. *FPC,* 12 December 1836, Nos. 36-37.
17. *Ibid.*
18. Tickell, *Events in Nepal,* 1836.
19. Shrestha, S., *op. cit.,* p. 38.
20. FPC, 20 March 1837, No. 88: Hodgson to Macnaghten. 4 March 1837.
21. *FPC,* 3 July 1837, No. 37: Hodgson to Macnaghten. 13 June 1837.
22. Tickell, *Events in Nepal,* 1937.
23. Nepali, C.R., *op. cit.,* pp. 36-41.
24. *Ibid.*
25. Tickell, *Events in Nepal,* 1837. Also Rana, Rumai expresses her view that the external factor the British representative at Kathmandu Residency had also contributed the fall of Bhim Sen Thapa. She writes "Hodgson as a factor for the fall of Bhim Sen Thapa" Ancient Nepal, pp. 13-20 (nd). She writes—"Hodgson resentment against Bim Sen Thapa were both personal and political. Personal because the restriction imposed on the British Residency at Kathmandu and political as the British was anxious to annex Nepal into British India", pp. 13-20.
26. Thapa, Sher Bahadur, *op. cit.,* pp. 161-162.
27. Dungel, G., *op. cit.,* p. 34.
28. *Ibid.,* p. 38.
29. Stiller, F.L., *op. cit.,* p. 271.
30. Landon, P., *op. cit.,* Vol. I, p.87
31. Thapa, S.B., *op. cit.,* pp. 150-162: Dungel, G., *op. cit.,* pp. 34-38.
32. *FPC,* 7 September 1837, No. 88: Hodgson to Macnaghten, 22 June 1873.
33. *FPC,* 12 June 1837, No. 35: Wade to Macnaghten, 27 May 1837: *FPC,* 21 August 1837, No. 35: Wade to Macnaghten, 20 July 1837.

34. *FPC,* 7 September 1837, No. 88: Hodgson to Macnaghten, 22 July 1837: Resident's Diary 1 to 23 June 1837.
35. Tickell's, *Events in Nepal,* 1837.
36. *FPC,* 27 December 1837, No. 57: Campbell to Macnaghten 8 December 1837.
37. Ramakant, *op. cit.,* pp. 156-157. Landon, P., *op. cit.,* 91.
38. Chhetri, Dil Bahadur., *Documents on Nepal,* Vol. I Pokhara 1998, p. 50.
39. *FPC,* 3 January 1838, No. 37: Campbell to Macnaghten 16 December 1837: Nepali, C.R., *op. cit.,* p. 47.
40. *Ibid.,* p. 122; Nepal Gyan Mani, *Nepal ko Mahabarat,* Kathmandu, (2052 BS).
41. Tickell, *Events in Nepal,* 1838.
42. *Ibid.*
43. *FPC,* 17 February 1838, No. 34: Campbell to Macnaghten, 30 December 1837.
44. Tickell, *Events in Nepal,* 1838.
45. *Ibid.,* Stiller, F.L., *op. cit.,* p. 277.
46. Pradhan, K.L., *op. cit.,* p. 94.
47. Rose, Leo E., *op. cit.,* p. 98.
48. Pradhan, K.L., *op. cit.,* pp. 95-97.
49. Majumdar, K., *op. cit.,* p. 36.
50. Nepali, C.R., *op. cit.,* pp. 61-62.
51. Tickell, *Events in Nepal,* 1838.
52. *Ibid.,* Also. *FPC,* 15 October 1838, No. 23.
53. Resident's Diary, 1st September to 31st October 1838.
54. Tickell, *Events in Nepal,* 1839.
55. Stiller, F.L., *op. cit.,* p. 281.
56. *Ibid.,* p. 282.
57. Jain, M.S., *op. cit.,* pp. 20-21.
58. Pradhan, K.L., *op. cit.,* p. 102.
59. Tickell, *Events in Nepal,* 1839.
60. Majumdar, K., *op. cit.,* pp. 39-45; Ramakant, *op. cit.,* pp. 154-156. Also see *FPC,* 6th February, 1839, No. 53: Hodgson to Torrens, 14th January, 1839.
61. Tickell, *Events in Nepal,* 1839.
62. Hunter, W.W., *op. cit.,* p. 174.: Sama, Balkrishna, *Bhim Sen ko Anta,* Kathmandu. (nd).
63. Tickell, *Events in Nepal,* 1839.
64. Nepali, C.R., *op. cit.,* pp. 62-63.

65. Landon, P., *op. cit.*, p. 91.
66. *Ibid.*, also Hunter, W.W., *op. cit.*, p. 176.
67. Dungel, G. *op. cit.*, p. 79; Gyanmani, *op. cit.*, p. 122: Nepali, C.R., *op. cit.*, p. 50.
68. Tickell, *Events in Nepal*, 1839.
69. Cf. Landon, P., *op. cit.*, p. 92: Yet, three years later the Thapas were recalled to power and descendants of that family have from that day to this enjoyed an exclusive and even autocratic authority in the State.
70. *Ibid.*, p. 91: Sama, Balkrishna, *op. cit.*, pp. 174.
71. Landon, P., *op. cit.*, p. 92.
72. Stiller, F.L., *op. cit.*, pp. 285-287.
73. Shrestha, S., *op. cit.*, p. 42.
74. Acharya, B., "Bhim Sen Thapako Pattan dekhi Jang Bahadur Ranako Prarambha Nabhaye Samma," year, 9 *Halchal*, p. 14.
75. Jain, M.S., *op. cit.*, p. 24.
76. Nicholett's, Narrative of Events, 1840-1851, vide *FPC*, 11 November 1853 No. 23: Pande, Bhim Bahadur., *op. cit.*, p. 187: Yogi, N.N., *op. cit.*, p. 45.
77. Oldfield, *op. cit.*, p. 347: Wheeler, J.T., *Diary of Events in Nepal*, 1841-1846, Simla (1878): Padma Jang, *Life of Jang Bahadur*, Allahabad, (1909), pp. 52-60.

IX

Conclusion

The 'Thapa' as a political faction in Nepal was little known prior to 1806. Few Thapas were in the service of Prithvi Nayaran Shah in the process of unification of the kingdom as Sardar and military commanders. These Thapas were not included in the policy-making body—the Thar Garh. It was in 1806 after the assassination of Rana Bahadur Shah that Bhim Sen Thapa had not only eliminated the opposition rivals but assumed the powers as Mukhtiyar and rule the country for thirty one years uninterrupted.[1] It is very surprising to note that how a simple Kazi became able to hold the highest post of civil and military administration of the kingdom. The reason is not far to seek. His recognition rested only on the measure of his ability, firm determination and resolution in controlling the politics of the period. Further, he clearly understood the importance of the army of Nepal. Most writers allege that Bhim Sen Thapa had monopolised the civil and military administration by appointing his own relatives. Yet a close study of the period reveals no such infiltration of his kith and kin into the civil or military hierarchy. Most of the Thapas who were holding the posts were appointed before 1806.[2] However, few Thapas were elevated to the ranks of Bharadars. Even if we suppose that the Thapa was given all inclusive powers from the time he was appointed general in 1811, the power was in fact limited. According to tradition of the state, the king had to be consulted before taking any decision. It seems that there were occasional instances where action was taken without consultations led to unrest and confusion.[3] Thus, Bhim Sen Thapa did not felt wise to isolate the Maharaja nor the Bharadars, but use his ability to persuade others to support and accept his resolution. During the period under the review, it is very much doubtful that Bhim Sen Thapa could have imposed his command even if he found deem fit to do so. In those days when the Darbar was under special strain, it is doubtful if Bhim Sen Thapa could have imposed his will even if had wanted to do so. That is why, whatever rules and regulations made were issued in the name of the Maharaja.[4]

Immediately after assumption of power, he undertook series of reforms and reorganised the standing army on the line of modern system. While pursuing the policy of expansion and consolidation of the kingdom, he adopted the essential principle of diplomacy in the post-1814 i.e., the policy of keeping Nepal isolation. In fact, there was the secret of Nepal's continuance as an independent state at a time when India was held under the clutch of expanding British imperialism. He was greatly influenced by Prithvi Narayan Shah in formulating Nepal's foreign policy. In his 'Dibya Upadesh' he advised his followers not to develop intimate relations with either Tibet-China or British India.[5] Bhim Sen Thapa followed his footsteps and tried to avoid any friction as far as possible. But due to unavoidable circumstances, he led a war with the British and faced the consequences. It has been said that the defeat of the Gorkhas in the late war and the loss of territories were considerable. However, if the Gorkha had not shown their valour and bravery, the English would have annexed Nepal completely, if not make her a puppet like Indian native states.[6] In spite of the defeat, Bhim Sen Thapa had shown profound farsightedness in keeping the British Resident cut off from all contacts with life in Nepal. Although the Treaty of Sagauli was implemented, he tried to evade the clauses as far as possible without antagonizing the British. He imposed restrictions to the Bharadars to meet the British Resident at any point of time. By sheer diplomacy Bhim Sen Thapa was abled to convince the Governor General for restoration of Tarai lands. This was a great achievement for Nepal.[7] He was skeptical of the British power, but now he realised that the era of conquest was over. For him the defence of Nepal lay in constant military preparation and sealing off the country hermetically to the European. Thus, according to him, peace was the best policy to preserve the independence of his country. Immediately after the war, Bhim Sen Thapa took bold steps to reorganise the judicial system of Nepal. In fact, he followed the judicial administrative system laid down by his predecessors.

In certain cases he modified the existing system. For smooth disposal of cases, Chief Justice at the capital and judges at the regional headquarters were appointed.[8]

The Thapa continued to maintain his authority in the Darbar. But the years 1832-33 were crucial for his position. Three important events—death of Regent Maharani from whom he got support, the attainment of majority by Maharaja Rajendra and the appointment of Brian Hodgson as Resident took place during these periods which affected his position in Nepali politics. In 1834, the restoration of family honours to the Pande faction further aggravated the Thapa's prestige. Thus the third decade of the nineteenth century a cloud of an unprecedented crisis gathered on the political horizon of Nepal. In the Darbar was now centre of internecine strife—the Maharaja, the senior and junior Maharani and the ambitious Bharadars belonging to rival groups scrambling for power.[9] The British Resident, who was very much annoyed of the Thapa's policy towards the Residency always, insisted to change the system. He played an important role to remove Bhim Sen Thapa from the Darbar politics. In the political crisis that followed, Resident sided with the royal family and the opposition faction headed by Ranjung Pande with selfish motives. Very soon the conspiracy was hatched against the Mukhtiyar. In spite of his non-involvement in poison case, he was removed from the office. Not contented with it, the opposition renewed the case to eliminate him permanently from Nepali politics. The final end came in 1839. On his tragic death, Landon writes, "his was a life of contrast and no Greek tragedy has ever presented a more dramatic catastrophe than his fearful end".[10] In spite of this, the political condition did not improve. The subsequent events testify political instability and insecurity in the country. It also paved the way for the British Resident to actively interfere in the internal affairs of the kingdom, which the late Mukhtiyar had always feared.[11]

Most writers regard Bhim Sen Thapa a 'war-time' Mukhtiyar. Yet, analysing his period under review, we can find the various significant and praiseworthy works undertaken by him, apart from expansions and consolidation of the kingdom. He understood that the main stumbling blocks of the national developments were the different set of laws, social evils, malpractice and nepotism in the administration. During his long reign of 31 years, he tried to reform these evils and establish a society on the line of modern system.

He got the inspirations from Prithvi Narayan Shah. He recalled "if the citizens are wealthy the country is strong. The king's storehouse is his people".[12]

The nineteenth century witnessed the widespread socio-religious reforms movement in the Himalayan sub-continents for the beginning and development of the process of all-round change, which contributed to the modernisation of the country. A series of reform movements engaged and affected different spheres of national life. Far from being merely political, they represented almost a scheme of social, religious and human value, which differed from and threatened traditional social value. Political subjection was accompanied by cultural confrontation. Ideas of human quality, contract and rationalism initiated catalysis within the heretical and authoritarian society. Efforts thus began to be made to reform the traditional structure of society and religion by removing the various evils that had crept into it over the century.[13] The need or change was compulsion. Yet, the most formidable difficulty of the reformers of which they were only partly conscious was that they had marginal control over the changes they were planning to bring about. Social customs, usage and institutions are complex phenomena, which evolve over a long period of time in response to a variety of forces. Human violation plays only a marginal role in this evolution. A whole scheme of rewards and threat, operating both in world and hereafter, is employed to ensure the adherence of people of those customs, usages and institutions. Mere intellectual conviction that these are bad and ought to be change does not go far in dislodging them. It is only a significant change in the forces responsible for a certain kind of institution that can modify or alter the institution. It is therefore essential to bear in mind the stupendous constraints within which the reforms had to operate. It is essential for appreciating the real, though limited significance of the modern social reform movements. It has been fashionable to stigmatic these reformers as cowards and hypocrites who were rarely prepared to go beyond passing pious resolutions and issuing stirring calls in favour of social reforms. But if we remember the time in which they were operating it should be possible for us to realise that daredevilry on the part of the reformers would have served no useful purpose. Their main concern was to remain at all costs within the society they were seeking to reform. Forcing the pace of reform beyond a point would have meant inviting the active hostility of those who had to be converted to the reformist way of thinking.[14]

Bhim Sen Thapa was fully aware of the fact that almost every customs, usages and institutions derive sustenance from religious injunctions and sanctions. This means that any serious attempt to reform the society could hardly be undertaken within reforming the existing religious notions, which sustained the prevailing social institutions. Thus social and religious reforms were intimately interlinked.

In spite of the existing constraints, he strongly opposed to the slavery system in Nepal. He had undertaken a measure of abolishing it and was working slowly towards it. While studying his efforts to reform the society the matter should be viewed from the context of prevailing social system and thinking pattern of the people of that time and judge accordingly. The administrative functioning in those days in Nepal was based on piecemeal pattern, considering a particular territory or community at a time. The laws enacted were also meant for particular community or caste only, based on its need due to the absence of data and proper national planning. The government ran on decentralised-centralisation system. As such Bhim Sen Thapa did not abolish 'Kariya' system at one stroke, but carried it out according to the needs of particular community. The other important factor too influenced the action, i.e., the political consideration. The feudal lords, who possessed slaves, strongly opposed to the idea of it. Even century later, when Dev Samsher Rana wanted to abolish slavery in Kaski and Lanjung, rebellion erupted. The most powerful Prime Minister of Nepal, Chandra Samsher had to be militarily prepared when he issued an order to abolish the slavery. So it is natural on the part of Bhim Sen Thapa to be apprehensive of the outcome.[15]

The first attempt made by him was the bold steps against the traders who used to acquire the children of debtors as slaves in lieu of accumulated interest of the capital borrowed and sell them on profit. At the same time the feudal lord regarded it derogatory to consider slave as human. It was considered unnatural to provide any legal facilities to them. Bhim Sen Thapa immediately challenged the attitude that had embedded deeply in the minds of people of contemporary Nepal. In 1830, he issued a Lalmohar strictly banning all Danuar traders residing with the seven villages of western Nepal from acquiring or selling the Kariya. The slaves under the custody of the landlords were also freed from their clutches. In fact he was deeply inspired by Prithvi Narayan Shah. As early as in 1773, he had opposed to the very system. His efforts towards abolition of this evil practice could be attributed more significant for the mankind than his conquests. His effort on this matter was given more realistic and broader shape later on by Mukhtiyar Bhim Sen Thapa. Thus the regulations aimed at providing legal rights and benefits to the slaves and treat them an human-being while boosting their morale. Six years later, he issued another Lalmohar to the Magar community of Marsiangadi, west Piuthan, who used to sell their children to trader for slave, proclaiming such practice illegal according to the law of the kingdom.[16]

It is established fact that Nepal was far more advanced as far as the idea of abolition of slavery is concerned. Nepal had, though partially declared slave trading as illegal while Wilberforce was trying to garner public's opinion in England against it. Even the powerful Prime Minister of that time, William Pitt seemed to be hesitant to bring an Act against it. Thus steps taken by Prithvi Narayan Shah and Bhim Sen Thapa may be considered a milestone in redemption of social evil like slavery in the history of mankind.[17]

Another significant contribution of Bhim Sen Thapa was on marriage practices of certain communities in Nepal. The prevailing system of marriage was against the concept of Hindu religion. Since Sati system was not in practice, widow remarriage was allowed in the society. It seems that there was no restriction to marry one's own brother's widow among the Magar community and daughter of maternal uncle among the Jaisi Brahmins of Thapoula and Salyan of western Nepal. Considering the negative implication of the system in the society, they urged the government to enact uniform law applicable to all community. Accordingly, Bhim Sen Thapa had issued a Lalmohar prohibiting such practices.[18]

Another community that attracted Bhim Sen Thapa to reform its socio-religious custom was the Newar of Kathmandu Valley. They had to spend huge amount of money during the ceremonies of birth and death of a person, which lead to indebtedness. The priest who performed the ceremony used to demand exorbitant amount as fees. Failure to offer such fees resulted in excommunication from the society. The plight of this community needs to be redressed. Therefore, in 1830-31, by issuing a Lalmohar,

Bhim Sen Thapa restricted the expenditures and fixed the minimum amount to be incurred by the individual family on such occasion. Failure to oblige the regulations, severe punishments were awarded to the wrong-doers.[19]

The social reform was not only the problems tackled by Mukhtiyar Bhim Sen Thapa. Though the administration ran on decentralised-centralised pattern, as already discussed in the preceding chapter, every effort taken by him were aimed at the progress and better administration. At that time neither was Nepal a democratic state nor Bhim Sen Thapa a democratic minded.

Yet, we can find the distinctiveness of the period. All royal orders, regulations and instructions were issued to an individual rather than to the frontier officials. It seems that Bhim Sen Thapa had given due importance to the wish and demand of the general public.[20]

During his early year of office, anarchy prevailed in the territories ceded by Prithvi Narayan Shah due to lack of mal-administration by his subsequent successors. It is true that they could not pay much attention towards the plight of the people as they were fully engaged with the conquest of territories, war with Tibet-China and mostly palace intrigues. The process of administrative stability thus began to take concrete shape only after Bhim Sen assumed the power. The Lalmohar issued by him to settle the problems in the Accham province clearly indicates his efforts. Here, the Zamindars, Amalis and traders treated the farmers with gross injustice. They revolted against them when they were forced to pay heavy interests on loans taken from them. Bhim Sen Thapa was deeply moved to the plight of those people. In his order, he directed that all outstanding dues against them be write off at once.[21]

Closely connected with this, he abolished the practice of free labour called 'jhara and beth-begari'—an outcome of feudal thinking. The Landlords, Zamindars, Amalis and other high government officials considered it as their right to engage labours free of wage. He already took restrictions as the official order to the people of Accham reveals. The government officials were debarred to make people carry their private belongings free of cost and such system was declared illegal except in the case of national interest to royal works, or to carry wounded soldier during war etc. Those officials, who engage these sections of people, require paying wages for the service rendered.

Bhim Sen Thapa was against nepotism, bribery and corruption in the central, provincial and village level administrations. It was reported that, the officials like Zamindars, Amalis and others posted in the far-flung districts were inhabited of accepting bribe from the people. Bribery is the first stage of corruption that encourages and leads to bigger corruption. Realizing the impact on the society, Bhim Sen Thapa prohibited and declared it illegal to give or take any kind of bribery or gift from the people.[23]

Another significant steps taken by him were the problems of the Mohi farmers. He firmly set rules with a view to free this category of people from the trouble related issue i.e., payment of taxes to the Zamindars. Due to scarcity of cash it was cheaper and easier for the farmer to their dues in kind. However, the Zamindars insisted that the taxes should be paid in cash whereas, the farmers preferred to pay in kind. As a result, the former always coerced the farmers. Here again, Bhim Sen Thapa had issued an order directing the Zamindars to accept foodgrains as tax and not to harass the farmer anymore. The order further stated that in case the Zamindar needs cash it was their responsibility to make an arrangement for it and not the farmer. Thus by such act, he freed the peasants from the atrocity of the landlords.[24]

Bhim Sen Thapa also undertook to reform the economic condition of the kingdom. In 1829, he issued a Lalmohar introducing uniform weights and measurements throughout the state. Prior to this there was no uniformity in weight and measurement system. Besides, he controlled the market through fixing the rates of commodities. He took further step in establishing towns, cities and markets. At that time, the individual property right was not granted. As such, they were hesitant to construct permanent residential houses or market places, they preferred to construct thatched house for market as well as dwelling purposes. It is reported that in 1829 shops at Riddi were completely destroyed by fire. In the following year, another trading centre, Tansen faced the similar fate and lost considerable amount of wealth. As a result of this, they urged the Government to allow them to construct concrete shopping and dwelling houses and also to grant them the property rights. The Mukhtiyar conceded their demand and accordingly permitted to build concrete shops and dwelling houses to avoid such incident in future and also extended the individual right to property, which helped the business community immensely.[25]

Similarly, he set a law on interest on borrowings for the benefit of traders and for equality in trade and commerce. The system was initiated by Ram Shah of Gorkha kingdom and Jayasthiti Malla of Kathmandu Valley respectively but was not practiced throughout Nepal. Therefore, Bhim Sen Thapa fixed the rate of interests as 10 per cent on cash and 25 per cent on goods borrowed. The system is still in vogue in the kingdom. Since agriculture was the main profession of the country, her national income also depended on its products. Bhim Sen Thapa who understood the importance of lands, measured and recorded them scientifically. Thereafter, assessed them accordingly for fixing annual taxation. Besides, he also increased the national income from the custom and transit duties through the Bhansar posted along the frontiers. It is recorded that in 1833, the revenue generated from these sources reached to two lakh and fifty thousand rupees. It naturally changed economic activities of the nation while adding the revenue to the kingdom' coffer. Besides, he successfully manipulated the Tibetan and reintroduced the Nepali coins for business transaction with Tibet. The later had banned the circulation of Nepali coins: Mahendra Mulli after the 1791 war. It was alleged that these coins were too debased to be accepted at par with the Tibetan. In 1836, he set up a national bank where considerable amount of Indian and Nepali rupees were deposited to be used at the time of national needs. Bhim Sen Thapa also advised Maharaja Rana Bahadur to confiscate the birta in 1805, to strengthen the economy of the state. In fact, he clearly understood that the political stability of nation wholly depended on the economic prosperity and proper planning. Thus, the period under review witnessed socio-economic development and political stability in Nepal.[26]

In those days, the postal system as we have today, was not in practice. However, Bhim Sen Thapa introduced a system appointing two to four persons from every village to carry the mails. For their services, they were allotted lands free of cost. Officials were detailed to see that the system run properly. For example, to ensure its proper maintenance in western regions (Bhinumati and eastern part of Mahakali) an investigation team under Subedar Jaikrishna and Jamadar Kalu Lama were instituted. They were in fact, empowered to decide the cases related to Hulak problems on the spot. As already explained, Nepal was meeting place of traders from both India and Tibet. And the Gorkhas always feared that these merchants might secretly acquire important information of the country and pass on them to the British. To check such events, he introduced the passport system in the kingdom. All frontier officials were instructed to allow to enter/leave the country, only on the production of passport duly signed and stamped by Mukhtiyar. Their belongings were thoroughly searched. Even private letters were censored.[27]

As already pointed out in the preceding pages, Bhim Sen Thapa took keen interest to reform the judicial system of the kingdom. In those days society was based on caste system and there prevailed unsociability. The conditions of the lower class people were pathetic. Thus, in 1826, he issued a Lalmohar in the name of Maharaja, directing Dalbhajan Pande to uphold the sanctity of the judiciary. It was further stated, "irrespective of castes, creeds or position in the society, all are same in the eyes of law". Justice should not be denied to the people of lower strata of the society on the basis of castes or creeds or untouchables. Thus, he laid down the principle of equality before the law in Nepal.[28]

From his character and personality, we can find Bhim Sen Thapa was a man of high ambition. Towards his early period of his Mukhtiyarship he followed a policy of imperialism. He organised a huge army through rotation system for extension and protection of the kingdom. He was the first person to model the Gorkha army on the line of modern line. He also introduced different ranks and files, e.g., general, colonel, captain, subedars, sardars etc., in the army. Through well-organised and disciplined soldiers, he planned a project to drive the British from Asian countries. He formed a well organised confederation with the Indian native princes against the British imperialism. Had Bhim Sen Thapa able to forge the alliance, the course of history would have been different. Further, he clearly understood the importance of the army to consolidate his position in the Darbar. In fact, he used them against the opposition Bharadars when his position was threatened. However, he never used the authority he had acquired for making him Mukhtiyar for life. Some writers even regard him a military dictator who had completely monopolised the system. Yet, throughout his Mukhtiyarship, no such indication is found nor he manifested for the authority. Indeed his own tenure of service depended in the Panjani where every individual service was renewed. Thus, the allegations are unfounded and baseless.[29]

He was severely criticised by some writers for his system of army. Despite fact that Nepal being economically backward, it could hardly afford such huge army enrolled through the rotation system. He saw the army as an important prop to his own design in the state and used them against the opposition whenever his position was threatened. Instead, he should have reduced the army and used them for national developmental works. As already mentioned, Bhim Sen Thapa had acquired considerable portion of lands for construction of the army headquarters, cantonments and barracks. Apart from these, he modernized the military administration through reforms. He was the first Mukhtiyar who was appointed to the post of the Commander-in-Chief of the Nepal Army. In this connection, he faced much criticism from the Bharadars. Yet he continued to follow the policy. Even if we assume that the Nepal army was his creation, he could have easily manipulated them. However, not a single soldier came forward in his support when he was removed from the Mukhtiyarship. Therefore, the accusation is unaccountable. In fact, in the political history of Nepal Bhim Sen Thapa's military administration was highly acclaimed. Thus Nepal has maintained her freedom, entity and sovereignty.[30]

Apart from this Bhim Sen Thapa's contribution can be seen in the field of arts and architectures. In spite of his routine works as civil and military, he had given due importance to the development of national treasures. There are ample evidences of constructions comprised of buildings, bridges, towers, canals, temples, gardens and the beautification of the Capital—Kathmandu. Prior to this, the constructions were confined to temples. In 1811, when he was appointed the General, he built Bag Darbar for his official residence. In the same year, he constructed Bagmati bridge. It has been said that Prithvi Narayan Shah had successfully amalgamated Kantipur and Lalitpur cities in his kingdom, but could not provide proper passage for the people. It was Bhim Sen Thapa who built a bridge across the Bagmati river. It is historically important.[31] A suspension bridge over the river Gandaki to connect Dhading and Gorkha district with Kathmandu were also constructed. In 1824 he erected a tower—Dharara near Tuddi Khel to commemorate the restoration of Tarai lands. Following the same tradition another tower was built in the instance of the Regent queen. However, the severe earthquakes destroyed them. The remains still exist. The

Ghanta Ghar (Watch Tower) constructed by him may be considered Nepal's symbol of hope and exultation of the Thapa period.[32]

He was also equally interested to develop the civil administration to provide daily needs of the people. For example, he dug wells, constructed water springs, fish ponds etc., and the most remarkable one is Sundhara in the capital. To meet the growing demands of the farmers, he constructed canal for irrigation at Raniban near Kirtipur. In 1829, a Lalmohar was issued to this effect that water should be equally distributed to the farmers on need base. A trust was constituted comprising seven members for proper management of the canal. They were empowered to collect fixed tax from the farmers. Violation of the system were awarded fine of five rupees.[33] Apart from these bridges, linking roads, travellers' inn were also constructed wherever necessary.

Nepal as a Hindu State, Bhim Sen Thapa gave due importance to Hindu religion. Although he professed Hindu religion, he was neither perverse in his belief nor forced any one to convert into Hindu fold. Within the Hindu religion, he found the atrocities of the gurus, pandits, purohits and religious leaders to the common people. His various reforms clearly reveal his intention to get rid of these evil systems from the society. While working on the matter, he converted his wealth into Guthi for construction of temples.[34] In 1817-1820, he built the Tripureswar temple in the capital. It is huge and systematically constructed. In 1825, in remembrance of his mother, Satyarupa Devi, a Satyaswar Mahadev temple was constructed at Riddi and donated a temple bell which still exists. In 1825 Bhimbireswar Temple was built at Bungkot near Gorkha district. He also renovated and decorated the famous Pasupati Nath Temple with gold and silver. For maintenance of the temples rules and regulations were laid down. The incomes from the Guthi were also spent for religious purposes. He was regarded as the defender of Hindu religion. During his period, we can find the growth and development of Nepali literature—poetry, prose, drama and folklore including social, historical, political and religious philosophies. Translations of different religious texts into Nepali were also found.[35]

Bhim Sen Thapa's contributions in the politics and various reforms are commendable. By sheer luck and fortune, he became the Mukhtiyar of the kingdom from a mere bodyguard and ran the country for thirty-one years. Yet, some recent writers blame him for his shortcomings. To them, he lacked vision and at a time he was an opportunist. He was concerned of his own position in the Darbar and a strong promoter of his own relatives and neglected the villagers. He was accused of monopolising the appointments of the Thapa family to various important and lucrative posts. A recent scholar writes "the essential failure of Bhim Sen Thapa administration was simply a lack of vision... He saw no greater goals to strive for. His administration and his own actions were all bound up maintaining the *status quo*."[36] Yet a closer study of the period reveals that his administrative system was based on people centric and upward mobility. As regards the filling up of the Bhardari, there was no such infiltration of the Thapa family into civil and military hierarchy at the level. Except few Bharadars who were appointed at senior level posts usually vacated by the death of the Thapa. Rests were appointed before 1816. Within the inner circle of the Darbar, no monopoly of any one family can be seen. In fact, he tried to maintain the balance required for any longer tenure of office by including representatives of the leading Kshatriya families in this group. Further the increased numbers of Chautariyas in the Darbar attributes that even Bhim Sen Thapa's monolithic administration was not proof against the use of influence to gain promotion. Since there was check and balance in the administration, the notion of monopoly of one family seldom arise.

He was also accused of his pro-British attitude after 1814-16 war. We was projected as friend of the English. But if we analyse his policy in details, we can find that from the beginning he adopted anti-British attitude. He was the first Nepali statesman who understood the basic principle of British imperialism and his policy was directed to save Nepal from her influence. He was compelled to wage a war against them. The defeat and loss of territories were immense, yet he never bow before the British influences. He tried to evade the clauses of the Treaty of Sagauli as far as possible without antagonising the British. He was skeptical of the British power, but now realized that the era of conquest was over. For him defense of Nepal was top priority and lay in constant military preparation and sealing off them hermetically to the European. Thus according to Bhim Sen Thapa peace was the best policy to preserve Nepal's sovereignty. His anti-British attitude can be seen as soon as the British Resident reached in Kathmandu. Restrictions were imposed on the Residency and the staff, irrespective of their positions. To gain British's favour he played a very clear diplomacy. Whenever he faced the problems from the British he turned towards the Chinese for help to gain his objectives. By sheer diplomacy, he achieved a great deal for Nepal when he succeeded in restoring most of the Terai land than the Governor General had planned to return in 1816. His understanding with the Governor General on various issues gave him the maximum opportunity to manoeuver in his conflicts with the Residents. Whenever the question of direct access to the Maharaja was sought by the Resident, he projected the monarch as a minor. At the same time, he refused to change the administrative system arguing that he did not have any authority to do so. He successfully avoided the Resident's overture.

Thus, Nepal owes his a debt of gratitude for skill in dealing with the East India Company in general and the Resident in particular. His foreign policy was directed to save Nepal from outside political domination throughout the period. Bhim Sen Thapa is often given credit for his various reforms. To eliminate the social evils like slavery and bondage, series of Lalmohar containing strict rules and regulations were issued to the different districts. He understood the real cause for the growth of these evils were rural indebtedness. Therefore, in spite of directly opposing the landlords, amalis, zamindars, he eradicated them from socio-economic and administrative reforms. His other reforms like price control of essential commodities, water management etc., are an example of his works.

During the period under review, I have tried to explore a great many aspects of the contributions of Bhim Sen Thapa. As a human being, he might have shortcoming one way or other in dealing with the people in general. His closed policy was alleged to be the real cause for the great massacre in 1845 and the rise of the Rana in the Nepali politics. The downfall of Bhim Sen Thapa accounts not only denigration of a personality in political system but also deterioration in administrative system. Infirmity in leadership can be traced due to political instability which resulted in feeble administration.[37] Whatever may be the subsequent events in the history of the kingdom, his contributions are universally accepted and recognized by rulers of Nepal as well as foreign writers. Oldfield, who spent more than a decade in Nepal writes on Bhim Sen Thapa that he loved his country whole-heartedly—"nothing is dearer and nearer to his heart than the independence of his country"[38] Hodgson, who was against Bhim Sen Thapa's attitude also affirms that he was a man of high calibre and only worthy to be compared with Ranjit Singh among the Gorkha leaders. Landon also remarks that "Nepal is Bhim Sen and Bhim Sen is Nepal". We can also find some interesting accounts on him as Maharaja Rana Bahadur Shah said that "if I die the nation will not die, but if Bhim Sen dies the nation will collapse". It was Karl Marx who praised Bhim Sen Thapa referring him the only man in Asia who braved to protest submission to the colonists. He is regarded as one of the national heroes of Nepal.

Thus from the above descriptions, one can find the essence of nationalism and patriotism in Bhim Sen Thapa. He can be regarded as the saviour of Nepal in true sense.

Notes

1. Chhetri, Dil Bahadur, *Documents on Nepal,* Vol. I, p. 40. Landon, *op. cit.,* p. 91.
2. Stiller, F. Ludwig, *op. cit.,* pp. 191-197.
3. Jain, M.S. *op. cit.,* pp. 6-9.
4. Ramakant, *op. cit.,* pp. 57-59.
5. Prithvi Narayan's *Dibya Upadesh, op. cit.,* p. 29.
6. Jaichandra, B., *op. cit.,* pp. 64-65.
7. See Chapter V and also Appendix-D.
8. See Judial Administion, Appendix-G.
9. Sharma Binaya Kumar, *op. cit.,* p. 19.
10. Hunter, W.W. *op. cit.,* n. Ch. I.
11. Pradhan, K.L. *op. cit.* see Ch.-VI on Tentative Intervention. pp. 113-138.
12. Prithvi Narayan Shah, translated from his *Dibya Upadesh* in Stiller, F. Ludwig, in the light of Dibya Upadesh, p. 43.
13. Natarajan, S., *A Century of Social Reforms,* Asia Publication, 1956. Also see Heimsath, *Indian Nationalism and Hindu Social Reform.* Oxford, 1970. (relevant chapters only).
14. *Ibid. Also* see Farquhar, J.N., *Modern Religious Movements in India,* New Delhi, 1967.
15. Nepali, C.R., *op. cit.,* pp. 140-141; Regmi, M.C., *op. cit.,* pp. 117-119.

16. *Ibid., Lalmohar,* March 1830.
17. *Ibid.*, Lalmohar, November, 1836.
18. Gyanu Dhungel, *op. cit.,* p. 42
19. *Ibid.*, Lalmohar, March 1830; Bhandari, D.R., *op. cit.*, p. 427.
20. *Ibid.*, Nepali, *C.R., op. cit.,* p. 241. Lalmohar, December, 1831.
21. *Ibid.*, Lalmohar, July 1836.
22. Gyanu Dhungel, *op. cit., p.* 43. Nepali, *C.R., op. cit.,* p. 148.
23. *Ibid., op. cit.,* pp. 186-195.
24. *Ibid.*, pp. 148-149.
25. *Ibid.*, pp. 147.
26. Nepali, C.R., *op. cit.,* pp. 161-163.
27. Regmi, M.C., *op. cit.,* pp. l04-105.
28. Stiller, F. Ludwig, *op. cit.,* pp. 34-47.
29. See Appendix-F.
30. Sharma, Binaykumar, *op. cit.,* p..5; Gyanu Dhungel, *op. cit.,* pp. 53-58.
31. *Bagmatiko Bhim Sen Thapako Stambhalekh,* No. 150., pp. 520-528, vide 'Sanskrit Sandesh', 1/7 pp. 1-14 by Nayaraj Pant.
32. Abhilekh Sangraha, p. 17; Manadhar, Sarala, *"Dharara"* (Bhim Sen Stambha).
33. Yadav, P., *op. cit.,* p. 139; Bhandari, D.R., *op. cit.,* p. 428.
34. Guthi Collections preserved in the National Archives of Nepal, Kathmandu.
35. Bajracharya, D.B., *Triratna Saundarya Gatha,* p. 259; Upadhaya, Kesau Prasad, *Prathmik Kalin Kavi ra Kabya Prabriti,* Kathmandu, 2032. BS. Bishwanath, *Sahitya Darpan,* New Delhi, 2034 BS, p. l54; Thapa, Mohan Himangshu, *Sahitya Parichaye,* Kathmandu, 2047, p. 20.
36. Stiller, F. Ludwig, *op. cit.,* p. 308.
37. Such incident was one of a phenomena in the history of oriental kingdoms. In the words of Theodore, H. White, "rudely but compellingly, every thirty or forty years, the ideas of one generation become the prison of the generation that follows. The more powerful the idea, the more confining the imprisonment". *The Making of the President,* New York, 1973, p. 498.
38. Oldfield, Henry Ambrose, quoted by Sharma, Binaykumar, *op. cit.* p. 14.
39. Sharma, B.K., *op. cit.* pp. 43-44; Regmi, Jagdish Chandra, *Kala Chetrama Bhim Sen Thapako Yogdan,* Amar Gatha, pp. 1-7.

List of Kings of Nepal and the Bharadars

A. Pre-Unification Period

Drabya Shah	–	1559-1570
Purendra Shah	–	1570-1605
Chatra Shah	–	1605-1606
Ram Shah	–	1606-1633
Damdar Shah	–	1633-1642
Krishna Shah	–	1642-1658
Rudra Shah	–	1658-1669
Prithwipati Shah	–	1669-1716
Bira Badra Shah	–	d.v.p.
Narbhupal Shah	–	1617-1742

B. Under Unification Period

Prithvi Narayan Shah	–	1742-1774
Singha Pratap Shah	–	1774-1777
Rana Bahadur Shah	–	1777-1799
Girwan Judda Vikram Shah	–	1799-1816
Rajendra Vikram Shah	–	1816-1847

C. List of Various Bharadars: From 1816-1839

The charts* appended below try to show the different political factions (family based) that dominated the politics of Nepal during the period under review. The following code has been used to distinguish their positions in the civil and military services.

G = General; K= Kazi; S = Sardar; C= Colonel; $ = Subba; C = Captain; s = Subedar.

*(vide Ludwig Stiller, F., The Silent Cry; The People of Nepal, Appendix-A)

BASNYAT

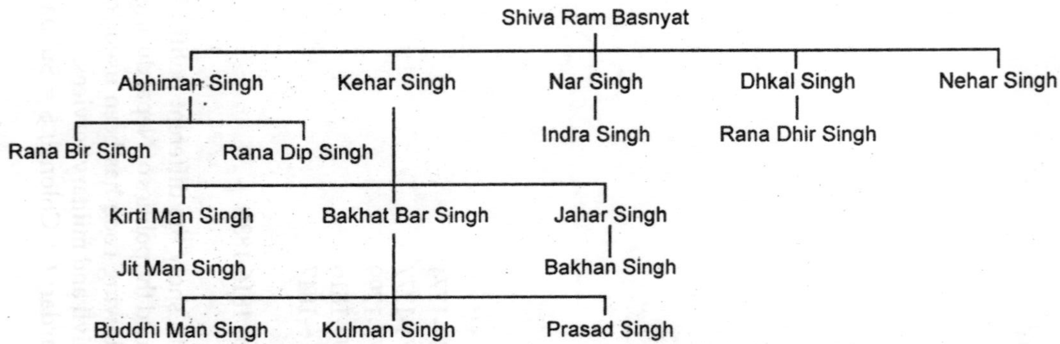

	1816	1817	1819	1819	1820	1821	1822	1823	1824	1825	1826	1827	1828	1829	1830	1831	1832	1833	1834	1835	1836	1837	1838	1839
Rana Bir Singh Basnyat											S	S	S	S			S		S		C			
Rana Dip Singh Basnyat			C									S	S	S	S	S	S	S	S			C		K
Indira Singh Basnyat												S												
Rana Dhir Singh Basnyat			K											K	K									
Kirti Man Singh Basnyat																	K							
Bhaktabar Singh Basnyat					K	K	K			K														
Jahar Singh Basnyat										K														
Jit Man Singh Basnyat			K	K															K	K	K	K		
Buddhiman Singh Basnyat										S													K	
Prasad Singh Basnyat	C	K	K							C	C	C	C	C	C	C	C	C	C	C	C	C	C	K
Kulman Singh Basnyat									K	K	K	K	K	K	K	K	K	K	K	K	K	K	K	K
Bakhan Singh Basnyat	S	S		C					S	S	S		C						C	C	C	C	C	

KUNWAR RANA

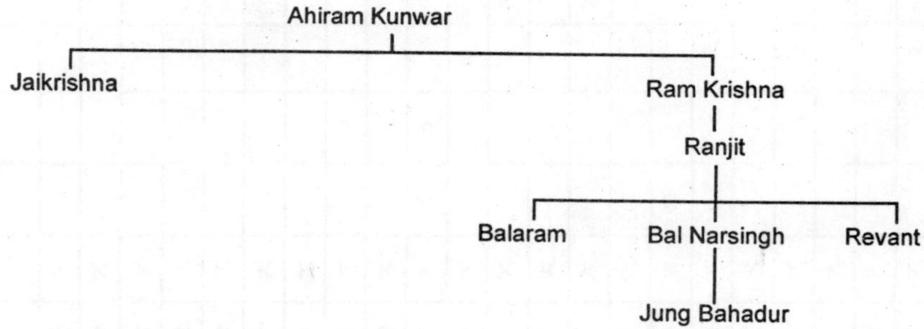

	1816	1817	1818	1819	1820	1821	1822	1823	1824	1825	1826	1827	1828	1829	1830	1831	1832	1833	1834	1835	1836	1837	1838	1839
Bir Bhadra Kunwar	S	S	C	C	C	C	C	C	C	C	C	C	C	C	C	C	C	C	C	C	C	C	C	
Balaram Kunwar											K	K	C	C	C	C	C	C	C	C	C	C		
Bal Narsingh Kunwar	K	K	K	K	K	K	K	K	K	K	K	K	K	K	K	K	K	K	K	K	K	K	K	
Revant Kunwar	K	K	K	K	K	K	K	K	K	K	K	K	K	K	K									

BHANDARI

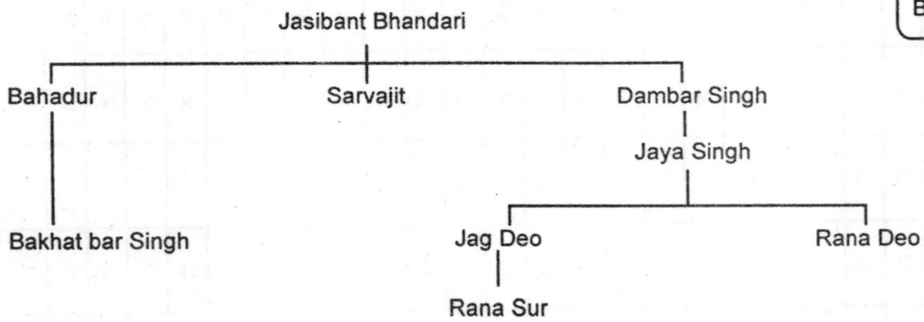

	1816	1817	1818	1819	1820	1821	1822	1823	1824	1825	1826	1827	1828	1829	1830	1831	1832	1833	1834	1835	1836	1837	1838	1839
Bahadur Bhandari	K	K	K	K	K	K	K	K	K	K	K	K	K	K	K	K	K	K	K	K	K	K		
Sarvajit Bhandari										s					S	S							C	
Dambar Singh Bhandari										s													s	
Bakhat bar Bhandari											S	S										C	C	C
Rana Sur Bhandari	s									s		$	$	$	$								s	C

THAPA
KAZI AMAR SINGH

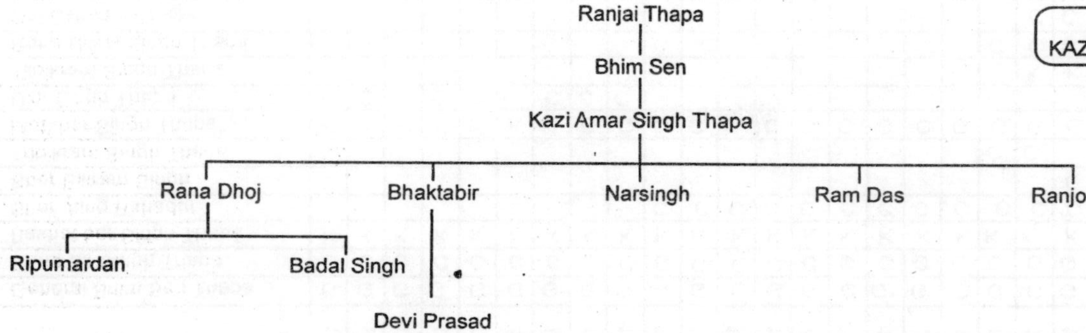

	1816	1817	1818	1819	1820	1821	1822	1823	1824	1825	1826	1827	1828	1829	1830	1831	1832	1833	1834	1835	1836	1837	1838	1839
Kazi Amar Singh Thapa	K																							
Rana Dhoj Thapa	K	K	K	K	K	K	K	K	K	K	K	K	K	K	K	K								
Bhaktabir Thapa	C	C	C	K	K	K	K	K	K	K	K	K	K	K	K	K	K	K						
Narsingh Thapa			C	C	K	K	K	K	K	C	C	C	C	C	C	C	C	K	K	K	K	K	K	K
Ram Das Thapa										s						K	K	K	K					
Ranjore Thapa												K	K	K	K	K	K	K	K	K	K	K	K	K
Ripumardan Thapa			$	$	$	$	K	K	K	K	K	K	K	K	K	K	K	K	K	K				
Badal Singh Thapa															K	K	K							
Surat Singh Thapa																	K	K	C	C	C	C	C	C

THAPA
BHIM SEN

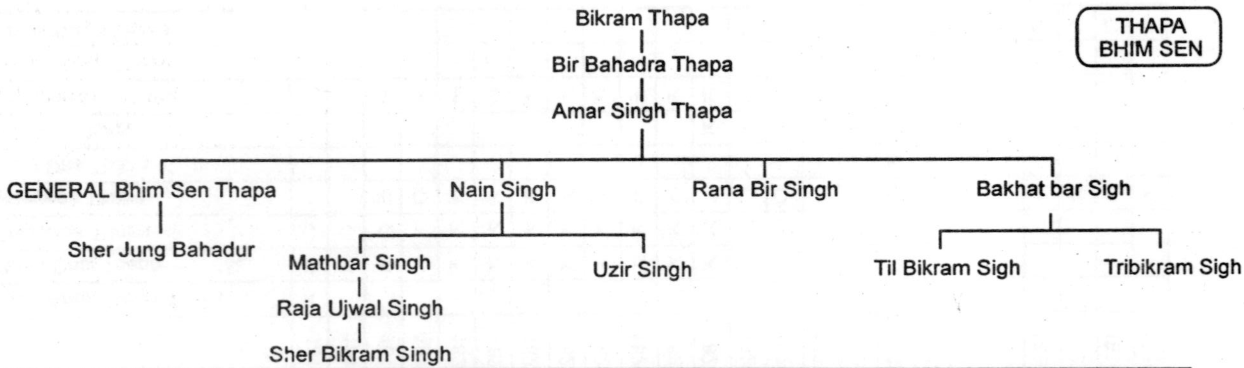

	1816	1817	1818	1819	1820	1821	1822	1823	1824	1825	1826	1827	1828	1829	1830	1831	1832	1833	1834	1835	1836	1837	1838	1839
General Bhim Sen Thapa	G	G	G	G	G	G	G	G	G	G	G	G	G	G	G	G	G	G	G	G	G	G		
Rana Bir Singh Thapa	C	C	C	C	C	C	C	C	C	C	C	C	C	C	C	C	C	C	C	G	G	G		
Bakhat bar Singh Thapa	K	K	K	K	K	K	K	K	K	K	K	K	K	K	K	K	K	K	K	K	K			
Sher Jung Bahadur										C	C	C	C	C	C	C	C	C	C	C	C	C		
Sher Bikram Singh																					C	C	C	
Tribikram Singh Thapa																			C	C				
Mathbar Singh Thapa	C	C	K	K	K	K	K	C	C	C	C	C	C	C	C	C	C	G	G	G	G	G		
Uzir Singh Thapa	C	C	C	C	C	C	C	C	C															
Tilbikram Singh Thapa																				K	K	K	K	
Rana Ujwal Singh Thapa																			C	C	C	C	C	C
Dal Bahadur Thapa																			C	C	C	C	C	C

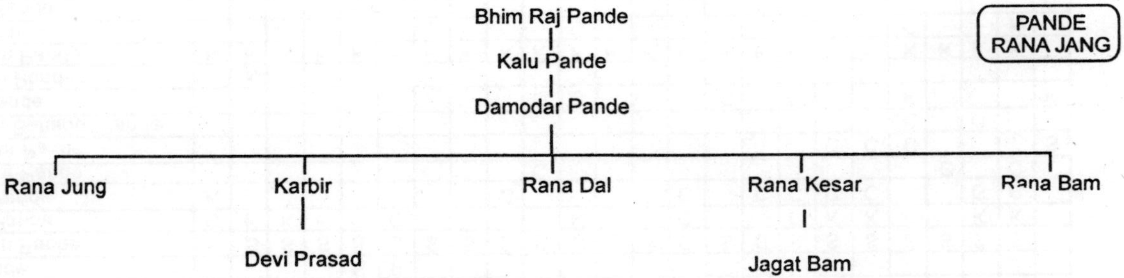

	1816	1817	1818	1819	1820	1821	1822	1823	1824	1825	1826	1827	1828	1829	1830	1831	1832	1833	1834	1835	1836	1837	1838	1839
Rana Jang Pande		S	S	S	S	S	S	S	C	C	C	C	C	C		C	C	C	C	K	K	K	K	
Kar Bir Pande			C	C		C	C	C	C	C		C	C		C	C	C		C	C	K	K	K	K
Rana Dal Pande								C		C	C	C	C				C		C	C	C	K	K	K
Jagat Bam Pande																		C	C	C	C		C	

PANDE

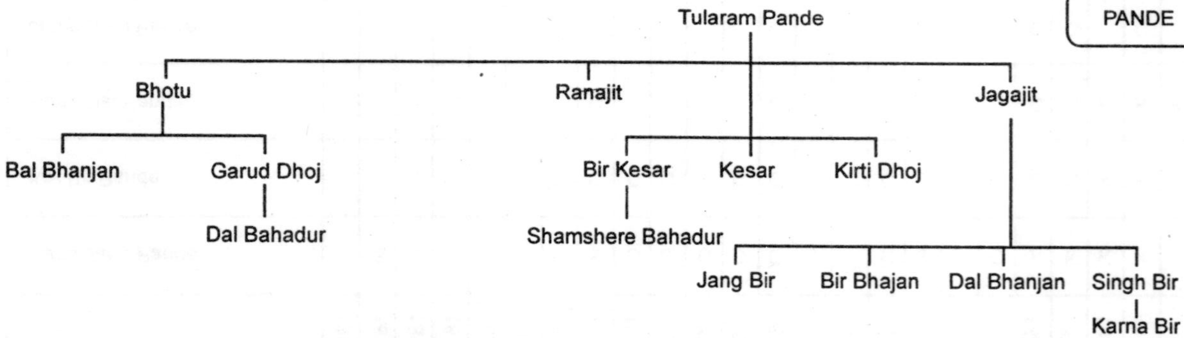

	1816	1817	1818	1819	1820	1821	1822	1823	1824	1825	1826	1827	1828	1829	1830	1831	1832	1833	1834	1835	1836	1837	1838	1839
Ranajit Pande										K														
Jagajit Pande					S	S																		
Bal Bhanjan Pande	S	S	S	S	S	S	S	S	S	S	S	S	S	S	S	S	S	S	S	S	S	S	S	
Bir Kesar Pande	C	K	K	K	C	C					K		C	C			C	K	K	C		K	K	
Kirti Dhoj Pande	K								C					C		C	C	C	C			C	C	
Bal Bahadur Pande										C											C		C	
Dal Bahadur Pande																		C	C	C				S
Shamshere Bahadur Pande																				C		C		
Jang Bir Pande										C	C			K	C		C			K				K
Bir Bhanjan Pande		K																						
Dal Bhanjan Pande	K	K	K	K	K	K	K	K	K	K	K	K	K	K	K	K	K	K	K	K	K	K	K	
Singh Bir Pande	L										C									C			K	
Karna Bir Pande																				C				C

Maps

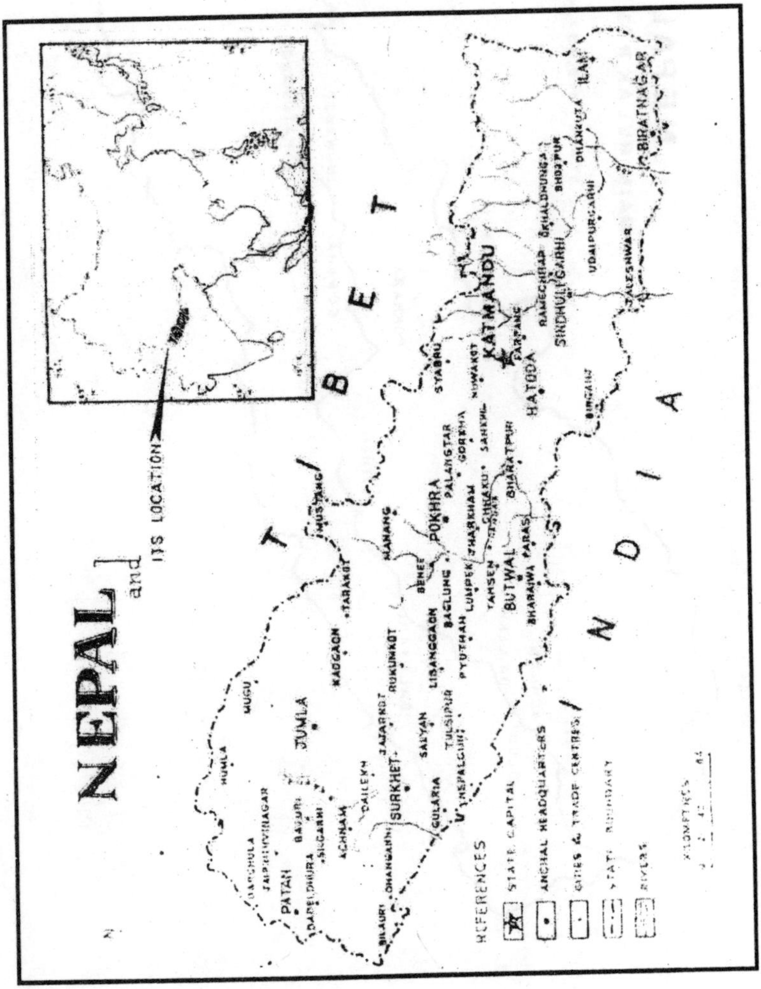
NEPAL and ITS LOCATION
TIBET
INDIA
KATMANDU
POKHRA
JUMLA
SURKHET
BUTWAL
HATODA
BIRATNAGAR
SINDHULI GARHI
PATAN
MUSTANG
MANANG
TARAKOT
KAGGAON
RUKUMKOT
JAJARKOT
SALYAN
TULSIPUR
PYUTHAN
LISANGGAON
BAGLUNG
BENEE
LUMPEK
TAMSEN
BHAIRAWA
PARASI
BHARATPUR
PALANGTAR
GORKHA
NUWAKOT
SYABRU
DAILEKH
GULARIA
ACHHAM
BAITADI
DANDELDHURA
MUGU
HUMLA
UDAIPURGARHI
DHANKUTA
ILAM
BHOJPUR
RAMECHHAP
BIRGANJ
JALESHWAR
REFERENCES
STATE CAPITAL
ANCHAL HEADQUARTERS
CITIES & TRADE CENTRES
STATE BOUNDARY
RIVERS
KILOMETRES

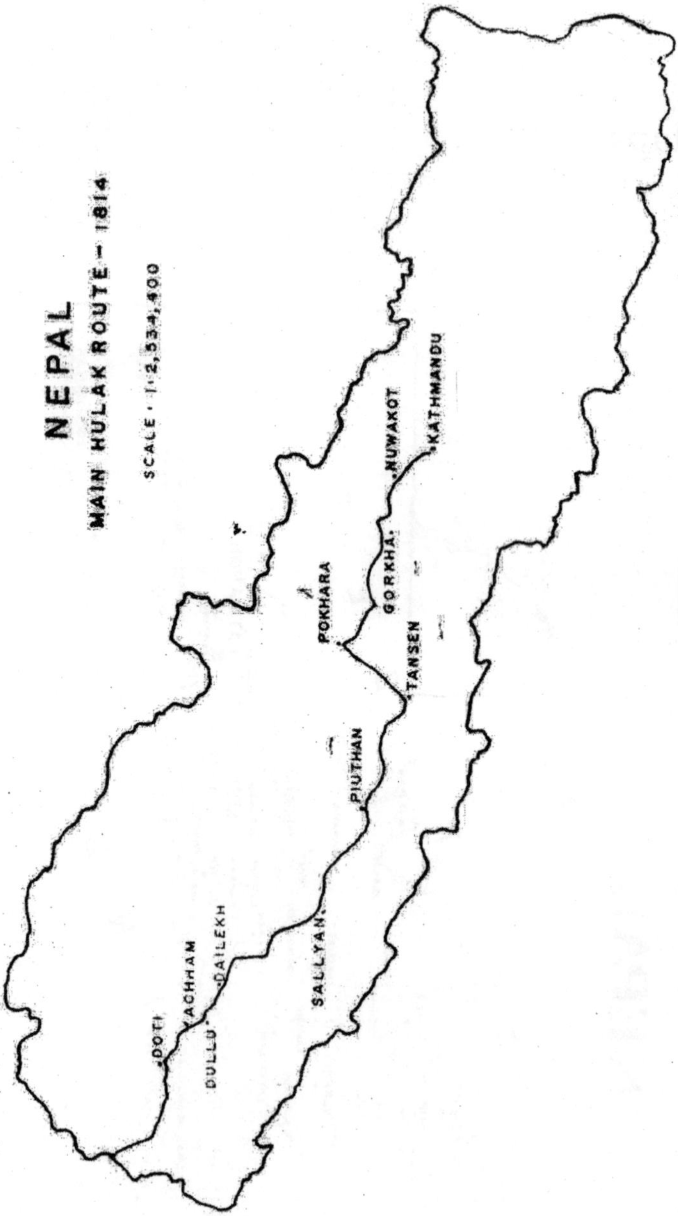
NEPAL
MAIN HULAK ROUTE – 1814
SCALE : 1:2,534,400
KATHMANDU
NUWAKOT
GORKHA
POKHARA
TANSEN
PIUTHAN
SALLYAN
DAILEKH
ACHHAM
DULLU
DOTI

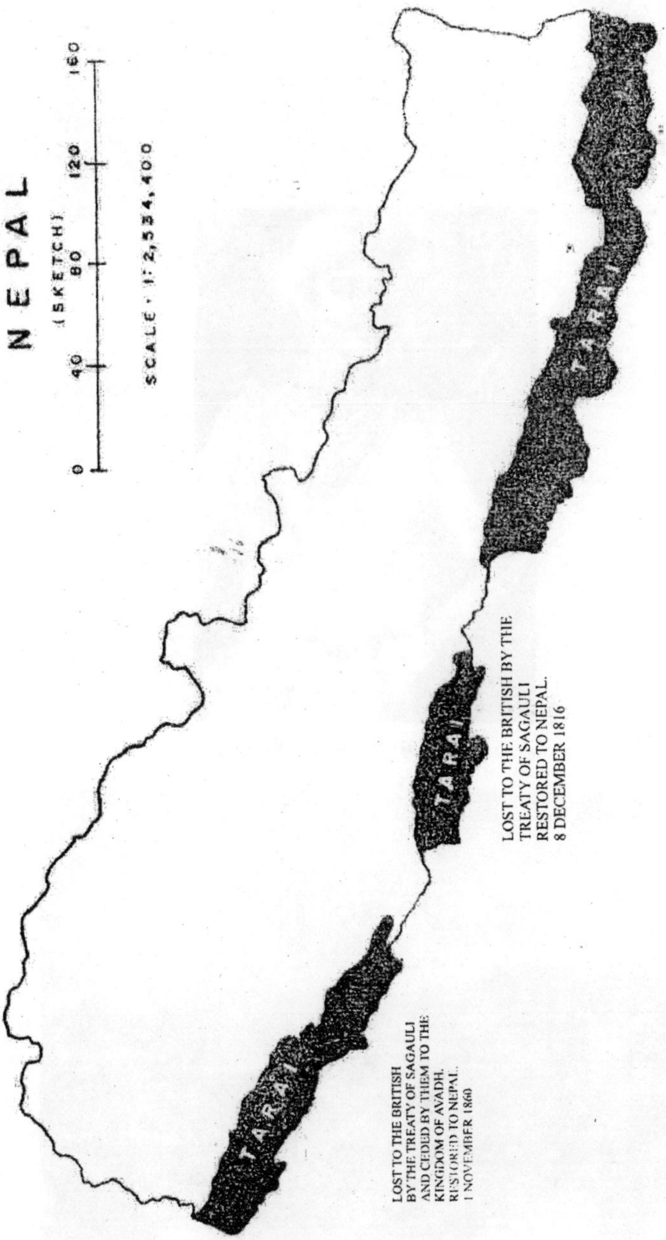
NEPAL
(SKETCH)
0 40 80 120 160
SCALE · 1: 2,534,400
TARAI
TARAI
TARAI
TARAI
LOST TO THE BRITISH BY THE TREATY OF SAGAULI RESTORED TO NEPAL. 8 DECEMBER 1816
LOST TO THE BRITISH BY THE TREATY OF SAGAULI AND CEDED BY THEM TO THE KINGDOM OF AVADH. RESTORED TO NEPAL. 1 NOVEMBER 1860

Photos

King Ran Bahadur Shah

The Royal Palace

Bagh Darbar at Kathmandu
(Residence of General Bhim Sen Thapa)

Sir Brian Houghton Hodgson

General Bhim Sen Thapa

Bhim Sen Temple at Patan

Girvan Judha Vikram Sah

Dharara at Kathmandu

Satyasawr Mahadev Temple at Riddi

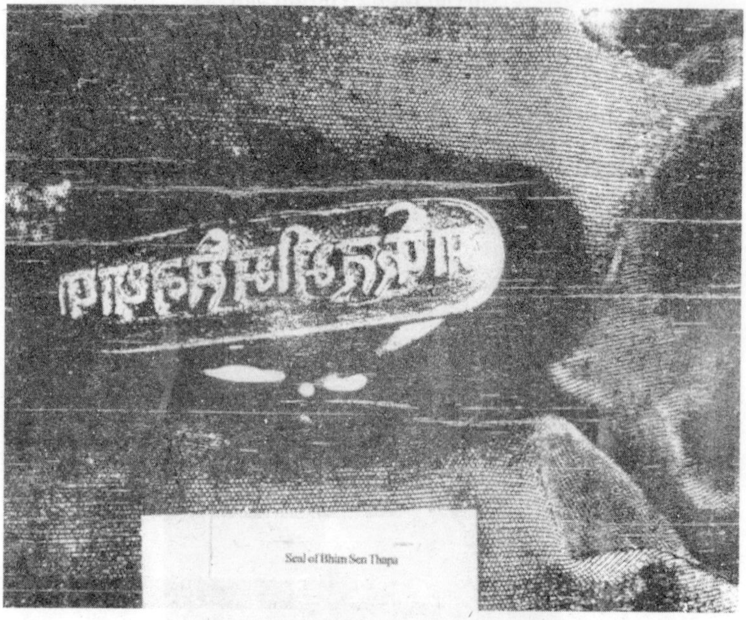

Seal of Bhim Sen Thapa

Thapathali, Kathmandu

The Bhimsenthan, Kathmandu

General Bhim Sen Thapa

Appendix-A

Treaty of Commerce with Nepal
1st March, 1792

"Treaty authenticated under the seal of Maharajah Run Behaudar Shah Behauder Shumshere Jung; being according to the Treaty transmitted by Mr. Jonathan Duncan, the Resident at Benaras, on the part of Right Honourable Charles, Earl Cornwallis, K.G., Governor General-in-Council, and empowered by the said authority to conclude a Treaty of commerce with the said Maharajah, and to settle and fix the duties payable by the subjects of the respective states of the Honourable English Company and those of Nepaul, the said gentleman charging himself with whatever relates to the duties thus to the company; in the like manner as hath the foresaid Maharajah, with whatever regards the duties thus to be payable by the subjects of the Company's Government to that of Nepaul; and The said Treaty having been delivered to me (the said Maharajah) by Mowlavy Abdul Kadir Khan, the aforesaid gentleman's vakkel, or agent, this counterpart thereof having been by the Nepaul Government, hath been committed to the said Khan, as hereunder detailed:

Article-I

Inasmuch as an attention to the general to welfare and to ease and satisfaction on the merchants and traders, tends equally to the reputation of the administrations of both Governments of the Company and of Nepaul; it is therefore agreed and stipulated, that 2½ per cent shall reciprocally be taken, as duty, on the imports from both countries; such duties to be levied on the amount of the invoices of the goods which the merchants shall have along with them; and to deter the said traders from exhibiting false invoices, the seal of the said customs houses of both countries shall be impressed on the back of the said invoices, and copy thereof being kept, the original shall be restored to the merchants; and in cases where the merchants shall not have along with him his original invoices, the custom house officers shall not in such instance lay down the duty of 2½ per cent on a valuation according to the market price.

Article-II

The opposite stations hereunder specified, within the frontiers of each country, are fixed for the duties to be levied, at which place the traders are to pay the same; and after having once paid duties and receiving rowannah thereon. On other of further duty shall be payable throughout each country of dominion respectively.

Article-III

Whoever among the officer·on either side shall exceed in his demands for, or exaction of duty, the rate here specified, shall be exemplarily punished by the Government to which he belongs, so as effectually to deter other from like offences.

Article-IV

In the case of theft or robberies happening on the goods of the merchants, the foujedar, or officer of the police, shall, advising his superiors or Government thereof speedily, cause the zamindars and proprietors of the spot of make the value, which is in all cases, without fail, to be so made good to the merchants.

Article-V

In cases wherein either country any oppression or violence be committed on any merchants, the officers of country wherein this may happen shall without delay, hear and inquire into the complaints of the persons thus aggrieved, and doing them justice, bring the offenders to punishment.

Article-VI

When the merchants of either country, having paid the established duty, shall have transported their goods into the dominions of one of other state if such goods be sold within such states, it is well; but if such goods not meeting with sale, and that the said merchants be desirous to transport their said goods to any other country beyond the limits of either of the respective states included in the Treaty, the subjects and officials of these latter shall not take thereon any other or further duty that the fixed one levied at the first entry; and are not to exact double duties, but are to allow such goods to deport in all safety without opposition. Demands for, or exaction of duty, the rate here specified, shall be exemplarily punished by the Government to which he belongs, so as effectually to deter other from like offences.

Article-VII

This Treaty shall be of full force and validity in respect of the present and future rulers of both Governments, and, being considered on both sides as a Commercial Treaty and a basis of concord between the two states, is to be, at all times, observed and acted upon in times to come, for the public advantage and the increase of friendship.

Appendix-B

The Treaty of "Commerce and Alliance" with Nepal 16th October, 1801

"Whereas it is evident as the noonday sun to the enlighten understanding of exalted nobles and of powerful Chiefs and Rulers, that Almighty God had entrusted the protection and Government of the universe to the authority of Prince, who make justice their principle, and that by the establishment of a friendly connection between then universe happiness and prosperity is secured, and that the more intimate the relation of amity and union the greater is the general tranquility; in consideration these circumstances, His Excellency the most Noble the Governor General Marquis Wellesley & c. & c. and the Maharajah have established a system of friendship between the respective Governments of the Company and the Raja of Nepaul, and have agreed to the following Articles:

Article-I

It is necessary and incumbent upon the principle and officers of that two Governments constantly to exert themselves to improve the friendship subsisting between the two States, and to be zealously and sincerely desirous of the prosperity and success of the Government and subjects of both.

Article-II

The incendiary and turbulent representations of the disaffected, who are the disturbers of our mutual friendship shall not be attended to without investigation and proof.

Article-III

The principals and officers of both Governments will cordially consider the friends and enemies of either states to be the friends and enemies of the other; and this consideration must ever remain permanent and in force from generation to generation.

Article-IV

If any one of the neighbouring powers of either state should commence any altercation or dispute, and design, without provocation, unjustly to possess himself of the territories of either country, and should entertain hostile intentions with the view of taking that country, the vakeels on the part of our respective Governments at either Court will fully report all particulars to the head of the state, who, according to the obligation of friendship subsisting between the two States after having heard the said particulars, will give whatever answer and advice may be proper.

Article-V

Whenever any dispute of boundary and territory between the two countries may arise, such dispute shall be decided, through our respective vakeels or our officers, according to the principles of justice and right; and a land—marked shall be placed upon the said boundary, and which shall constantly remain, that the officers both now and hereafter may consider it as a guide, and not make any encroachment.

Article-VI

Such places as are upon the Frontiers of the dominions of the Nobab Vizier and of Nepaul, and respecting which any dispute may arise, such dispute shall be settled by the mediation of the vakeels on the part of the Company, in the presence of one from the Nepal Government, and one from His Excellency the Vizier.

Article-VII

So many elephants on account of Muchwanpoor, are annually sent to the Company by the Raja of Nepaul, and therefore the Governor-General with a view of promoting the satisfaction of the Raja of Nepaul and in consideration of the improved friendly connection, and of the new Treaty, relinquishes who, according to the obligation of friendship subsisting between the two States after having heard the said particulars, will give whatever answer and advice may be proper and forgoes the tribute above-mentioned, and directs the officers of the Company, both now and hereafter from generation to generation, shall never, during the continuance of the engagement contracted by this Treaty (so long as the condition of this Treaty shall be in force), exact the elephants from the Raja.

Article-VIII

If any of the dependents or inhabitants of either country should fly and take refuge in the other, and a requisition should be made for such persons on the part of the Nepaul Government by its constituted vakeel in attendance of the Governor-General, or on the part of the Company's Government by its representative residing at Nepaul, it is in this case mutually agreed that such person should have fled after transgressing the laws of his Government, it is incumbent upon the principals of both Governments immediately to deliver him up to the vakeel at their respective courts, that he may be sent in perfect security to the frontier of their respective territories.

Article-IX

The Maharajah of Nepaul agrees, that a pergunnah with all the lands attached to it, excepting privileged lands and those appropriated to religious purposes, and to jaghirer & c., which are specified separately in the account of collections, shall be given up to Sames Jee are, that if he should remain at Benaras, or at any other places within the Company's provinces, and should spontaneously farm his jagire to the officers of Nepaul, in that event the amount of collections shall be punctually paid to him, agreeably certain kists which may be hereafter settled; that he may appropriate the same to his necessary expenses, and that he may continue to religious abstraction, according to his agreement, which Benarahe may had engraved on brass, at the time of his abdication of the Raj and of his reigning it my favour. Again, in the event of his establishing his residence on his jagire, and of his realizing the collections through his own officers, it is proper that he should not keep such a one and other disaffected persons in his service, and besides one hundred men and main servants, & c, he must not entertained any person as soldiers, with a view to the collections of revenue of the pergunnah; and to protection of his persons he may take two hundred soldiers of the forces of the Nepaul Government, the allowances of whom shall be paid by the Rajah of Nepaul. He must be cautious, also of commencing altercation either by speech or writing; neither must be committing plunder and devastation upon the subjects of Nepaul. In the event of such delinquency being proved to the satisfaction of the two Governments, the aid and protection of the Company shall be withdrawn from him, and in the event also it shall be at the option of the Rajah of Nepaul whether or not he will confiscate his jagire.

The Maharajah also agrees, on his part, that if Sames Jeo should take up his residence within the Company's provinces and should farm out his land to the officers of Nepaul, and that the kists should not be paid according to agreement, or that he should fix his residence on his jagire, and any of the inhabitants of Nepaul should give him or the ryots of his pergunnah any molestation, a requisition shall be made by the Governor-General of the Company, on this subject, to the Rajah. The Governor-General is security for the Rajah's performance of this condition, and the Maharajah will immediately as quit himself of the requisition of the Governor- General, agreeably to what is above written, if any profit should arise in the collection of the said pergunnah, in consequences of the activity of the officers, case, the Rajah of Nepaul will be totally unconcerned.

Article-X

With the view of carrying into effect the different objects contained in this Treaty, and of promoting other verbal negotiation the Governor-General and the Rajah of Nepaul, under the impulse of their will and pleasure, depute a confidential person to each other as vakeel, that remaining in attendance upon their respective-Governments, they may effect the objects above specified, and promote whatever may tend to the daily improvement of the friendship subsisting between the two States.

Article-XI

It is incumbent upon the principals and officers of the two states that they should manifest the regard and respect to the Vakeel of each others Government, which is due to their rank, and is prescribed by the laws of nations; and that they should endeavour, to the utmost of their power, to advance any object which they may propose and to promote their case, comfort, and satisfaction, by extending protection to them, which circumstances are calculated to improve the friendship subsisting between the two Governments, and to illustrate the good name of both states throughout the universe.

Article-XII

It is incumbent upon the vakeels of both States that they should hold no intercourse whatever with any of the subjects or inhabitants of the country, excepting with the officers of the Government, without the permission of those officers; neither should they carry on any correspondence with any of them and if they should receive any letter or writing from any such people, they should not answer it, without the knowledge of the heads of the state, and acquainting him of the particulars, which will dispel all apprehension or doubt between us, and manifest the sincerity of our friendship.

Article-XIII

It is incumbent upon the principals and officers mutually to abide by the spirit of this Treaty, which is now drawn out according to their faith and religion, and deeming it in force from generation to generation that they should not deviate from it; and any person who may transgress against it will be punished by Almighty God, both in this world and in a future state."

Ratified by the Governor-General and council, 30th October, 1801, and by the Nepaul Darbar on 28th October, 1801.

Appendix-C

The Treaty of Sagauli, 1816

Treaty of Peace between the Honourable East India Company and Maha Rajah Bikram Shah, Rajah of Nepaul, settled between Lieutenant-Colonel Bradshaw on the part of the Honourable Company. In virtue of the full powers vested in him by his Excellency the Right Honourable Francis, Earl of Moira, Knight of the Most Noble Order of the Granter, one of His Majesty's most honourable Privy Council, appointed by the Court of Directors of the said Honourable Company to direct and control all the affairs in the East Indies, and by Shree Gooroo Gujrat Misser and Chunder Seekur Opedeea on the part of Maha Rajah Girmukh Jode Bikram Sah Bahauder Shumsheer Jung, in virtue of the power to that effect vested in them by the said Rajah of Nipal—2nd December, 1815.

Article-I

There shall be perpetual peace and friendships between the Honourable East India Company and the Rajah of Nipal.

Article-II

The Rajah of Nipal renounces all claims to the lands which were the subject of discussion between the two states before the war; and acknowledges the right of the Honorable Company to the sovereignty to those lands.

Article-III

The Rajah of Nipal hereby codes to the Honourable East India Company in perpetuity all the undermentioned territories, viz. First, The whole of the low lands between the River Kali and Rapti. Second, The whole of the low-lands (with the exception of Bhootwal Khass) lying between the Rapti and the Gunduck. Thirdly, the whole of the lowlands between the Gunduck and

Coosah in which the authority of the British Government has been introduced, or is in actual course of introduction.

Fourthly, All the lowlands between the River Mechee and the Teestah. Fifthly, All the territories within the hills eastward of the River Mechee, including the fort and lands of Nagree and the pass of Nagarocote, leading from Morung into the hills, together with the territory lying between the pass and Nagree, the aforesaid territory shall be evacuated by the Gorkha troops within forty days from this date.

Article-IV

With a view to indemnify the Chiefs and Bharadars of the State of Nipal, whose interests will suffer by the alienation of the lands ceded by the forging Article, the British Government agrees to settle pensions to the aggregate amount of two lakhs of rupees per annum on such chiefs as may be selected by the Rajah of Nipal, and in the proportions which the Rajah may fix. As soon as the selection is made, Sunnuds shall be granted under the seal and signature of the Governor-General for pension respectively.

Article-V

The Rajah of Nipal renounces for himself, his heirs, and successors, all claims to or connexion with the countries lying to the west of the River Kali and engages never to have any concern with those countries or the inhabitants thereof.

Article-VI

The Rajah of Nipal engages never to molest or disturb the Rajah of Sikkim in the possession of his territories; but agrees if any difference shall arise between the states of Nipal and the Rajah of Sikkim, or the subjects of either, that such difference shall be referred to the arbitration of the British Government, by whose award the Rajah of Nipal engages to abide.

Article-VII

The Rajah of Nipal hereby engages never to take or retain in his service any British Subject, nor the subject of any European and American States, without the consent of the British Government.

Article-VIII

In order to secure and improve the relations of amity and peace hereby established between the two states, it is agreed that accredited Minister from each shall reside at the Court of the other.

Article-IX

This Treaty, consisting of nine Articles, shall be ratified by the Rajah of Nipal within fifteen days from this date, and the ratification shall be delivered to Lieutenant Colonel Bradshaw, who engages to obtain and delivered to the Rajah the ratification of the Governor-General within twenty days or sooner, if practicable.

Appendix-D

Memorandum Regarding the Restoration of the Eastern Terai

8th December, 1816

Adverting to the amity and confidence subsisting with the Rajah of Nepal, the British Government propose to suppress, as much as is possible the executing of certain Article in the Treaty of Segowlee, which bear hard upon the Rajah, as follows:

2. With a view of gratify the Rajah in a point which he has much at heart, the British Government is willing to restore the Terai ceded to it by the Rajah in the Treaty to wit, the whole Terai lands lying between the River Coosa and Gunduck such as appertained to the Rajah before the late disagreement: excepting the disputed lands in the Zillahs of Tirhoot and Sarun, and excepting such portions of territory as may occur on both sides for the purpose of settling a frontier upon investigation by the respective commissioners; and excepting, such lands as may have been given in possession to any one by the British Government upon ascertainment of his rights subsequent to the cession of Terai to that Government. In case they may be exchanged for others, and let it be clearly understood that, notwithstanding the considerable extent of the lands, in the Zillah of Tirhoot, which have for long time been a subject of dispute, the settlement made in the year 1812 of Christ, corresponding with the year 1869 of Bikramjit shall be taken and everything also relinquished, that is to say, that the settlement and negotiations, such as occurred at that period, shall in the present case hold good and be established.

3. The British Government is wailing likewise to restore Terai laying between the Rivers Gunduck and Rapti, that is to say from the Rivers Gunduck to the western limits of the Zillah of Goruckpore, together with Pootwal and Seoral, such as appertained to Nipal previous to the disagreements, complete, with the exception of the disputed places in the Terai, and such quantity of

ground as may be considered mutually to be requisite for the new boundary.

4. As it is impossible to establish desirable limits between the two states without survey, it will be expedient that Commissioner be appointed on both sides for the purpose of arranging in concert as well defined boundary on the basis of the proceeding terms, and of establishing a straight frontier, with a view to the distinct separation of the respective territories of the British Government to the south and of Nipal to the north; and in case any indentations occur to destroy the even tenor of the line, the Commissioners should effect and exchange of lands so interfering on principles of clear reciprocity

5. With a view to prevent continual dispute and discussion between the Governments, the respective Commissioners should effect in mutual concurrence and cooperation the exchange of such lands, so as to render them subject to one dominion alone.

6. Whensoever the Terai should be restored; the Rajah of Nipal will cease to require the sum of two lakhs of rupees per annum, which the British Government agreed the advance for the maintenance of certain Bharadars of his Government.

7. Moreover, the Rajah of Nipal agreed to refrain from prosecuting any inhabitations of the Terai, after its revertance to his rule, on account of having favoured the cause of the British Government during the war, and should any of those persons, excepting the cultivators of the soil, be desirous of quitting their estates, and of retiring within the Company's territories, he shall not be liable to hindrance.

8. In the event of the Rajah's approving the foregoing terms, the proposed arrangement for the survey and establishment of boundary marks shall be carried into execution, and after the determination in concert of the boundary line, Sunnuds conformable to the foregoing stipulations drawn out and sealed by two States shall be delivered and accepted on both sides.

Seal (Signed) Edward Gardner,
Resident

(A true translation)

Assistant (Signed) G. Wellesley

Appendix E

Hulak Service Ordinances (Extract) From: King Girbana Yuddha Bikram Shah

To: Subedar Bal Bhadra Khatri and Subedar Dharmananda Khabas

We hereby issue ordinance for the direction of your work in the area west of Dharma Thali and west of Jamuna River. Carry out your work according to these ordinances, without favouritism, and remain true to our salt. Be alert in carrying out the assigned task, which we have entrusted to you.

1. Find out whether those recruited for the *hulak* mail service according to our earlier directives are at their posts or not. In our earlier directives we granted hulak mail carriers exemption from the labour tax and the household tax (*serma*) and from half the *saune-fagu* tax. We also ordered that the fields worked by *hulak* mail carriers should not be taken from them. From the 1866 (1809 A.D.) harvest onwards we also grant exemption from remaining half of the *saune-fagu* tax. We have also made land allotments so that each *hulak* family should have rice land [in proportion to the size of the family]. Send details of whatever arrangements you make according to these instructions and our earlier directives, and we will issue the necessary official documents.
2. From Dharma Thali westward to the Bheri River establish *hulak* porterage centres. Four such centres should be set up for each stage of the road. Twenty families should be assigned to each *hulak* porterage centre. Families doing *hulak* porterage services are exempt from *saune-fagu* taxes and the labour tax. Send us details of the arrangements you make there, and the labour tax. Send us details of the arrangements you make there, and we will issue the necessary official documents.
3. No one, whether he be guru, chautariya, kazi, sardar, subba, subedar, jamindar, sipahi, or anyone else, should

ask hulak porters to carry loads other than military loads or the wounded in either direction along the road unless they have an authorization signed by Kazi Bhim Sen Thapa. If anyone falsely claims that the goods for which he is demanding transport facilities are for the palace, seize him and the goods, and inform us. We will send instructions for his punishment.

4. We have sent special directives to all the bharadars, subbas, and subedars in the undermentioned taluks with orders that anyone who has committed any act contrary to the terms contained in our directives regarding the *hulak* mail service and porterage service should be apprehended and full particulars sent to us. You should, therefore, promulgate this order in each of these taluks:

    Pokhara (from the Marsyangdi river to the Kali River)
    Puithan (from the Kali River to the Sakhi River)
    Salyan (from the Sakhi River to the Bheri River)
    Dullu-Dailekh (from the Bheri River to the village of Kadha in Doti)

    Doti (from Kadha village in Doti to the Mahakali River) Almora (from the Mahakali River to the border of Garhwal) Srinagar (from the Kumaon border to the Bhagirathi River) Doon (from the Bhagirathi River to the Jamuna River)

14. In allotting land on an *adhiya* basis to *hulak* carriers, assign from twenty-five to forty *ropanis* to each family according to the size of the family. Since four porterage centres are to be set up for each stage of the road, verify yourselves the distance *hulak* carriers are expected to cover in one day, and assign three or four carriers per load according to the length of each stage of the road. Send us particulars of your arrangements, and we will issue the necessary official documents.
15. We have granted remissions [in revenue assessments] to the concerned *amalis* for the *hulak* carriers who have been settled on the land earlier. Send us a list of those officers whose emoluments will be reduced because of the

remissions that are granted in accordance with these instructions and the amount of each officers reduction in emoluments, and we will make the necessary adjustments.

16. Each household of hulak carriers is entitled to a remission of up to one rupee in homestead taxes. Send us particulars, and we will issue the necessary official documents.

Dated: B.S. 1866, 1 Ashad, Sudi 4, Roj 7
Bhim Sen Thapa Documents: 1/367/325.

Appendix-F
Judicial Regulations

Prasasti of king Girbana Yuddha Bikram Shah

To:

Subba Madhav Sahi, Srinath Panth, Jagganath Ghimire, Ram Sunder Thapa, Gajadhar Panth, Krishna Ananda Lohani, Krishna Ananda Padhya, Ram Chandra Thapaliya, Ram Chandra Sibakoti, Sribilas Padhya, Karna Bir Adhikari, Hani Narayan Dotyal, Radha Ballabh Padhya and Srikrishna Panth.

We issue these instructions to direct your work in the administration of law and justice in the area of our kingdom lying between the Kanak-Teesta River on the east and the Mahakali River on the west. Show no favouritism. Accept no bribes. Remain true to our salt. Carry out your investigations in accord with these instructions. If any person within these areas of your jurisdiction, regardless of his rank, should file a complaint or a report against you, we shall not act until we have heard your side of the case, and then we will punish the one on whose side we see the fault to lie. Carry out your investigations with full assurance.

1. If anyone has accepted a bribe from the months of Falgun 1860 (February 1804 A.D.) onwards, he shall be made to confess and a fine equivalent to three times the amount of the bribe shall be imposed. If anyone has accepted a bribe before that date and in doing so has caused harm to the king, you shall carry out an investigation and obtain a confession. The one taking the bribe shall be fined three times the amount of the bribe.
2. If, without orders, anyone has evicted an innocent person and taken possession of his house, the pertinent documents shall be scrutinized and the house restored to the rightful owner. After inquiries into the expenses incurred by the tenant for repair of the house and the rent,

deduct the cost of repairs and give the remainder of the rent to the owner of the house. Exacting the *salami* fee from the owner of the house and remit this to the palace.

3. Conduct a full investigation and send us particulars in writing of instances in which *bharadars* of *amalis* have remitted *sirto* or other sums due to the government without authorization; instances in which these have been reduced or suppressed on the basis of bribery, nepotism, or favouritism; or instances in which such sums have been misappropriated.
4. Punish anyone who has enslaved the children of our subjects without our order. Set those who have been enslaved free.
5. Lands that have been developed on the basis of a grant of tax exemption shall be turned over to military companies on the expiry of the tax exemption period stated in the grant. If there is evidence that anyone has promised to develop lands, received on the basis of this promise a letter of authorization, and then allowed the land to lay fallow, enquire into the details of the case. If there appears to have been no obstacle to his development of the land, exact rents at the rate of twenty-five rupees per *khet* per year.
6. Investigate the income from *sera* lands, cattle farms, etc., that are managed for the palace and find out how much of this income has actually come to the palace. Enquire into the reasons for any delay that had occurred in remittances; and fine the one responsible for withholding remittances triple the amount involved.
7. If there is evidence that *amalis, ijaradars* and other revenue functionaries have not made required payments to *jagirdars* and have had their accounts approved despite not having presented receipts for these payments, calculate the sum due to the *jagirdar* and make payment. If the *jagirdar* had abandoned his claim to the money, the sum should be collected and sent to the palace. The *ijaradar* and the *bharadar* who so cleared the accounts without our authorization shall be fined double the amount involved.
8. Enquire into instances where individuals have made unauthorized appropriations of judicial fines for major offences. Collect this money and send it to the palace.

9. Investigate the amounts that those responsible for revenue collections have collected from the new *pota* tax. the *salami* fee, the *puchali* tax on buffaloes, fine on *jaisis*, the fee for copper plate inscriptions, the fee for the scrutiny of *guthi* endowments, fines adulterating milk with water, the *gadi mubharak* levy, the fine on profiteering on currency transactions, *walak* levies, and revenue from *Mahant Mandalis*. Ascertain how much has been collected, how much has been misappropriated, and how many tenant farmers have been dispossessed. Obtain a confession if misappropriated sums to the palace, and fine the offender triple the amount involved.
10. If there is evidence that *adais*, officials of the Hitichowk, and others who are responsible for the management of *sera* lands have been using counterfeit *mana* and *pathi* measures and have thereby profited for themselves from collections and disbursements, collect the sums so misappropriated and send them to the palace. Warn the *adais* and the officials at Hitichowk not to use in the future *mana* and *pathi* measures that do not have an official seal on them.
11. If anyone has appropriated for his own use goods either purchased for the palace or sent as gifts to the palace, obtain a confession from him, punish him, gather the gifts, and distribute them to those for whom they were intended. Those who have misappropriated such gifts or concealed them should be punished.
12. If there is evidence that priests have accepted ritual gifts from the palace for other Brahmins and failed to distribute them, obtain a confession, gather the gifts, and distribute them to those for whom they were intended. Those who have misappropriated such gifts or concealed them should be punished.
13. Obtain a confession from anyone who has misappropriated things given for worship or the ornamentation of temples. Repossess the misappropriated items and inform us. Give the items to the temples for which they were intended. Punish the guilty party.
14. If there is evidence that anyone has misappropriated either

money or property that belonged to the Malla Kings, or, without spending it, has sent it to another party for safekeeping, obtain a confession, repossess the goods, and send it to the palace. Punish the guilty party.

15. If anyone has taken as wife the daughter of a Kasai, a Kusle, a Dhobi, or a Kulu and allowed others to use water, which he has touched, he shall confess his offence and be punished.
16. If anyone destroys a rent-house, a roadside shelter, a temple, or a bridge without our authority and uses the materials for his own purpose, he shall confess his offence and be punished.
17. Audit the accounts of the Office of Mines. If there is evidence that anyone has misappropriated or concealed revenue or suppressed information concerning income, the guilty party shall confess his offence and be punished.
18. If anyone in our kingdom who belongs to the four caste and thirty-six sub-castes, in disregard of the traditions of his caste, takes a relative as wife, he shall confess and be punished according to the gravity of his offence.
19. Ascertain what levies the tenant-farmers throughout our kingdom paid to their former rulers, which of these levies were suppressed and which maintained after these territories came under our rule which levies were increased and who the *amalis* were who increased them. Gather full details and send them to us. Take such action in the matter, as we shall order.
20. Obtain a confession from anyone guilty of taking *chares* and *bhang* or gambling after the year 1860 (1804 A.D.). Punish those who have not yet been punished. Issue a proclamation that in the future anyone who takes *chares* or *bhang* or gambles will be subjected to corporal punishment according to his caste.
21. If any *ijaradar* or revenue official has appropriated for himself judicial fines in excess of Rs. 100.00, he shall confess his fault and be punished.
22. If anyone is guilty of killing cows or bulls (except yaks) in the area between the Teesta River and Garhwal after the territory came into our possession, pays the fines which he had not previously paid, and again is caught killing

cows or bulls, obtain a confession and send him to us. Punish *amalis* and villagers who conspire to suppress information regarding the killing of cows and bulls. From this time let there be no killing of cows and bulls. Let it be known that in the future anyone who kills cows and bulls will have his property confiscated and suffer capital punishment. From this time forward the *amali* should put to death anyone who is guilty of killing cow or bull.

23. Take possession of escheat property of Magars which has been concealed up to this time, unless the right to this property is granted to the *ijaradar* in his contract.
24. In the area between the Teesta River and Garhwal, including Palpa, Gulmi, Argha, and Khanchi, have all *khet* lands which were scrutinized in 1862 (1805 A.D.) and assigned to the army surveyed. If there is evidence that the area is greater than the area mentioned in the official allotment, send us full particulars in writing and take action according to the orders we send to you.
25. Whatever *khet* land remains after making allotment to the army should be surveyed and assigned as we shall direct.
26. If the ownership of *birta, guthi,* or other *khet* lands for which there was no documentary evidence was confirmed by inspectors on the basis of the sworn testimony of a person who claimed to be the owner of a neighbouring plot of land, and if there is evidence that this testimony was false and that the inspectors and owners conspired in producing this false witness, confiscate these lands, have them surveyed, and assign them to the army. Punish the owner, the inspectors, and the one who took the oath.
27. Confiscate all lands that inspectors have confirmed after accepting bribes or lands which they have permitted to remain in the possession of the others on the basis of nepotism or favouritism. Have these lands surveyed and assign them to the army. Punish those who have confirmed such lands on the basis of bribery or nepotism.
28. Scrutinize *khuwa* and *chhap* land grants and send us particulars of each holding.
29. If anyone has occupied more land than is authorized by his grant, inspect the boundaries of his grant and confiscate the land he is holding in excess of his authorization. Have

the land surveyed and assign it to the army. Punish the one who occupied land in excess of his authorized holding.

30. Survey all lands being held on the claim that they are held on mortgage from former kings. If there is evidence that more land is being utilized than is authorized by their documents, send us full particulars concerning the amount of mortgaged land held and the amount of money involved. We will send orders specifying further action.
31. If there is evidence that officials sent to inspect lands, have held fields for their own use. claiming that they are *sera* lands, have such fields surveyed and assigned them to the army.
32. Send us full particulars regarding the amount of *salami* fees taken by land inspectors on the occasion of the confirmation of landowner's rights to their holdings. We will send orders specifying further action.
33. If anyone should file a case claiming that a debtor has failed to pay his creditor sums that are due and for which the creditor is holding promissory notes, or that a creditor has exacted interest in excess of the rate of ten per cent, investigate and decide the case. Deduct from the principal any amount taken in excess of ten per cent and send one-fourth of this amount to us.
34. Prepare separate records of the land that has been confiscated since 1861 (1804 A.D.) and 1862 (1805 A.D.) for each *thum*, town and village. Send us full particulars stating who received the harvests of these two years and to whom they were assigned. Also send particulars stating which military companies were assigned the 1863 (1806 A.D.) harvest and, if it was taken by someone other than the army, who took it. Send these details to us and we will provide instructions for further action.
35. If Brahmins or Chettris have taken liquor, confiscate their goods and deprive them of their caste. If members of other castes who wear the sacred thread other than Brahmins and Chettris have taken liquor, punish them severely and deprive them of their caste.
36. If anyone held lands as *jagir* from the Malla Kings and after these lands came under our rule, continued to use such lands, paying the *pota* tax and claiming them as *birta*

lands, punish him. Confiscate the land and assign it to the army.

37. If anyone files a complaint in the Shrestha Adalat (court of administrative appeals) to the effect that any *amali* or other local official in our kingdom has committed an injustice, hear the case, obtain confessions, and settle the case. The fine imposed on the loser and fees from the winner of the case should be sent to us.
38. If any officer has excused citizens from their labour obligation (compulsory and unpaid) and taken money from them, the amount taken shall be determined and sent to us.
39. If anyone holds land granted originally by the Malla Kings as *jagir, manachamal,* or *sera* and, after our conquest, claimed that these lands were purchased as *suna birta,* paid the *pota* tax on them, and continued to use them, file a complaint against him, obtain a confession, and confiscate the lands. Such a person should also be punished according to our instructions.
40. Investigate any report that goods have been removed from the palace without our approval. Seize the goods, obtain a confession, and forward the goods to us.

Dated: 1863 B.S., Baishakh, Badi 3, Roj 1 (April 1806)
countersigned on the reverse by:

Bhim Sen Thapa	Sher Bahadur Shah
Bahadur Bhandari	Pran Singh
Bal Narsingh Kunwar	Ranadhoj Thapa
Ranajit Pande	Narsingh

Appendix-G

The Documents on Judiciary

From King Rajendra

Instructions for the *bicharis* ('judges') who go annually through the territory lying between the Mahakali River on the west and the Bheri River on the east, to direct the conduct of their work in the courts.

List of Instructions

1. If anyone should come with a complaint that he has suffered injustice from the *amali* ('head of village council') [in his decision of a quarrel], bring the *amali* and the plaintiff together and hear each of them. If the *amali* is guilty of injustice, punish him in proportion to the gravity of his offence. If the plaintiff confesses that his charge is false, impose a fine equal to half of the punishment the *amali* had imposed on him, and allow the amali's decision to stand. If the *amali* does not come for the confrontation, set aside his decision in the dispute, make enquiries, and decide. Send the fine imposed on the loser and the tax on the winner (*jitauri*) to us.
2. In places where disputes arise, place the documents and Lal Mohars from both parties to the dispute before the *Panchayat*. Ratify whatever decision they reach. In a case too complicated for you to decide, send the documents to us. Decide the case according to our instructions.
3. In cases concerning the payment of debts, explain that the interest rate is ten per cent for cash loans and twenty-five per cent for loans in kind. If anyone comes with a complaint that someone has collected interest at rate higher than this, bring the two parties together and hear each of them. If a higher interest rate has been charged, punish the offender. Give him ten per cent in cash or twenty-five per cent in kind. Collect ten per cent (*dasaud*) and send it here.
4. In areas where cases involving the five principal offences arise, hear the case. If the guilty one confesses, punish him

in accordance with directives that have been issued in regard to these offences. Punish him according to the gravity of his offences. If the crime deserves the death penalty, put the culprit in chains and refer the case to us. Carry out whatever instructions we issue.

5. If anyone complains that he has been compelled to pay taxes higher than authorized, bring the two sides together and hear each of them. If it appears that the *amali* or whoever is in charge of accounts has been guilty of injustice, punish him. Return to the farmer whatever has been taken in excess of the prescribed tax.
6. If anyone is caught gambling except during the five days of *Tihar*, whether before or after that time, get a confession from him and punish him.
7. If a farmer comes to the court with a complaint, the amali or *thekdar* ('tax contractor') can go to settle the matter. If the *amali* does not go and the court send someone to bring the plaintiff [to the court], let the *amali* not interfere.
8. If anyone comes with accusation that someone has found and secreted treasure trove, let the accused and the accuser be brought together. Hear each of them and investigate. If the accuse confesses, take the treasure and punish him. If the accuser confesses that his accusation is false, punish him severely.
9. If there has been incitement to insurrection, put the accused before the *panchayat* and investigate the matter. If the accused confesses, imprison him and send details of the case to us. Settle the case according to our instructions. If the strength of the *bicharis* alone is not adequate for this, let the people and the *amalis* assist in this work.
10. If someone from a caste that requires a *Brahman* to perform the rites for birth or death does not have a *Brahman* perform these rights and afterwards touches water to be used by others, punish him and send those who have been pollute by using this water to the *dharmadhika*'s man for purification.
11. In places where land has been mortgaged to a moneylender and the moneylender refuses to return the land even after the money has been repaid. Punish the moneylender and return the deed to the landowner. Take only *pan-phul* ('small fees') from him.

12. When hearing a case that has been brought to the court, whatever districts it may be in, consideration should be given not only to the Lal Mohars in force for that areas but also the regulations that, after careful investigation, have been established by the *Bharadars* according to the local caste differences and customs. Use this guideline in settling dispute.
13. Whenever anyone is apprehended travelling, without a passport in places where a passport is required or travelling by trails and passes that have been officially closed, get a confession from him and punisn him. Do not allow trails that have been officially closed to be opened.
14. If anyone comes to you claiming to be a free man, publicize the case and investigate the matter. If it is decided that he is a free man, punish the one who sold him [into slavery, the one who purchased him, and those who acted as witnesses to the sale]. Restore him to the status of a farmer (raiti). If the one claiming to be free man found to be lying, however, punish him.
15. If someone files a case over a commercial transaction that took place under laws that maintained before the district came into our possession, find out when the transaction took place and send us a complete description. Dispose of the case according to our instructions.
16. Pay the men required to carry out the work of the court according to the schedule given here out of the proceeds of the court. Send any sums over and above this to us through the *dittha* of the four courts [in Kathmandu]. Carry out the work of the court and be true to our salt.
    Bicharis (2)
    Bahidars ('accountant') (1) [no allowance is stated]
    Tahabildar ('treasurer of the court') (1)
    Pyada (14)
17. Let the two *bicharis* take half of the income from *dasaud* ('ten per cent of the value of goods involved in a case'), *beri, dunga,* and *karpan* as their share of the income derived from their labour.

Dated: 1884, Chaitra, Sudi 15, Roj 2
[Monday, 9th April, 1828 A.D.].
Bhim Sen Thapa Documents: 28/265/372-80

Appendix H
Coinage Systems

Kirkpatrick writes[1],

"The currency of Nepaul consists, principally, of silver pieces of eight *annas*, there are also some struck of sixteen *annas*: but the circulation of this last coin, which is called a *Sicca*, is confined to Nepaul proper, and is far from being common even there...

"Besides the silver coins abovementioned, they have one of so low value as the two hundred and eighty-eight parts of *Sicca*, which is called a *Cheedum*. It may be easily conceived, however, that the pieces of this denomination are not in ordinary or general use, any more than the very minute gold coins which are sometimes struck at the mint at Kathmanda, and occasionally sent as presents by the Rajah to foreign powers. Even the *ushrupee*, or gold rupee, of Nepaul is to be considered rather in the light of a medal than a current coin...

"Besides the gold and silver coins enumerated above, they have a copper currency in Nepaul of two or three denominations, such as *Chardams*, *Dodums* & c, thirty-six of the former usually going to the *mohr*, or eight-*anna* piece."

According to Hamilton[2], "In Nepal accounts are kept thus: 4 *Damas* = 1 *Paisah*; 4 *paisah* = 1 *Ana*; 8 *Anas* = 1 *Mohur*. The *Ana* is an imaginary money. The coin called a *Mohur* varies in its rate of exchange, but is commonly worth 34 *Paisahs*. The *Paisah* always exchanges for 4 *Damas*."

The *anna* was synonymous with *ganda*. The Nepali rupee usually consisted of 16 *gandas* or 64 *paisas*.[3] According to the one source, 22- and 27-*ganda* rupees also were in circulation[4], but no documentary evidence is available.

The different denominations and weights of copper coins minted at the Beni Mint in Baglung district in 1806 were as follows[5]:

Denomination	*Weight*
Paisa	2 tolas
Adha-Paisa	1 tola
Chhakani	½ tola
Dam	2.8 tolas
32 Paisas	1 Rupee

It is possible that these denominations were not uniform in all areas where Nepali coins were in circulation.

Notes

1. Kirkpatrick, *op. cit.*, pp. 217-218.
2. Hamilton, *op. cit.*, p. 214.
3. *Order to Traders of Palpa to Use 16-Ganda Rupee,* Falgun Sudi 9, 1853 (March 1797). (25/322).
4. Gopaldatta Pande, *op. cit.*, p. 1.
5. *Order to Ijaradar Jitaram Newar to Mint Copper Coins at Beni Mint,* Chaitra Sudi 6, 1862 (March 1806). (16/753).

Appendix-I

Administrative Regulations of the Government of Nepal, 1793

Regulations promulgated at Nuwakot on Wednesday, Falgun Badi 4, 1849 (February 1793) for administrative arrangements in the country, including the capital and the provincial areas.

1. The Malik[1] shall get up at 4 *ghadis* and complete his bath, worship and meal by 12 *ghadis*. He shall then sleep for 6 *ghadis*. For 1 *ghadi*[2] thereafter, he shall have confidential talks with the *Bharadars*. He shall hold court for 9 *ghadis* and listen to and keep him self-acquainted with developments both inside and outside the country. At the end of 30 *ghadis*, after the evening greetings and obeisances have been exchanged, he shall dismiss the court. The court shall sit only up to the early hours of the evening, after which it shall be dismissed and everybody shall recreate himself as he likes. This shall be the daily routine.
2. Official functions shall be allocated separately to the *Chautariya, Kaji, Sardar, Khajanchi, Taksari, Dittha, Jethabudha, Kharidar, Kaptan, Subedar, Dware, Bichari, Chhebhadel, Itachapli, Tusal, Kapardar, Adai*[3], etc. The functions of one official shall not be discharged by another. The functions to be allocated to any official may be increased or reduced in consultation with him.
3. A strong fort shall be constructed in Nepal (i.e. Kathmandu Valley). Forts, outposts, barricades etc. shall be constructed at strategic places. Arrangements shall be made for their proper repair and maintenance.
4. Current customs lead to injustice while it will not be possible to follow the tenets of the *Dharmashastras.* so, in consultation with the *Guru, Purohit, Dharmadhikar,* and a few other *Pandits, Bharadars, Tharghars,* respectable persons and merchants, punishments for different crimes shall be prescribed keeping in view the customs of the country. These shall be inscribed on a copper-plate. A good person

shall be given (judicial) authority. *Bicharis* shall be appointed in the number recommended by this person. 4 *Pandits* and 16 *Tharghars* shall be placed under him. Summonses of the *Adalat* shall be honoured by all. Fines shall be imposed for ignoring such summonses. A company (of troops) shall be assigned (to the *Adalat*). Cases shall be referred to us and punishment as prescribed in the copper-plate inscription shall be awarded. Justice will then be insured.

5. Persons who are to be appointed as officials shall be given temporary appointment for 3 years. If they render satisfactory service, they shall be confirmed in their posts; otherwise, they shall be dismissed.
6. The different grades of officials and their Khangi emoluments shall be prescribed. Promotion shall be given to persons rendering satisfactory service, but their Khangi shall not be increased.
7. Lands in Nepal, the hill regions and the Tarai shall be surveyed. Records of such surveys shall be kept with the government and land grants shall be made, if necessary, on the basis of these records.
8. In case unauthorized collections are made in excess of prescribed rates the revenue collector shall be punished.
9. Our Tarai region is desolate since large areas are given on *Ijara* to one person, as there are no *Zamindars*. If tenants want to lodge complaints in Kathmandu, they will have to spend 10 to 20 rupees for travel expenses. Those who get lands give 2 or 4 rupees more to the revenue collector to keep him happy. Those who do not get (lands) become homeless and migrate abroad. The *Zamindari* system shall therefore be introduced. If tenants become homeless, the *Zamindar* will lose. If injustice is done in the country, *Zamindars* can come here to complain.
10. Areas shall not be joined together under *Ijara* or *Amanat*. They shall be kept separate. No changes shall be made during the stipulated period. No remission shall be given in respect to the stipulated amount. Both profits and losses belong to the *Ijaradar*. While issuing *Ijaras*, area shall be surveyed and (necessary) remissions granted. The amount payable (under the *Ijara*) shall be fixed and collected in

12 monthly instalments. In the event of default, interest shall be charged.

11. *Guthis* shall be endowed to provide for major expenses of the royal palace. Transit duties to be collected in the Tarai and Nepal, places where the area of rice land of good quality is small in proportion to the total area, mines and mints shall be surveyed, and assessments thereon shall be made in cash.
12. Reclaimable lands in the hills and other areas, including Tumlingtar and Arghu-Phant, shall be reclaimed and assigned as *Jagir*. Soldiers and *Bharadars* shall be given cash salaries only if such lands are not available.
13. *Chaudharis* shall be appointed to control the prices of cloths, foodgrains and other commodities. Principalities which have been retained in our Kingdom shall be under obligation to supply male buffaloes for the Dasham festival and *Salami* levy for the Fagu festival.
14. Brahmans shall be allotted as priests for different classes. Only Brahmans thus authorized shall perform priestly duties at the allotted household. No person shall perform such functions at households other than those allotted to him.
15. Four persons shall be appointed to scrutinize royal orders to be issued in any matter, such orders shall be issued only if they give their approval. If they do not give their approval, no order shall be issued. Once a royal order is issued, it shall be complied with. Those who violate royal orders shall be punished. If royal orders are found inadequate in content, persons scrutinizing them shall be punished.
16. Fees payable to *Bharadars* shall be prescribed. Those who accept bribes in addition to such fees are tampered with justice shall be punished.
17. *Subbas* shall be appointed only in areas beyond the Bheri and in *Vijayapur.* Musketeers shield-bearers and soldiers shall be stationed in areas which are under the jurisdiction of *subbas*. Areas where Dwares have been appointed shall be surveyed and placed under *Ijara*.
18. The administration of the country shall be put under different *Bharadars* in separate sections, so that confusion may not be created.

19. Details of administrative duties assigned to different officials shall be incorporated in regulations which they will draft themselves.

Falgun Badi 4, 1849
(February 1793)
(1A/13)

Notes

1. Lit. lord or master. The term has obviously been used to denote the King.
2. 1 *ghadi* is equal to 24 minutes. The king was apparently expected to get up approximately 1½ hours before day-break.
3. See Glossary for definitions.

Appendix-J
Saptari-Mahottari Administrative Regulations, 1793

From King Ran Bahadur,
To Subba Laxmi Narayan Pandit.

You are hereby commenced to make arrangements as follows in Saptari and Mahottari districts:

1. Expenditure shall be incurred in the construction of dams and irrigation channels in order to promote land reclamation. Remission shall be granted on the basis of the *Munsiff's* recommendations.
2. *Bhota* and *Tagabi* loans shall be issued with reliable persons as surely for promoting resettlement.
3. Lands shall be measured according to the unit mentioned in royal orders. Revenue shall be transmitted to the treasury on the basis of the assessments thus fixed, the *Jammabandi* records of the *Munsiff* and the collections actually made in that region.
4. Lands which are already under cultivation shall be measured and tax assessments prescribed thereon. *Pattas* of 3 to 5 years, providing for increments in revenue, shall be issued to responsible persons. The *Mokaddam*'s emoluments shall be debited from the total amount. Bonds shall be obtained from *Makaddams* to insure that collections in excess of the prescribed amounts are not made from *ryots*.
5. Rewards given to *Chaudhari's, Kanugoyes, Mokaddams, Jethraiyats, Saidars* etc. shall be debited from the total amount. *Salami* payments collected thereon shall be credited to the accounts.
6, Reasonable expenses incurred during Dashain, Fagu, and other functions and in entertaining respectable foreign visitors shall be debited. Presents received from foreign visitors shall be submitted to us.

7. Salaries shall be paid to the *Subba, Fouzdar, Peskar, Munsiff, Nausinda, Kathait* and soldiers stationed in forts at rates prescribed by royal orders. Such expenses shall be debited from the total amount.
8. Gun powder, flints and cartridges shall be obtained from the palace and used when necessary. They shall not be misused. Reserve stocks of such supplies shall be maintained at the fort.
9. Remissions shall be given for expenses incurred for customary religious functions.
10. (Lands) assigned to *Chaudharis, Kanugoyes* and *Mokaddams* shall be confiscated and the matter shall be reported to us.
11. Complaints received from the district against the revenue collector shall be disposed of after hearing both sides and the guilty shall be punished.
12. The *Munsiff* shall affix his signature on the tax assessment register *Chaudharis* and *Kanugoyes and Mahaldars* shall affix their signatures on records relating to customs and other miscellaneous taxes and levies.
13. Remuneration shall be paid to ryots and traders who bring Sal or Catechu timber to the *Kathmahal*. The *Amil* shall punish who use force for this purpose.
14. Remission shall be given for responsible expenditure incurred on paper, ink, oil, and cushions for use at the *Kachahari,* the monthly salary paid to clerks employed for correspondence in Persian, and expenditure incurred in cash, in addition to *Begar* labour, for repairing forts.
15. Raikar lands which are found in the course of investigations to have been appropriated as *Birta* or *Jagir* without authority shall be confiscated.
16. Water from rivers flowing through different *moujas* and *Pargannas* shall be supplied to all villages, whether, situated in the *Sira* or in the *Bhatha* region. Any person who use force in this matter shall be punished and his land shall be confiscated.
17. Collections of land taxes and other levis made after Baisakh Badi 1, 1850 (April 1793) by the outgoing *Amil* shall be recovered from him according to statements signed by *Chaudharis, Kanugoyes,* etc. In case he does not refund such collections, report the matter to us and we shall give a reply.

18. Remission shall be given for reasonable expenses incurred on *Gumastas, Patuwaris* and peons for collecting *Kathmahal, Sair* and other revenue according to the amount collected.
19. Land taxes shall be collected in instalments as follows:

Month	*Annas in the Rupee to be Collected*
Aswin	1
Kartik	1
Marga	2
Poush	3
Magh	3
Falgun	3
Chaitra	2
Baisakh	1
	16 *annas*

Collection shall not be made except in instalments as mentioned above. In case default is made in the payment of any instalment, additional amounts as mentioned below shall be collected:

2 *annas* (for each peon) per day for provisions.

4 *annas* per day for each expenses.

One-third of the daily salary of (peon).

The amount (thus collected) shall be adjusted against the salaries of peons.

20. Employees shall be paid their salaries in instalments. They shall maintain themselves through their own resources till they receive their salaries.
21. Cases of appropriation of taxable lands without authority by *Chaudharis, Kanugoyes, Mokaddams* and *Jethraiyats* shall be detected and appropriate punishment shall be awarded. The *Munsiff* shall receive provisions from the *ryot* during the time when surveys are underway.
22. Cases shall be disposed of in the presence of *Chaudharis, Kanugoyes, Mokkadams, Birta* owners and other respectable persons. Fines shall be imposed in consultation with *Panchas* and in the presence of ryots on the basis of the nature of the offence.
23. A *Kotwal* shall be appointed in *Mahottaris* to apprehend thieves and dacoits. Riots shall provide emoluments to him at rates prevalent in *Saptari*. 1 *Mauja* of wastelands shall be granted as *Jagir* to the *Kotwal*.

24. *Kanugoyes* shall compile record containing particulars of land and other revenue, as well as cultivated and waste-lands in their areas, submit them to the palace every year and obtain receipts. Failure to submit such records shall be punished with dismissal.
25. *Nankar* land shall be granted to *Chaudharis* and *Kanugoyes* in proportion to the revenue accruing from the *Parganna* under their jurisdiction. Wastelands shall be granted as *Nankar* to those who have no such lands. A tax on the income accruing from such lands shall be collected.
26. *Jagir, Istamrar, Mokarri* and other lands shall be measured and revenue due thereon assessed. These records shall be signed by *Chaudharis* and *Kanugoyes* and submitted to us. We shall scrutinize them and issue orders for granting possession.
27. Soldiers stationed in Tistung and Palling have been deputed there. On the day they reach there, pay salaries due to the *Thanedar* and soldiers of the fort and dismiss them.

Marga Sudi II, 1850
(December 1793)
(36/40)

Appendix-K

Jumla Administrative Regulations, 1796

From King Ran Bahadur Shah,
To Bhayaharan son of Subba Prashram Thapa

We hereby issue the following regulations regarding the work to be done by you in Jumla:

1. Religious ceremonies during Dashain, Fagu and other festivals shall be conducted as usual. The *Kachahari* building shall be repaired as done by previous *Subbas.* Clothes shall be given to maid-servants and other menials at the palace during the Dashain festival.
2. Salaries in cash and in kind according to the revenue collected there shall be paid to the personnel of 18 military companies according to regulations, and receipts shall be obtained against such payments. Offenses committed by *Subedars* and *Jamadars* shall be reported to us, and action shall be taken as ordered.
3. In the event of attack by enemies from any quarter, additional troops shall be recruited for repulsing them. Such troops shall be paid reasonable salary.
4. Appropriate expenses for correspondence with foreign countries shall be incurred. Presents received from foreign countries shall be submitted to us.
5. Rs. 30 each shall be paid as monthly salaries to the *Munshi* and the *Peshkar.* The *Munshi* shall scrutinize (whether collections have been made) according to the tax assessment records, appropriate expenses shall be incurred for repairing forts, manufacturing gunpowder and cannon balls maintaining reserves thereof and constructing wooden bridges.
6. Arrangements shall be made to operate mines. Income therefrom shall be collected and expenses incurred as prescribed. After making arrangements for operating

mines, report the matter and dies for minting paisa coins shall be supplied. Stamps for weights and measures have been sent. Revenue from fees in consideration thereof shall be submitted to us.

7. *Birta* and *Fakirana* land grants made by former *Rajas* during their reign, or *Birta* lands purchased from others, shall be scrutinized. Such grants is valid, shall be confirmed when the matter is presented to us. *Salami* shall be collected in consideration of such confirmation. *Birta* or *Fakirana* land grants made by persons other than reigning *Rajas* shall be confiscated.
8. People of all the 36 castes in Jumla shall display their loyalty to us by complying with the orders of the Subba. Cases of disobedience shall be judged by *Panchas* and punishment shall be awarded according to caste status. Men guilty of treason and rebellion shall be beheaded if their caste status so warrants and if they are above 12 years of age. The member of their families shall not be enslaved but shall be sent to a distant place. Those who cannot be beheaded shall be punished with loss of caste or exile.
9. Persons guilty of immoral offences shall be granted expiation in accordance with local usage and in consultation with a representative of the *Dharmadhikar.*
10. The previous land tax assessment rates, as well as those now introduced in *Jumla,* shall be reported to us. The schedule of rates sanctioned by us shall then be enforced.
11. The land tax assessment system on the basis of blocks, which is customary in Jumla, shall be abolished and assessment shall be made on the basis of individual holdings. Reliable and honest persons shall be appointed as officials and frequently transferred.
12. Counterfeiters shall be punished with amputation or otherwise according to their caste status as ordered by us in offences committed after the region was annexed by us.
13. Allowances shall be given to Jagirdars and military personnel according to regulations.
14. You have been deputed far from the palace. You shall remain there as long as our favour lasts. In case any evil

person submits complaints against you, we shall award justice after hearing both sides. We shall not hear only one side.

Ashadh Sudi 4, 1853
(July 1796)
(5/322)

Appendix L

Timber Export Regulations, 1811

From King Girban
To Padmapani Pandit.

We hereby promulgate these regulations for transporting timber cut in Belod, Chituan, and selling it in Calcutta, as well as for constructing a temple in Kashi. Act according to these regulations:

1. After the timber reaches the Tribeni river, south of Chituan, make arrangements for its transportation to Calcutta by boat or by floating it in stacks, whichever costs less, is more convenient and does not result in loss of timber. Charges for boats from Tribeni to Calcutta, as well as wages of boatmen and the cost of rope and provisions shall be paid as by other merchants. Remissions shall be granted for such expenses in the same manner as granted by other merchants.
2. Maintain the soldiers accompanying the timber under your control and guard the timber day and night. Appoint capable persons as employees and pay them monthly salaries as prescribed in these regulations. Dismiss those who do not obey your orders, and replace them by others.
3. After the timber reaches Calcutta, kept it there for a few days. Ascertain prices from respectable persons in the neighbouring areas. If it is possible to sell the timber soon at reasonable prices, do as soon as you reach there. If prices are not favourable, wait for a few days and sell the timber when prices become favourable. If the timber is not sold out within six months after it had left Tribeni, retain employee as long as necessary. Sell the timber and bring (the proceeds) along with you. The account shall be cleared off after ascertaining the reasonable prices.
4. If any timber is lost in streams and rivers on the way, make efforts to recover it. If you cannot do so through your own

resources, employ labourers on payment of wages, if necessary, and maintain records of the expenditure thus incurred. The accounts shall be cleared off accordingly. If it is not possible to recover the lost timber even through your efforts and through expenditure of money, the loss shall be remitted. If favourable prices can be obtained by paying some money to anybody while selling the timber, make such payments, which shall be remitted.

5. After the timber is sold and the price collected, prepare a statement of income and expenditure and submit it to us. Make an estimate of the amount required to go to *Kashi* and construct a temple there with this money, and submit it to us. Incur expenses as ordered and have the temple constructed.
6. Persons who are deputed to sell timber shall get salaries and emoluments as follows. They shall perform the work assigned to them in a profitable manner without causing us any loss, with due consideration to their morality and integrity:

Padmapani Pandit	Rs. 500
Salaries of 8 peons at Rs. 4 per month for 6 months	Rs. 192
Salaries of 2 peons at Rs. 7 per month, for 6 months	Rs. 84

7. An order has been issued to the *Subba* and *Fouzdars* of Belod, Chituan, to exact *Jhara* labour from the *ryots* of all the four *Pargannas* comprising that district for transporting timber to *Tribeni.* If the entire stock cannot be transported through *Jhara* labour, employ hired labourers. While transporting the timber have religious ceremonies performed through a *Dhami* according to the rites current in Chituan. Remission shall be regarded for reasonable expenses incurred for both these purposes.

Bhadra Sudi 5, 1868
(September 1811)

Appendix-M

Mining Regulations, 1813

From King Girban
To Hanumat Singh

We hereby promulgate the following regulations for the operation of an *Ijara* for exploiting copper deposits and minting *Paisa* coins in the regions between Sanga and the Dudhkoshi river, other than mines assigned to (State) markets and the Army. Act faithfully in accordance with these regulations and the *Ijara* deed:

1. In case any trader smuggles copper, obtain a confession from him, and if he is proved to be guilty of smuggling, confiscate the copper and punish him according to the nature of his offences. The copper brought by him shall be stamped and the customary duties shall be collected thereon.
2. If any trader voluntarily offers to sell his copper, purchase it at reasonable price. If a mine-worker pilfers copper and sells it elsewhere, confiscate, and punish him according to the nature of his offense. Do not treat traders and mine-workers unjustly on the ground that you have been granted a monopoly, but conduct transactions in the customary manner.
3. Collect fees from mine-workers at the same rates as previous *Ijardars.* Do not inflict injustice on the subjects, and do not oppress them. Confirm those mine workers who work faithfully for you, and dismiss those who do not do so, and cannot work efficiently.
4. Copper and Paisa coins to be supplied to the royal palace shall be dispatched by *Hulak*. These shall be delivered at the royal palace, and receipts obtained thereagainst. Accounts shall be cleared on the basis of these receipts.
5. Metal workers in mines shall make copper according to the prescribed manner. Any metal worker who debases the metal shall be punished. Any person who forges dies

and makes counterfeit coins shall suffer punishment on his life and property.

6. Mine workers in the regions between Sanga and the Dudhkoshi river shall prospect for new deposits. Extract metal from old mines and mint coins. *Mukhiyas* of mines shall continue to enjoy the customary perquisites.
7. The metal workers of Bhadgaun and Patan, who go to the Nagre mines to manufacture dies for minting coins, shall be exempted from *Jhara* and other forced labour obligations.

Falgun Sudi 10, 1869
(March 1813)
(39/532)

Appendix-N

On the Military Tribes of Nepal

ORIGIN AND CLASSIFICATION OF THE MILITARY TRIBES OF NEPAL

(*Read before the Bengal Asiatic Society, 9th January,* 1833)

The great aboriginal stock of the inhabitants of these mountains, east of the river *Káli,* or in *Népál,* is Turanian. The fact is inscribed, in characters so plain, upon their faces, forms, and languages, that we may well dispense with the superfluous and vain attempt to trace it historically in the meagre chronicles of barbarians.

But from the twelfth century downwards, the tide of *Mussulmán* conquest and bigotry continued to sweep multitudes of the *Brahmans* of the plains from *Hindústán* into the proximate hills, which now compose the western territories of the kingdom of *Népál.* There the *Brahmans* soon located themselves. They found the natives illiterate, and without faith, but fierce and proud.

Their object was to make them converts to *Hindúism,* and so to confirm the fleeting influence derived from their learning and politeness. They saw that the barbarians had vacant minds, ready to receive their doctrines, but spirits not apt to stoop to degradation, and they acted accordingly. To the earliest and most distinguished of their converts they communicated, in defiance of the creed they taught, the lofty rank and honours of the *Kshatriya* order. But the *Brahmans* had sensual passions to gratify, as well as ambition. They found the native females—even the most distinguished—nothing loath, but still of a temper, like that of the males, prompt to repel indignities. These females would indeed welcome the polished *Brahmans* to their embraces, but their offspring must not be stigmatised as the infamous progeny of a *Brahman* and a *Mléchha*—must, on the contrary, be raised to eminence in the new order of things proposed to be introduced by their fathers. To this progeny also, then, the *Brahmans,* in still greater defiance of their creed, communicated the rank of the second order of *Hindúism;* and from these two roots, mainly, sprung the now numerous, predominant, and extensively ramified, tribe of the *Khas*—originally the name of a small clan of creedless barbarians, now the proud title of the *Kshatriya,* or military order of the kingdom of *Népál.* The offspring of original *Khas* females and of *Brahmans,* with the honours and rank of the second order of *Hindúism,* got the patronymic titles of the first order; and hence the key to the anomalous nomenclature of so many stripes of the military tribes of *Népál* is to be sought in the nomenclature of the sacred order. It may be added, as remarkably illustrative of the lofty spirit of the *Parbattias,* that, in spite of the yearly increasing sway of *Hindúism* in *Népál,* and of the various attempts of the *Brahmans* in high office to procure the abolition of a custom so radically opposed to the creed both parties now profess, the *Khas* still insist that the fruit of commerce (marriage is out of the question) between their females and males of the sacred order shall be ranked as *Kshatriyas,* wear the thread, and assume the patronymic title.

The original *Khas,* thus favoured by it, became soon and entirely devoted to the *Brahmanical* system.* The progress of *Islám* below daily poured fresh refugees among them.

They availed themselves of the superior knowledge of the strangers to subdue the neighbouring tribes of aborigines, were successful beyond their hopes, and, in such a career continued for ages, gradually merged the greater part of their own habits, ideas, and language (but not physiognomy) in those of the *Hindús.*

The *Khas* language became a corrupt dialect of *Hindí,* retaining not many palpable traces (except to curious eyes) of primitive barbarism.

An authentic anecdote told me at Káthmándú confirms the origin above assigned to the modern Khas tribe of Népál. In the reign of Ram Sáh of Górkhá, an ancestor of the present dynasty of Népál, an ambassador was sent from the Durbar of Gorkha to that

* That is, they agreed to put away their old gods, and to take the new; to have *Brahmans* for *Gurus;* and not to kill the cow: for the rest they made, and still make, sufficiently light of the ceremonial law in whatever respects food and sexual gratification. Their active habits and vigorous character could not brook the Restraints of the ritual law, and they had the example of licentious *Brahmans* to warrant their neglect of it. The few prejudices of the *Khas* are useful, rather than otherwise, inasmuch as they favour sobriety and cleanliness.

of Méwár, to exhibit the Górkháli Rajah's pedigree and to claim recognition of alleged kindred. The head of the renowned Sesodians, somewhat staggered with the pedigree, seemed inclined to admit the relationship, when it was suggested to him to question the ambassador about his own caste as a sort of test for the orthodoxy or otherwise of the notions of caste entertained in the far distant, and, as had always at Chitor or Udaypur been supposed, barbarous Himalaya. The ambassador, a Khas, who had announced himself as belonging to the martial tribe, or Kshatriya, thus pressed, was now obliged to admit that he was nevertheless a Pándé, which being the indubitable cognomen of a tribe of the sacred order of Hinduism, his mission was courteously dismissed without further enquiry.

The *Ektháriahs* are the descendants more or less pure of *Rájpúts* and other *Kshatriyas* of the plains, who sought refuge in these mountains from the *Moslem,* or merely military service as adventurers. With fewer aims of policy, and readier means in their bright swords of requiting the protection afforded them, than had the *Brahmans,* they had less motive to mix their proud blood with that of the vile aborigines than the Brahmans felt the impulse of, and they did mix it less. Hence, to this hour, they claim a vague superiority over the *Khas,* notwithstanding that the pressure of the great tide of events around them has, long since, confounded the two races in all essentials. Those among the *Kshatriyas* of the plains, who were more lax, and allied themselves with the *Khas* females in concubinage, were permitted to give to their children, so begotten, the patronymic title only, not the rank. But their children, again, if they married for two generations into the *Khas,* became pure *Khas,* or real *Kshatriyas* in point of privilege and rank, though no longer so in name ! They were *Khas,* not *Kshatriyas,* and yet they bore the proud cognomina of the martial order of the *Hindús,* and were, in the land of their nativity, entitled to every prerogative which *Kshatriya* birth confers in *Hindústán!*

Such is the third and less fruitful root of the *Knas* race.

The *Ektháriahs* speak the *Khas* language, and they speak no other.

The *Thádkuris* differ from the *Ekthários* only by the accidental circumstance of their lineage being royal. At some former period, and in some little state or other, their progenitors were princes.

The *Sáhi* or *Sáh* are the present royal family.

The remaining military tribes of the *Parbattias* are the *Mayor* and *Gúrung,* who now supply the greater number of the soldiers of this state.

From lending themselves less early and heartily to *Brahmanical* influence than the *Khas,* they have retained, in vivid freshness, their original languages, physiognomy, and, in a less degree, habits.

To their own untaught ears their languages differ entirely the one from the other, and no doubt they differ materially, though both belonging to the unpronominalized type of the Turanian tongues. Their physiognomies, too, have peculiarities proper to each, but with the general caste and character fully developed in both. The *Gúrungs* are less generally and more recently redeemed from *Lamáism* and primitive impurity than the *Magars.*

But though both the *Gúrungs* and *Magars* still maintain their own vernacular tongues, Tartar faces, and earless manners, yet, what with military service for several generations under the predominant *Khas,* and what with the commerce of *Khas* males with their females*, they have acquired the *Khas* language, though not to the oblivion of their own, and the *Khas* habits and sentiments, but with sundry reservations in favour with pristine liberty. As they have, however, with such grace as they could muster, submitted themselves to the ceremonial law of purity and to *Brahman* supremacy, they have been adopted as *Hindús.* But partly owing to the licenses above glanced at, and partly by reason of the necessity of distinctions of caste to *Hindúism,* they have been denied the thread, and constituted a doubtful order below it, and yet not *Vaisya* nor *Sudra,* but a something superior to both the latter—what I fancy it might puzzle the *Shastrís* to explain on *Hindú* principles.

The *Brahmans* of *Népál* are much less generally addicted to arms than those of the plains; and they do not therefore properly belong to our present subject. The enumeration of the *Brahmans* is nevertheless necessary, as serving to elucidate the lineage and connexions of the military tribes, and especially of the Khas.

The martial classes of *Népál* are, then, the Khas, *Magar* and *Gúrung,* each comprising a very numerous race, variously ramified

---

* Here, as in the cases of the *Brahman* and *Khas,* and *Kshatriya* and *Khas,* there can be no marriage. The offspring of a *Khas* with a *Magarni* or *Gurungni* is a titular *Khas* and real *Magar* or *Gurung*. The descendants fall into the rank of their mothers and retain only the patronymic.

and sub-divided in the manner exhibited in the following tabular statement.

The original seat of the Khas is ordinarily said to be *Górkha**, because it was thence immediately that they issued, some years ago, under the guidance of Prithvi Narayan, to acquire the fame and dominion achieved by him and his successors of the *Górkhali* dynasty.

But the Khas were long previously to the age of Prithvi Narayan extensively spread over the whole of the *Chaubísya,* and they are now found in every part of the existing kingdom of *Népál,* as well as in Kùmuná, which was part of *Népál* until 1816. The Khas are rather more devoted to the house of *Górkhá,* as well as more liable to *Brahmanical* prejudices than the *Magars* or *Gúrungs;* and, on both accounts, are perhaps somewhat less desirable as soldiers for our service than the latter tribes. I say somewhat, because it is a mere question of degree; the Khas having, certainly, no religious prejudices, nor probably any national partialities, which would prevent their making excellent and faithful servants in arms; and they possess preeminently that masculine energy of character and love of enterprise which distinguish so advantageously all the military races of *Nèpál*. The original seat of the *Magars* is the *Bára Mangránth,* or *Satahung, Páyung, Bhírkót, Dhor, Garahúng, Rísíng, Ghiring, Gálmi, Argha, Khâchi, Músikót,* and *Isma;* in other words, most of the central and lower parts of the mountains, between the *Bhéri* and *Marsyándí*** Rivers. The attachment of the *Magars* to the house of *Górkhá* is but recent, and of no extraordinary or intimate nature. Still less so is that of the *Gúrungs,* whose native seats occupy a line of country parallel to that of the *Magars,* to the north of it, and extending to the snows in that direction. Modern events have spread the *Magars* and *Gurúngs* over most part of the present kingdom of *Népál,* The *Gúrungs* and *Magars* are, in the main, *Hindús, only because it is the fashion;* and the *Hindúism* of the Khas, in all practical and soldierly respects, is free of disqualifying punctilious.

These highland soldiers, who dispatch their meal in half an hour, and satisfy the ceremonial law by merely washing their hands

---

* Gorkha, the town, lies about sixty miles W.N.W. of Káthmándú. Górkhá, the name, is derived from that of the eponymous deity of the royal family, *viz.* Górakshanáth or Gorkhánáth, who likewise has given his name to our district of Górakpur.

** The *Marichangdi* of our maps.

and face, and taking off their turbans before cooking, laugh at the pharisaical rigour of our *Sipáhis,* who must bathe from head to foot and make *puja,* ere they begin to dress their dinner, must eat nearly naked in the coldest weather, and cannot be in marching trim again in less than three hours.

In war, the former readily carry several days' provisions on their backs: the latter would deem such an act intolerably degrading. The former see in foreign service nothing but the prospect of glory and spoil: the latter can discover in it nothing but pollution and peril from unclean men and terrible wizards, goblins, and evil spirits. In masses, the former have all that indomitable confidence, each in all, which grows out of national integrity and success: the latter can have no idea of this sentiment, which yet maintains the union and resolution of multitudes in peril, better than all other human bonds whatever; and, once thoroughly acquired, is by no means inseparable from service under the national standard.

I calculate that there are at this time in *Népál* no less than 30,000 *Dakhreahs* of soldiers off the roll by rotation, belonging to the above three tribes. I am not sure that there exists any insuperable obstacle to our obtaining, in one form or other, the services of a large body of these men; and such are their energy of character, love of enterprise, freedom from the shackles of caste, unadulterated military habits and perfect subjectibility to a discipline such as ours, that I am well assured their services, if obtained, would soon come to be most highly prized.*

In my humble opinion they are by far the best soldiers in Asia; and if they were made participators of our renown in arms, I conceive that their gallant spirit, emphatic contempt of Madhesias (people of the plains,) and unadulterated military habits, might

---

* Since this paper was written the value and the availability to us of the Górkháli soldier tribes have been well tested; and it is infinitely to be regretted that the opinions of Sir H. Fane, of Sir C. Napier, and of Sir H. Lawrence, as to the high expediency of recruiting largely from this source, were not acted upon long ago. So long as my voice carried any weight, I often pressed the subject on the attention of those in authority. But the then prejudice in favour of Brahman and Kshatri Sipáhis neutralized all my efforts, though the danger of so homogeneous an army of foreign mercenaries was, among other arguments, earnestly dwelt upon. (1857)

be relied on for fidelity; and that our good and regular pay and noble pension establishment would serve perfectly to counterpoise the influence of nationality, so far as that could injuriously affect us.

The following table exhibits a classified view of the *Brahmanical* and military tribes, with their various sub-divisions:

TABULAR VIEW OF THE TRIBES

BRAHMANS

Arjal.	Dohál.	Dhákal.	Bikrál.
Pondyál.	Lamsál.	Adhikári.	Ukniyál.
Khanál.	Kimál.	Doeja.	Bhattwál
Begmi.	Dêvakotya.	Rukái.	Gajniyál.
Bhattrái.	Parbatya, Vash.	Sywál.	Ohavala Gái.
Niróla.	Parbatya Misr.	Rijál.	Vast a Gái.
Achárya.	Davári.	Dhúngyál.	Banjára.
Bhatt.	Koikyál.	Loiyál.	Dági.
Sápankotya.	Nepálya.	Dotiyál.	Sôti.
Maharáshtra.	Barál.	Kandyál.	Osti.
Kôirála.	Pokaryál.	Katyál.	Utkulli.
Pakonyál.	Rúpákheti.	Dangál.	Kandariah.
Sattyál.	Khativára.	Singyál.	Ghart mél.
Ghartyál.	Timil Sina.	Panêru	Dulál.
Nivapánya.	Káphalya.	Loityál.	Parajuli.
Temrákoti.	Gaithoula.	Sigdhyál.	Bajgái.
Uphaltopi.	Gairaha Pipli.	Barál.	Satôla.
Parijai Kavala.	Ghimirya.	Gotamya.	Ghúrchóli
Homya Gái.	Simkhára.	Ghorasaini.	Kéláthoni
Champa Gái.	Phûnwál.	Risyál.	Gilal.
Gûra Gái.	Chamka Saini	Chálîsya.	Lahóni.
Subêri.	Pûra Saini.	Dhôngána.	Muthbari
Pandit.	Dhurári.	Bharári.	
Têvâ pánya.	Bhúrtyál.	Bágalya.	

KHAS

1st Sub-division of the Khás, called Thápa

Bagyál	Gágliyá	Powár	Khapotari
Takuryál	Súyál	Ghimirya	Parájuli

Palámi Maharáji Khulál Deoja
Gûdar Lámichanya Sunyál

2nd Sub-division of the Khás, called Bishnyát

Khulál Khaputari Sripáli Puwár

3rd Sub-division, called Bhandari

Raghubansi Láma Sijapati

4th Sub-division, called Kárki

Sutár Láma Múndala Khûlál

5th Sub-division, called Khánka

Powár Mahárji Partyal Lakánggi Lámichanya
Khulál Kálikotya Khaputari Palpáli

6th Sub-division, or Adhikari

Thámi Tharirái Pokriál Musiah
Dhámi Khadhsena Thákúri

7th Sub-Division, or Bisht

Kálikotya Puwár Dahál

8th Sub-division, or Kunwár

Bagálya Khulál Khanka Arjál

9th Sub-division, or Baniah

Sijapati

10th sub-division, or Dáni

Sijapati Powár

11th Sub-division, or Gharti.*

Kalikotya	Sijapati

12th Sub-division, or Khattri

Pánde	Khulál	Lámichánya	Tewári	Suveri
Dhakál	Panth	Poryál	Phanyál	Adhikári
Sakhtyál	Burál	Arjál	Sápkotya	Silwal

TRUE KHAS NOT YET CLASSIFIED

Dhongyál	Sijal	Satouya	Rûpakhetí
Loyál	Parsái	Khatiwata	Chouvala Gái
Chalatami	Bhatt Rai	Lamsál	Am Gái
Kilathoni	Naopánya	Khukriyal	Baj Gái
Dangál	Dahál	Satya Gái	Muri Bhús
Sikhmiyál	Deakota	Alpháltopi	Sóti
Bhiryál	Garhtóla	Osti	Parijái Kawala
Pouryál	Sèóra	Bhatt Ojha	Bamankotya
Bikrál	Bálya	Tewári	Kadariah
Kanhál	Gilál	Porseni	Kála Khattri
Batyál	Chonial	Homya Gái	Dhúngána
Ganjál	Regmi	Túmrakot	Pungyál

EKTHARYA, OR INSULATED TRIBES RANKING WITH KHÁS

Búrathoki	Chohan	Bohara	Kutál	Ráya	Boghati
Chiloti	Dikshit	Ravat	Khatit	Dángi	Pandit
Katwál	Bávan	Raimanjhi	Parsái	Kháti	Mahat
Bhusal	Chohara	Bhukhandi	Chokhál	Maghati	Barwál
Chohara	Durrah				

THAKURI, OR ROYAL LINEAGES, RANKING WITH KHÁS

Sáhi	Singh	Chand	Jiva	Malla	Maun
Hamál	Rakhsya	Séna	Chohan	Ruchál	

---

* Manumitted slaves are called Párgharti, if of Khas lineage. They form a separate and rather numerous class, and so also do the Khawás or manumitted slaves of royalty.

MAGARS

I. Sub-division of the Magars, called Ráná

Bhusál	Gyángmi	Byángnási	Kyápcháki	Aslámi
Pulámi	Phyúyáli	Durra Lámi	Yahayo	Gácha
Lámichanya	Máski	Sárû	Pusál	Ghandharma
Charmi	Arghounlé	Tháda	Dûtt	

II. Sub-division of Magars, called Thápa

Gránjá	Chumi	Keli	Bareya	Namjali
Lúngeli	Jhángdi	Máski	Darrlámi	Sunári
Yángdi	Phyûyali	Marsyangdi	Chitouriah	Jhári
Arghounli	Gelung	Sinjali	Sárû	Rijái

III. Sub-division of Magars, called Alaya

Yángmi	Sarángi	Púng	Lamjál	Súrya Vansi
Gónda	Sripáli	Sûyál	Kháli	Dukhcháki
Sijapati	Panthi	Thokcháki	Méng	Gharti
Rakhál	Sithûng	Maski	Lámichánya	Palámi
Lahakpá	Arghounle	Khaptari	Phyûyáli	Kyapcháki
Dûrrá	Khulál	Chermi	Pacháin	

GURUNGS

Gúrúng	Lámichánya	Khaptari	Tangé
Ghalle	Siddh	Ghúndáne	Ghónyá
Byápri	Karámati	Dhárén	Paindi
Vumjan	Gósti	Jimel	Méngi
Láma	Bagálva	Lopáte	Dal Láma
Chandú	Tháthúng	Lotháng	Kurángi
Góthi	Chárki	Bûlûng	Khulál
Gondúk	Kháti	Shakya Láma	Surya Vansi Láma
Gohori	Guáburi	Golángya	Madán
Baráhi	Pengi	Khangva	Palámi
	Ghárti	Dhakaren	

Bibliography and Source Materials

A. Primary Sources

I. Unpublished

Government Records and Documents: English.

A. In the National Archives of India, New Delhi.

a. Foreign Political and Secret Consultations and Proceedings.
b. Foreign Miscellaneous Political Records.
c. Political and Secret Letters to and from the Court of Directors.
d. The Governor General's Dispatches to and from the Court of Directors.
e. The Governor General's Confidential dispatches to and from the Court of Directors.
f. Nepal Residency Records.
g. Resident' Diary Hodgson manuscripts. Cleaveland Microfilm, No. 77 Roll-8.

B. In the National Archives of Nepal, Kathmandu, Nepali.

a. Government Regulations. Bhim Sen Thapa' Documents.
b. Land grants and assignment under Birta, Jagir, Guthi and Kipat.
c. Jangi ko Kitab.
d. Jang Bahadurko Ain of 1910.
e. Revenue Settlement Reports.

II. Published Documents

A. English

Aitchison, C.U., *A Collection of Treaties, Engagement and Sunnads relations to Indian and Neighbouring Countries,* 10 Vols. Calcutta, 1931.

Bajracharya, B.R., *Diary of Events in Nepal,* New Delhi, 1996.

Campbell, A., Campbell's Sketches, published in Bikramjit Hasrat's *History of Nepal,* Punjab, 1971.

Cox, J.L., *Papers* Respecting the Nepaul War, Lodon, 1924, Reprinted as Military History of Nepal, New Delhi, 1983.

Ganguly, D.C., Select Documents of the British period of Indian History, Calcutta, 1958.

Hodgson, B.H., *Essay on the Language, Literature and Religion of Nepal and Tibet,* London, 1874 (Reprint, New Delhi, 1972).

— —, "On Administration of Justice and Some Account of the System of Law and Police as Recognised in the State of Nepal", *Asiatic Research,* Vol. xxii. 1836.

Kshetri, D.B., *Documents on Nepal,* Pokhara, 1998.

Markham, Clements, *Narratives of the Mission of George Boggle to Tibet and of the Journey of Thomas Manning to Lhasa,* London, 1876.

Nicholetts, C.H., Narratives of Events in Nepal from 1840 to 1850. vide Bikramjit Hasrat, *History of Nepal,* Punjab, 1971.

Pemberton, R.B., *Reports on Bootan,* Calcutta, 1839.

Princep, H.T., *History of the Political and Military Transactions in India during the Administration of the Marques of Hastings, 1813-1823,* 2 Vols., London, 1825.

Sinha, N.R., and Dasgupta, A.K. (Ed.), Selections from Ochterlony Papers (1818-1825), Calcutta, 1825.

Tickell, J.R.,. Excerpts from the Letters of the Resident at Kathmandu to the Government, from 1830-1840, vide Bikramjit Hasrat, *History of Nepal,* Punjab, 1971.

Wheeler, J.T., *Diary of Events in Nepal, 1841-1846,* Calcutta, 1878.

B. Nepali

Bajracharya, D., *Aitihasik Patra Sangraha,* Part I, Kathmandu, 2014 BS.

— —, *Itihas Sansodhanko Pramey,* Kathmandu, (nd.).

Bir Pustakalaya, *Aitihasik Chitthipatra Sangraha*, 2 Vols., Kathmandu, 2022 BS.

Mandal, Itihas Prakash, *Itihas Prakash*, 4 Vols., Kathmandu, 1955-56.

Narhari Nath Yogi, *Itihas Prakashma Sandhipatra Sangraha*, Parts I and II, Banaras, 2022 BS.

Nepal, J.B., *Aitihasik Patra Sangraha*, Kathmandu, 2014 BS.

Puratattva Patra Sangraha, 3 Vols., Kathmandu, 1960-63.

Regmi, M.C., Regmi Research Series: A Translation of Nepali Documents, *Monthly Issue*, Mimeograph.

Shahkalin Aitihasik Chitthipatra Sangraha, 2 Vols., Kathmandu, 1966.

Tewari, Ramji, *Aitihasik Patra Sangraha*, Part 2, Kathmandu, 2016 BS.

— —, (Ed.) *Abhilekha Sangraha*, Vol. I., Kathmand, 2018 BS.

Secondary Source Materials: English

Adam, Leonhard, "Criminal Laws and Procedures in Nepal in a Century ago", Note left by B.H. Hodgson, *The Far Eastern Quarterly*, February, 1960, Vol. 9, No. 2.

Agarwal, Hemnarayan, *The Administrative System in Nepal: From Tradition to Modernity*, New Delhi, 1976.

— —, Pre-Gorkha Administrative System of Nepal, *Patna University Journal*, Vol. 23, No. 1, 1968

Aitkinson, Edwin, T., *The Himalayan Districts of the North-Western Provinces of India*, 2 Vols., Allahabad, 1882.

Bahadur, Purna, "The Strategic Importance of Nepal," *Nepal Today*, April, 1953.

Baid, T. and Manadhar, T.R., *Crimes and Punishments in Nepal*, Centre for Nepal and Asian Studies, Tribhuvan University, Kathmandu, 1985.

Bajpai, G.S., "Nepal and Indo-Nepalese Relations", *Indian Year Book of International Affairs*, Madras, 1954.

Ballantine, Henry, *Our India's Frontiers on Nepal: The Gurkhas Mysterious Land*, New York, 1895.

— —, "The Land of the Gurkhas," *Harper's New Monthly Magazine*, No. 78, 1889.

Basnet, Lal Bahadur, Nepalese or Gorkha ? (A Pamphlet), Sikkim, (nd.)

Bell, Charles, *Tibet, Past and Present*, Oxford, 1924.

Bendall, C., *A Journey of Literary and Archaeological Research in Nepal and Northern India*, Oxford, 1886.

Barat, Amitya, *The Bengal Native Infantry: Its Organisation and Discipline*, 1796-1965, Calcutta, 1962.

Baylay, S.F., *Kathmandu, the Capital of Nepal*, Calcutta, 1918.

Banerjee, N.N., *Nepal—The Hindu Kingdom: The Himalayas in and Across*, Calcutta, 1937.

Benadach, W., *An Inquiry into the States of the Indian Army*, London, 1826.

Bishop, R.N.W., *Unkown Nepal*, London, 1952.

Bista, Dor Bahadur, *People of Nepal*, Kathmandu, 1967.

Bolt, David, *Gurkhas*, London, 1967.

Bredin, A.E.C., *The Happy Warriors*, Dorset, 1961.

Brown, Percy, *Picturesque Nepal*, London, 1912.

Bruce, C.G., *Nepal and Sikkim, Twenty Years in the Himalaya*, London, 1910.

Buchanan (Hamilton) Francis, *An Account of the Kingdom of Nepal*, New Delhi, Reprint 1971.

Buckland, C.E., *Dictionary of Indian Biography*, London, 1906.

Bose, S.C., *Geography of Himalayas*, New Delhi, 1983.

Camman, Schuyler, *Trade through the Himalayas*, Princeton, 1951.

Candler, E., *Bengal Native Army*, Calcutta, 1903.

Caplan, Lionel, *Land and Social Change in East Nepal: A Study of Hindu-Tribal Relations*, London, 1970.

Cavenagh, Orfeur, Rough Notes on the State of Nepal: Its Government, Army and Resources, Calcutta, 1851.

——, *Reminiscences of an Indian Official*, London, 1884.

Chaudhuri, K.C., *Anglo-Nepalese Relations*, Calcutta, 1960.

Choudhury, Roy, P.C. "Early Indo-Nepal Relations", *Bengal Past and Present*, 74, July-December, 1955.

Das, S.C, *The Commerce of Tibet*, Calcutta, 1883.

Datta, K.K., "Some Unpublished Letters Relating to Anglo-Nepalese Relations in the beginning of the 19th Century", *The Journal of Bihar and Orissa Research Society*, September-December, 1939.

Davis, Hassoldt, *Nepal, Land of Mystery: Adventure in Burma, China, India, and the Kingdom of Nepal*, London, 1942,

Dhanalaxmi, R., *British Attitude to Nepal's Relations with Tibet and China, 1814-1914*, New Delhi, 1981.

Duncan, Forbes, *Johney Gorkhas*, New Delhi, 1972.

Edgar, J.W., *Report on a visit to Sikkim and the Tibetan Frontier*, Calcutta, 1874.

Farwell, Byron, *The Gurkhas*, London, 1985.

Fisher, Margarent and Rose, Leo E., *England, India, Nepal, Tibet, China, 1765-1958*, Berkeley, 1963.

Fortesque, J.W., *History of the British Army*, Vol. IX, London, 1930.

Gaige Frederick, H., *Regionalism and National Unity in Nepal*, California, 1975.

Gibbs, H.R.K., *The Gurkha Soldiers*, Calcutta, 1944.

Gimlette, G.H.D., *Nepal and the Nepalese*, London, 1928.

Gruseppe, Father, "An Account of the Kingdom of Nepal", *Asiatic Researches*, Vol. 2, 1790 (Reprinted 1983).

Ghose, L.N., *The Modern History of Indian Chiefs, Rajas and Zamindars*, Calcutta, 1819.

Gupta, Aniruddha, *Politics in Nepal*, New Delhi, 1964.

Hagen, Toni, Nepal, *The Kingdom in the Himalayas*, Berne, 1961.

Hau, W.E., *A Treaties and International Law*, London, 1924.

Harsat, B.J., *History of Nepal: As Told by the Own and Contemporary Chronicles*, Punjab, 1970.

Hooker, Sir Joseph Dalton, "On Notes of a Naturalist", *The Himalayan Journal*, 1891.

Hunter, W.W., *Life of Brian Houghton Hodgson*, London, 1896.

— —, *The Imperial Gazetteer of India*, XIX Vols., Oxford, 1908.

Hussain, Asad, *British India's Relations with the Kingdom of Nepal*, London. 1970.

— —, Imdad, *Problems of Defence of North-East Frontier: 1822-1866*, Guahati University, 1975.

Jain, M.S., *The Emergence of New Aristocracy in Nepal*, Agra, 1972.

Joshi, H.R. and Joshi, Indra, *The First German to Visit Nepal, Kathmandu*, 1997.

Karan, P.P., and Jenkins, M.M., *The Himalayan Kingdoms: Bhutan, Sikkim and Nepal*, Lexington, 1963.

Kaye, J.W. (Ed), *The Life and Correspondence of Charles Metcalf*, 2 Vols. London, 1858.

— —, Selections from the Papers of Lord Metcalf, London, 1875.

Kirkpatrick, W., *An Account of the Kingdom of Nepal*, London, 1911.

Land, Alister, *Britain and Chinese Central Asia: The Road to Lhasa*, London, 1960.

— —, "Tibet in Anglo-Chinese Relations, 1767-1842", *The Journal of the Royal Asiatic Society of Great Britain and Ireland*, December 1957 and April 1958.

Landon, P., *Nepal*, 2 Vols, London, 1928,

Lingat, Robert, *The Classical Law of India*, Translated by J. Duncun and M. Derett, Berkeley, 1973.

Loraine, R.E., *The 1st King George's Own Gurkha Rifles: The Maulana Regiment, 1815-1921*, London, 1925.

MacMunn, George, *The Martial Races of India*, New Delhi (reprint) 1972.

Mason, K., "A Note on the Nepal Himalaya", *The Himalaya Journal*, 1934.

Mitra, K.P., "Anglo-Nepalese Treaty of Commerce, 1792", *Bengal: Past and Present*, July-December, 1941.

Mojumdar, K., *Political Relations between India and Nepal: 1877-1923*, New Delhi, 1972.

— —, *Anglo-Nepalese Relations in the Nineteenth Century*, Calcutta, 1972.

Morris, C.J. *The Gurkhas: A Handbook for the Indian Army*, Delhi 1933.

— —, and Northy, W.B., *The Land of the Gurkhas*, Cambridge, 1937.

Morrion, J.L., *Lawrence of Lucnow*, London, 1934.

Munshi, D.N., *Foreign Policy of Nepal*, Delhi, 1973.

Narayan, S., *India and Nepal*, Bombay, 1970.

Nepali, G.S., *The Newars*, Bombay, 1965.

Nevill, H.R. (Ed), *District Gazetteer of the United Provinces of Agra and Oudh, Vol. XLIV. 1909, and Gorakhpur, Vol. XXXI, 1902.*

O'Mally, L.S.S. (Ed.), *Bengal District Gazetteer, Champaran, 1907; Saran, 1908; Purnea, 1911.*

Oppenhiem, L., *International Law: A Treatise*, 1955.

Pannikar, K.M., *The Relations of the Indian States with the Government of India*, London, 1927.

— —, *The Evolution of British Policy towards Indian States, 1774 -1858*, Calcutta, 1929.

Pemble, John, *The Invasion of Nepal*, Oxford University Press, 1971.

Philips, C.H., *The Correspondences of Lord William Bentinck*, 2 Vols, Oxford, 1977.

Poynder, F.S., *The 9th Gurkha Rifles: 1817-1936*, London, 1937.

Pradhan, K.L., "Brian Hodgson at Kathmandu Darbar (1825-1843)", *The Quarterly Review of Historical Studies*, Calcutta. Vol. XXXIV. April-September, 1994, Nos. 1 and 2.

— —, *Brian Hodgson at the Kathmandu Residency: 1825-1843*, New Delhi, 2001.

— —, "The Gorkhas of Mizoram", *The Nepalis in North East India-A Community in search of Indian Identity*, edited by A.C. Sinha and T.B. Subha), New Delhi, 2003.

Rahul, Ram, *The Himalaya Borderland*, New Delhi, 1970.

——, *The Himalaya as a Frontier,* New Delhi, 1978.
Ramakant, *Indo-Nepalese Relations 1816-1877,* New Delhi, 1968.
——, *Nepal-China and India,* New Delhi, 1976.
Radhakrishnan, S., *The Heart of Hinduism,* Madras, 1936.
Rana, Padma Jung Samser, *Life of Jang Bahadur Rana of Nepal,* Allahabad, 1909. (ed. A.C. Mukherjee).
Rawat, P.C., *Indo-Nepal Economic Relations,* New Delhi, 1974.
Regmi, D.R., *A Century of Autocracy in Nepal,* Kathmandu, 1958.
——, *Political and Economic History of Nepal,* 4 Vols., Calcutta, 1959.
——, *Modern Nepal,* Calcutta, 1960.
Regmi, M.C., *Land Tenure and Taxation in Nepal,* Berkeley, 1968.
——, *A Study in Nepali Economic History,* New Delhi, 1971.
——, *Land Ownership in Nepal,* Berkeley, 1976.
Riesman, David, *et al., The Lonely Crowd,* New Haven, Conn. 1961.
Rose, Leo E., *Nepal: Strategy for Survival,* Berkeley, 1971.
——, and Scholz, J.T., *Nepal: Profile of Himalayan Kingdom,* New Delhi, 1980.
Sanwal, B.D., *Nepal and the East India Company,* Bombay, 1965.
Satis Kumar, *Rana Polity in Nepal: Its Origin and Growth,* New Delhi, 1967.
——, "The Nepalese Monarchy from 1769 to 1951", *The International Studies.*
Sen, Jahar, *Indo-Nepal Trade in the Nineteenth Century,* Calcutta, 1977.
Shah, Ikbal, *Nepal: The Home of Gods,* London, n.d.
Shah, Rishikesh, *Nepali Politics: Retrospect and Prospect,* Delhi, 1975.
——, *Nepal and the World,* Kathmandu, 1955.
——, *An Introduction of Nepal,* Kathmandu, 1976.
Spake, O.H.K., Learmouth, A.T.A. and Farner, B.H., *India, Pakistan and Ceylon: The Regions,* Part IV, New Delhi, Reprint, 1967.
Shakespeare, L.W., *History of the 2nd King Edward's Own Gurkha Rifles, (Sirmoor Rifles),* 2 Vols., London, 1912.
Sherring, Charles A., *Western Tibet and British Borderland,* London, 1906.
Shrestha, B.P., *An Introduction of the Nepalese Economy,* Kathmandu, 1974.
——, M.K., *A Handbook of Public Administration in Nepal,* Kathmandu, 1975.
Sinha, A.C., *Studies in the Himalayan Communities,* New Delhi, 1983.
——, N.C., Asian Law and Usages in European Expressions: Some Illustration from Tibet, *Man in India,* Vol. III, No. i, 1971.

——, S.N. "A Survey of Internal History of Nepal, 1767 - 1847", *Journal of Historical Research*, Bihar University, Vol. II, 1960.

Stiller, Ludwig, F., *The Rise of the House of Gorkha*, Patna, 1973.

——, *The Silent Cry: The People of Nepal, 1816-1839*, Kathmandu, 1976.

Temple, R., *Journals Kept in Hyderabad, Kashmir, Sikkim and Nepal*, 2 Vols, London, 1887.

The Imperial Gazetteers, Vol. IV, 1908; Vol. XIX, 1909.

Thompson E., *Life of Lord Metcalf*, London, 1937.

——, *The Making of the Indian Princes*, Oxford, 1943.

——, and Garratt, G.T., *Rise and Fulfilment of British Rule in India*, London, 1935.

Tucci, Giuseppe, *Nepal: The Discovery of the Mall* (translated by Edward Lovett), London, 1962.

Tucker, Francis, *Gorkha: The Story of the Gorkhas in Nepal*, London, 1957.

——, *While Memory Serves*, London, 1950.

Tyagi, Sushila, *Indo-Nepalese Relations: 1858-1914*, New Delhi, 1974.

Vansittart, E., *Notes on Gurkhas*, Calcutta, 1890.

——, *Gurkhas: Handbook for the Indian Army*, Calcutta, 1915.

Waddell, L.A., *Among the Himalayas*, London, 1900.

Wheeler, J.T., *A Short History of India and the Frontier States of Afghanistan, Nipal and Burma*, London, 1889.

Westlake, J., *International Law*, Cambridge, 1910.

Wood, H.B., *Nepal Bibliography*, Oregon, 1959.

Woodyatt, N.G., *Regimental History of the 3rd Queen Alexadra's Own Gurkha Rifles*, London, 1923.

Wright, D. (Ed.), *History of Nepal*, Cambridge, 1877.

Yule, H., and Burrel, A.C., Hobson-Jobson, London, 1969.

B. Nepali

Acharya, Babu Ram, *Nepalko Sangchhipta Britanta*, Kathmandu, 2022 BS.

——, *Aba Yesto Kahile Nahos*, Kathmandu, 2055 BS.

——, "Bhimsen Thapako Atmahatya ra Hadkhod", *Rooprekha*, 2, No. 8.

——, "Bhimsen Thapako Utthan", *Rooprekha*, I, No. 4.

——, "Bhimsen Thapako Pattan", *Pragati*, 2, No. 4.

——, "Bhimsen Thapako Pattan Dekhi Jang Bahadur Ranako Utthan Nabhaye Sammako 9 Barsa Samma Halchal", *Rooprekha*, 3, No. 5.

——, "Janaral Bhimsen Thapako Parakram ra unle Samarjung . Kampani lai Diyeko Danda", *Arti*, 2004 BS.

——, *China ra Tibet sita Nepalko Sambandha*, Kathmandu, 1958.

——, *Sri Panch Maharajadhiraja Prithvi Narayan Shah (Sangchhipta Jiwani)*, Kathmanu, 2024 BS.

——, Yagyanath, *Nepalko Itihas (1977-2007 BS)*, Kathmandu, 2039 BS.

Aryal, B.B., *Nepalko Parichaye*, Kathmandu, 2044 BS.

——, Ramji P., *Nepal Itihas ra Aryal Pariwar*, Kathmandu, 2047 BS.

Baid, R.K., *Sarbajanit Prasanka Siddhanta*, Kathmandu, 2033 BS.

Bajracharya, D. (Ed.), *Galima Phyakiyeka Kasingar*, Kathmandu, 2018 BS.

——, *Triratna Saundarye Gatha*, Kathmandu, 2019 BS.

——, and Shrestha, T.B., *Shahkalin Abhilekh*, Kathmandu, 2023 BS.

——, *Dolkhako Itihas Ruprekha*, Kathmandu, 2031 BS.

——, *Nuwakotko Itihas Ruprekha*, Kathmandu, 2032 BS.

——, and Baaid, T.R., *Gorkhako Aitihaasik Samagri*, Kathmandu, 2029 BS.

—— "Licchavi Kalma Chaleko Pnchali Sashan Paddatiko Parichaye", *Purnima*, 2023, CNAS, TU, 2035 BS.

Bagale Thapa Kalyankari Parisad, *Amar Gatha*, Kathmandu, 2054 BS.

Bam, Lalit Bahadur, *Sri Panch Maharajadhiraja Rajendra ra Tatkalin Nepal*, Kathmandu, 2023 BS.

Baniya, K.B. and Shrestha, R., *Uzir Singh Thapa*, Kathmandù, 2054 BS.

Bhandari, D.R., *Nepalko Aitihasik Vivechana*, Banaras, 1959.

——, *Nepalko Udbhao Ratha Bikasko Bilesanatmak Itihas*, Kathmandu, 2046 BS.

Chenzong, Iman Singh, *Kirat Kalin Bikyapur ko Sangchhita Itihas.*

Dhahal, Ram Kumar, *Nepalko Parichaye*, Kathmandu, 2051 BS.

Dixit, Kamal, (Ed.) *Jang Bahadur ko Vilayat Yatra*, Kathmandu, 2014 BS.

Dungel, Gyanu, *Mukhtiyar Bhim Sen Thapa ra Tatkalin Nepali Sahitya*, Kathmandu, 2056 BS.

Duvedi, B., *Nepalko Naveen Itihas*, Birganj, 1955.

Ghimire, B.R, *Palpa Rajyako Itihas*, Chitwan, 2045 BS.

Gyawali, Surya V., *Amar Singh Thapa*, Darjeeling, 1943 BS.

——, Min Prasad, *Nepalko Sangchhipta Itihas*, Kathmandu, 2043 BS.
Khanal, M.P., *Madhye Kalin Abhilekh*, Kathmandu, 2030 BS.
Lama, Buddhabir, *Rajnitik Sanskriti Antargat Mukhtiyar Bhim Sen Thapako Pattan*, (Unpublished Thesis), 2044 BS.
Limbu, P.B. and Dungel, B.N., *Sangchhipta Nepalko Itihas*, Lalitpur, 2011 BS.
Malla, Govinda, *Prajatantra Udaye ra Panchayati Prajatantra Pradurbhao -Nepal Parichaye*, TU, 1970.
Malla, M.B., "Bum Shah ra Bhim Sen Thapa", *Madhuparka*, 10, No. 5.
Manadhar, T.R., *Nepal Ayekakiran, Nepal Parichaye*, TU, 1970.
Nepali, C.R., "Mukhtiyar Rangnath-Ek Jhalak", *Sharada*, 20 , No. l, 2012 BS.
——, "Nepal Aur British Samrajya", *Sharada*, 21, No. l, 2013 BS.
——, "Sri Panch Rana Bahadur Shahko Hatya Kanda", *Rooprekha*, 2, No. 9, 2018 BS.
——, *General Bhim Sen Thapa ra Tatkalin Nepal*, Kathmandu 2035 BS (Reprint).
——, *Sri Panch Rana Bahadur Shah*, Kathmandu, 2047 BS.
Nepal, Gyan Mani, *Nepalko Mahabharat*, Kathmandu, 2052 BS.
Ojha, B.N., *Ranbir Singh Thapako Jiwani* (Unpublished Thesis) 2052 BS.
Pande, Atmaram, *Bhim Sen Thapako Sasankalma Nepal* (Unpublished Thesis) 2052 BS.
——, *Sardar Bhim Bahadur, Rastrabhaktako ek Jhalak*, Kathmandu 2041 BS.
——, T.R. and Pant, N.R., *Nepalko Sangchhipta Itihas*, Banaras, 2004 BS.
Pant, Naya Raj, "Thapa thaliko Bhim Sen Thapako Stambha Lekh" *Sanskriti Sandesh*, 1, No. 7, 2010 BS.
——, "Bhim Sen Thapa", *Poornima*, 8, No. 4. 2031 BS.
——, and others, *Sri Panch Prithvi Narayan Shahko Upadesh*, Kathmandu, 2035 BS.
——, D.R., "Asrit Rajya Upar Bahadur Shahle Lieko Niti", *Purnima*, No. 6.
——, "Swami Rana Bahadur Shahko 1862 ko Bandobast" *Purnima*, No. 24, 2028 BS.
——, Mahesh Raj, "Nepal-Angrez Yudhako Doshro Charan", *Purnima*, No. 6, 2022 BS.
——, "Bir Bakhta Thapa", *Purnima*, No. 17, 2025 BS.

Pokhrel, Balkrishna, *Panch Saye Barsa,* Kathmandu, 2048 BS.
Poudel, Nayanath, *Bhasha Vamshavali,* 2 Vols, Kathmandu, 2023 BS.
Rajbansi, S., *Aitihasik Kundali,* Kathmandu, 2033 BS.
Ram Bahadur Pahadi, (Trans.) *Jiudo Singh-General Amar Singh Thapa,* Kathmandu, 2058 BS.
Regmi, M.C., *Prachin Nepalko Rajnitik Itihas,* Kathmandu, 2035 BS.
— —, *Nepalko Adhunik Bhugol,* TU., Kathmandu, 2039 BS.
Rana, Rumani, "Hodgson as a factor for the downfall of Bhimsen Thapa", *Ancient Nepal* (nd).
Sijapati, G.V., *Nepali Prashasan Vyavastha Vikasko, Ruprekha,* Kathmandu, 2019 BS.
Sharma, Balchandra, *Nepalko Aitihasik Ruprekha,* Banaras, 2033 BS.
— —, *Nepali Sahityako Itihas,* Kathmandu, 2039 BS.
— —, Devi Prasad, *Adhunik Nepalko Itihas,* Kathmandu, 2047 BS.
— —, Binay Kumar, *Bhim Senlai Niyalda,* Kathmandu, 2059 BS.
— —, Shiva Prasad, *Nepalko Sainik Itihas,* Kathmandu, 2042 BS.
Shrestha, H.L., *Naya Nepal Parichaye, Kathmandu,* 2035 BS.
— —, K.B., "Ma Mari Muluk Dubneya Chhaina", *Madhuparka,* 15, No. 3.
— —, Sangita, Mathbar Singh Thapa, Kathmandu, 2046 BS.
Singh, Yuraraj, *Viswa Parichaye-Kathmandu,* Okhaldunga, 2031 BS.
Surendra, K.C., *Nepalko Kutnitik Itihas,* Taplejung, 2046 BS.
Subedi, R., "General Bhim Sen Thapako Kanun", *Nepal Kanun Paricharcha,* 9, No. 1, 2040 BS.
Thapa, Ramesh Jung (ed.), *Nepal Deshko Itihas: Prachin Nepal,* Kathmandu, 2030 BS.
— —, *Samsher Bahadur, Ranbir Singh Thapa,* Kathmandu, 2023 BS.
— —, *Sagauli Sandhi ke ho*?Kathmandu, 2048 BS.
Upadhya, A.P., *Nepalko Itihas,* Banaras, 1979.
— —, Ramji, *Nepalko Itihas arthat Digdarshan,* Banaras, 1950.
— —, S.P., *Nepalko Prasasanit Byabasta,* Kathmandu, 2029 BS.
Vidyalankar, Jaichandra, *Gorkhali Itihaski Mukhya Dharaya* (Hindi), Jallandar, 1962.
Yadav, Pitambar Lal, *Nepalko Rajnitik Itihas,* Kathmandu, 2040 BS.
Yogi, N.N., *Gorkhaliruko Sainik Itihas,* Kathmandu, 2011 BS.
— —,(ed.), *Gorkha Vamshawali,* Vananasi, 2021 BS.
— —, and Acharya, B., *Rastrapita Sri Panch Bada Maharaja Prithvi Narayan Shah ko Dibye Upadesh,* Kathmandu, 2014 BS.

Index